Control
Your
Overheads

Control Your Overheads

A Practical Programme to Improve Performance and Reduce Costs

RUPERT BOOTH

FINANCIAL TIMES

PITMAN PUBLISHING

PITMAN PUBLISHING
128 Long Acre, London WC2E 9AN

A Division of Longman Group Limited

© Rupert Booth 1994

First published in Great Britain 1994

British Library Cataloguing in Publication Data
A CIP catalogue record for this book can be obtained from the British Library.

ISBN 0 273 03859 1

Typeset by PanTek Arts, Maidstone.
Printed and bound in Great Britain by Biddles Ltd, Guildford and King's Lynn.

It is the Publishers' policy to use paper manufactured from sustainable forests.

To my mother and father,
Pauline and John,
who appreciated the value of their children,
before counting their cost.

CONTENTS

PREFACE

The ability to control overhead structures is now one of the key competencies for major corporations. Overheads are not only a burgeoning cost but their performance is also crucial to satisfying customers through quality and timeliness. Control of these overheads is no longer simply concerned with monitoring departmental budgets, but involves:

● putting in place an overhead structure which will benefit the organisation by optimising the processes which add value to its products and services;
● identifying the activities which are undertaken, measuring their value and their cost, and relating these activities to the outputs of the organisation;
● acting to obtain improvements, both individually and as part of a continuous process, which depends on the right information and attitudes being present in the organisation.

These benefits can be obtained through a five-step programme and the bulk of this book is concerned with defining the execution of this programme. The programme is not prescriptive, requiring every component to be carried out, but is generic, reflecting many years' experience in management consultancy of specifying and implementing programmes to control overhead functions. While engaged in this work, it became apparent that that many of the individual programmes followed a common theme, and in the words of the source, which is quoted liberally later in the book, that indeed 'All is vanity . . . There is no new thing under the sun'. On this basis it seemed possible to define a generic programme.

Every book gives a view from the perspective of the author. In this case the author is typically engaged for a short time to undertake a project during which there are a number of 'deliverables'. This has had several influences on the programme given in this book:

● The deliveries for each step of the programme are highlighted, as is the information flow between each step.
● The underlying assumption is that to control overheads requires an initial programme to *bring them under control*, i.e. specific action is required, rather than gradual adjustment.
● There is an emphasis on fact, not judgement, so that potentially controversial conclusions can be objectively justified.

The array of objective techniques described is very broad, taking a view far wider than is typically taken when considering overhead control. In particular there is an unusual emphasis on:

- relating the overhead structure to the business strategy of the organisation's customers;
- carefully establishing the requirements of the customers of the organisation, with examples given of specialist techniques such as conjoint analysis and quality function deployment;
- simultaneously considering the operational and the information technology issues of overhead control to avoid the common tendency to develop these aspects independently;
- describing the principles of procurement as a prelude to discussing outsourcing.

On the other hand little room has been found for some 'old favourites', e.g. budgetary control. The primary reason is that since the traditional aspects of overhead control are usually in place, even in situations where overheads are not under control, there is no need to include them within the programme; also there are so many texts on these subjects; repetition would be futile.

It needs emphasising that hardly any of the techniques contained within the book are new. There has, however, been a deliberate transfer of expertise from:

- product design to process design. Product design has well-developed techniques to ensure the designs are relevant to customer needs, their costs are justified by the value attached to them and the consequences of failure are understood. These techniques are equally applicable to process design;
- manufacturing to service industry. Manufacturing industry has established methods for improving its operations, which have already been deployed in the area of repetitive clerical operations. Now, as manufacturing operations become more complex and flexible, new techniques (some of which contradict the old) have been developed. These new techniques are especially relevant to the control of overheads.

Finally, and most importantly, I want to thank some of the many people with whom I have worked and who have shared their expertise with me. In particular Mike Fradette and Ken Parekh from the Boston office of Deloitte and Touche introduced me to the concepts of activity-based management techniques and a structured interview methodology which has influenced the 'Activity Analysis' step; within the London office of Touche Ross, Mark Musgrave worked with me on developing many of the concepts of the cross-allocation of costs between products and customers and Pearse Reynolds introduced me to the concept of challenge groups; thanks too to Peter Bould, who provided advice on the final text. Similar comments apply to many others within Touche Ross who are too numerous to name and to many managers within client firms whom I would like to mention but for maintaining the anonymity of the case studies (whose details have also been altered for this purpose). The case studies are drawn primarily from the utility and manufacturing sectors from around the world. The case studies which follow the chapters describing the five step programme do not just relate to that chapter alone.

Needless to say, any errors are my own responsibility.

1

RESPONDING TO CHANGE

What profit hath a man of all his labour he taketh under the sun?

ECCLESIASTES 1:3

A CHANGING WORLD

Oversupply of the markets

For the first half of this century there was a shortage of consumer and durable goods. In this situation, the emphasis was on production. Companies were organised so as to maximise production efficiency and, to survive, a company had to have an efficient production facility, relative to the competitors in its market.

In this environment the voice of the customer was not generally heard. This is perhaps epitomised by Henry Ford's comment 'Any colour, so long as it's black'. This is a view that is ridiculed today, but at the time it was a sound summary of the market conditions: consumers hungry for goods and grateful (usually) for what they got. It was a time when the view was that those involved in the design and manufacture of products needed to be insulated from the customers' demands. Today this is heresy, but at the time it made sense: customers change priorities and this lowers production efficiency.

The situation has now changed. Consumers are offered a vast supply of alternative goods. There is a limit to the amount that can be consumed, as a result there are three effects:

- The original exporting nations (e.g. the United States and the United Kingdom) have come under intense competition as the new manufacturing nations (e.g. Japan) have increased their export drives, after having satisfied their own domestic markets.
- Consumers no longer view a product as a commodity. They seek differentiation of the product from similar products which gives rise to complexity.

- Consumers seek good service, i.e. manufacturers of products have to acknowledge they do operate, to some extent, in a similar way to a service industry. In terms of Maslow's hierarchy, consumers now have their physiological and security needs satisfied and are seeking the less tangible belonging and esteem needs which are met more by service than specification.

These three effects, namely global competition, complexity and customer service, and their further consequences are discussed below and illustrated in Figure 1.1.

Global competition

The advent of global competition is one of the main reasons for the new interest in overhead control. In the past, when markets were localised, a company only had to be as competitive as those in the locality. If a potential competitor with a better way of doing things existed elsewhere, it did not present a challenge.

This has now changed. Obviously if a company is choosing to export into a foreign market it must be competitive in terms of cost, quality and timeliness, compared to its rivals in that country. It is equally true for a domestic concern; while it may not have international aspirations, its customers will receive the attentions of foreign companies who do. In these circumstances only 'world-class' performance will suffice.

If all this seems too depressing, there is a positive side. Not only are there threats from overseas, there are also opportunities. If a company can attain world-class performance its rewards are now on a global scale.

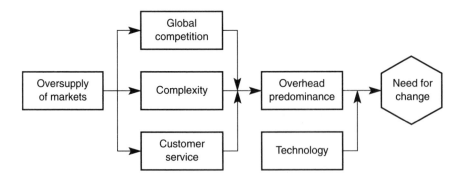

Figure 1.1 Pressure for change

Complexity

Increased competition alone, however, would not have led to the renewed interest in the control of overhead activities. If companies were similar to those which prevailed during the Industrial Revolution, the emphasis would be on minimising the cost of materials and direct labour. At that time companies offered a relatively small range of products, with long product life cycles. This had two effects:

- The administrative demands of such a company were not great and therefore the overheads were relatively easy to control.
- The overheads themselves were therefore not the predominant portion of cost and therefore the issue of their efficiency of operation or economy of the resources consumed was not a major issue.

The situation is now completely changed. Complexity has now permeated all levels of the business, including:

- *Markets and customers*. Different customers and markets have different requirements, in terms of buyer behaviour, packaging and distribution. Supporting this diversity within the company is costly and places large demands on the control systems of the company.
- *Products*. To differentiate themselves from competitors or to avoid focus on particular markets and competing on price alone, the product portfolio of most companies is broadening. This obviously leads to an increase in complexity in the design and manufacturing areas, but this is only part of the infliction. Wide product variety imposes demands on forecasting, scheduling, purchasing, inventory holding and, of course, general management time.
- *Operations*. Capital investment has greatly reduced the number of operators who are directly involved in producing a product or service. In parallel there has been a proliferation of support activities, ranging from maintenance to sophisticated scheduling. The control of an array of support activities is more demanding than a few manually intensive operations with large numbers of people doing the same thing.

In fact this growth in complexity has progressed to the point where it must be reversed. An important part of the approach to controlling overheads which is advocated in this book is the identification of the underlying reasons for complexity, namely the products and customers which cause it to happen. This is then carried forward to the quantification of the costs through activity-based costing so a rational view can be taken on whether the revenue from a particular product or customer justifies its support; in parallel with this, opportunities for reducing complexity through reorganisation often present themselves.

Furthermore, there is a desire to define the organisation's business and, from this definition, understand its key competences. The organisation then concentrates on these competences alone and contracts out the peripheral activities. In this way, the management avoids being swamped by complexity and can focus on the processes which really matter.

Customer service

The production of a product or a service can no longer proceed protected from the demands of its recipients. As a consequence of having to increase the quality of service delivered for the various markets and customers, we see additional demands on the overhead functions from:

- more complex scheduling of operations to provide flexibility;
- the introduction of new dimensions, other than cost, to customer satisfaction, namely time and quality.

The first of these points follows the removal of the barriers between the customer and the company's operations. All other things being equal, an increase in flexibility leads to an increase in the need for support functions, though in response to this there is now a drive to rearrange the operations of organisations to make them inherently more flexible, often through the reduction of inventory and lead times.

The second item is both an opportunity and a problem. If customers are no longer simply interested in obtaining the lowest price, it is possible for the company to obtain higher prices through the provision of superior quality or delivery times. Nonetheless, competing on these additional parameters requires changes to systems and performance measures. It can also lead to a growth in overhead functions.

The increase in overhead functions means that overhead costs now exceed the labour costs of most organisations.

Overhead predominance

Most overhead functions involve skilled white-collar tasks, which are usually difficult to define closely and consequently are difficult to measure. They require developed skills and as a result the human resource is expensive.

The trend in productivity improvement in this area has not been encouraging. The most optimistic research has suggested that white-collar productivity can increase at a rate of perhaps two per cent per year, though this compares unfavourably with an average blue-collar rate of increase of some four per cent per year. However, much of this productivity improvement is concentrated in the more mundane clerical tasks and not in the higher skill functions. Furthermore the disappointing increases in productivity have occurred despite large investments in information technology.

One reason for the inability of traditional approaches to deliver improvements in the skilled white-collar areas is that departments and even individuals have multiple roles. This makes pinning down what people actually do, let alone measuring and improving it, very difficult. For this reason there is a new interest in 'activity-based management' techniques which seek to closely define the activities of an organisation prior to their improvement. One of these is activity-based costing, which has received particular prominence.

We now discuss how the role of the white-collar worker has been affected by advances in information technology.

Technology

The increased rate of technological change places additional demands on the task of controlling overheads. Changes in product technology shorten product life cycles and this demands adaptability and speed of response from the overhead functions.

In addition there are changes in process technology. For overhead processes the relevant technology is, of course, information technology. The technology can appear to be a blessing, though, in a competitive environment, if the technology is not properly managed the organisation will be at risk from better-equipped competitors.

Advances in technology can provide incremental benefits, which arise from doing the same work more efficiently. More radically, they allow an entirely new approach to be taken to a current task or even make a task feasible, where previously it was impossible.

Traditionally information technology has been used to eliminate clerical labour from tasks, thereby reducing staff costs, or for computation and analysis. However, when combined with advances in communication, new opportunities present themselves:

- *Better scheduling and monitoring*. It now becomes possible to plan and track the position of an item in far closer detail, perhaps through a factory or a distribution network.
- *Removal of 'middle-men'*. Rapidity of communication can remove entire stages of a process, threatening those who have created brokerage positions.
- *Reduction of lead time*. In the past the transmission of information was time consuming, especially over large distances. Transmission time need not now be a major obstacle to transacting business.

- *Artificial intelligence.* This is the most recent opportunity offered by information technology, in the form of expert systems and neural networks. Information systems have always been used for the storage of data, but the drawing of inferences from these data in ambiguous circumstances is a new facility, which allows the dissemination of expertise throughout the organisation.

These factors are leading to greater integration of an organisation, as information is captured at one point and on one occasion and is then accessible to all, no matter where they are situated. Given the waste and lack of co-ordination associated with poor and inconsistent management information, the potential rewards are large, even if they have been elusive in the past. Some of these past failures have been due to faulty implementation, which has led to the full potential of the system not being realised. In other cases the failure has been due to the installation of technology on top of an imperfect organisational system.

To deal with the last point the proposed programme considers both the organisational and information technology issues in tandem.

RESPONSES

Overview

The impression that will have emerged from the previous section is that the world is getting to be a more complicated and competitive place. Previously, organisations were relatively simple; certainly, they may have employed large numbers of people, but these people were engaged on simple tasks that were easy to measure. Furthermore, it seemed that the demand for goods was insatiable; customers counted themselves lucky to own the products and were not too demanding in their expectations of customer service.

By contrast, today companies have to offer a wider variety of products to customers who are willing to go elsewhere if they are not satisfied, and there is no shortage of competitors to offer an alternative. As if this were not enough, the internal operations of the company are far more difficult to define. A smaller number of more expensive people carry out a variety of tasks that are difficult to monitor.

Given this shift it is not surprising there has been a major drive to understand overheads and to bring them under control. For example, successful companies do not place a high premium on the tight cost control of direct labour; instead they raise productivity through superior design of products and services and in their use of overhead functions to add value.

To respond to these changes, companies must change. This change is occurring on three fronts:

- *new analysis tools*, to allow the more complex overhead structures to be understood;
- *better costing and performance measurement systems*, to ensure the new complex organisations work in unison to satisfy the customer and take full advantage of the improvement in information technology;
- *cultural change*, to maximise responsiveness and ensure the better information systems allow delegation of responsibility to the lowest possible level to avoid needless checking and authorisation.

These three factors follow in sequence, in that the new analysis tools guide the design of the new information systems, which in turn allow changes to the way people assume responsibilities. To bring these changes about requires traditionally separate disciplines, such as marketing, activity-based costing, information technology and human resource skills, to be combined. We now discuss how the use of these disciplines can bring about the necessary change, starting with a brief summary of the contemporary problems in each of these areas, and conclude with a discussion of 'outsourcing', which is a further response to the new competitive conditions.

Analysis tools

The roots of the previous difficulty in managing overheads are, first, a lack of understanding on how the overhead structure relates to a customer's need and, second, the inability to relate resource input to individual activities and outputs. These points glare out when the prime tool for traditional overhead control is considered: the annual budget. Much of a departmental manager's time is spent in the ritual activity of making 'bids' for budgeted expenditure from the bottom, defending attempts to trim the budget imposed from the top and finally explaining 'variances' from the budget, many of which are outside his control.

The blindfolds in this corporate 'egg-dance', which is generally performed with more panache in the public than the private sector, are impenetrable. The bid for expenditure is based on the need to maintain or increase the expenditure of a department; the function of a single department has little relevence to a customer and therefore the value of the expenditure cannot be easily evaluated. For the same reason, when the corporate centre seeks to reduce expenditure to a sustainable level it has no mechanism for considering the relative priority of various areas and consequently applies across the board cuts or is swayed by personal advocacy. Finally, the inability to relate resource input to output, or even individual activities, frustrates the ability to monitor efficiency.

Much of the remainder of this book is concerned with describing a co-ordinated set of analysis tools to overcome these shortcomings.

Costing and performance measurement systems

'You get what you measure' is a familiar adage. This should be encouraging, since it suggests that the control of overheads can be reduced to the selection of an appropriate set of performance measures, though of course life is not so simple. The reverse side of the coin is that the wrong set of measures can cause havoc. Before considering the changes required to the existing information systems, it may be worthwhile to take stock of their most common problems.

The most benign problem is the simple absence of the information necessary to take decisions. In these cases the manager falls back on the bounded rational approach to decision making and uses his intuition. He may often comment on the need for sound judgement or preface assertions with 'I believe' or 'In my opinion'. Phrases such as these are sure signs of a lack of knowledge; no one says 'I believe two plus two equals four', instead it is an accepted fact. The lack of management information in some organisations can appear bizarre to an outsider; for example, product rationalisation exercises are carried out without access to product profitability information, price negotiations are carried out without access to customer profitability information and budgets are set without reference to activity levels. Those on the inside are supported in the belief of their own judgement, though of course good judgement must be based on fact.

A further common problem is inconsistent information or information presented in an inconvenient form. The symptoms are a proliferation of inefficient and inconsistent PC spreadsheet and database applications, usually supported by manual rekeying of information. Such a situation arises when the information needs of the managers have not been assessed and they therefore have to resort to developing their own systems. The solution is to determine the information requirements in a systematic way and invest in the technology to support coherent systems, e.g. data links between the corporate systems and managers' PCs are a relatively simple way of encouraging consistency of data and avoiding manual re-entry of data.

A more subtle problem is where an opportunity to carry out tasks in a different way has been missed because of outdated technology. The managers of the organisation may not be aware of the technology currently available. To address this issue requires a fresh look at the organisation's business processes and a 'green field' solution to be developed, often by outsiders who are familiar with current technology. In some cases the use of advanced technology, such as knowledge-based systems, can yield massive improvements, e.g. an order of magnitude reduction in lead time or staffing levels.

The final and the most common shortcoming in most cost and performance measurement systems is the inappropriate use of proxies. The organisation as a whole will have a set of top-level targets on which the senior management measure their success, e.g. return on capital, market share. These however cannot be used directly to measure middle management, so a different set of parameters is used; examples might include machine utilisation, proportion of on-time deliveries or budget variances. Two problems can arise from this substitution:

- the subsidiary targets are incompatible with top-level targets, with the result that the actions of middle management are incompatible with the aspirations of top management;
- the subsidiary targets are incompatible with themselves, with the result that the middle managers of the organisation are not working in concert.

Reform of the cost and performance measurement systems begins with the process perspective which was described previously. Once the organisation and its component activities have been related to the business processes which support a customer's requirement, it is then possible to define a set of process measures which work in unison to meet that requirement; in some cases the measures will simply be the customer's eventual requirement broken down into small parts and applied to individual activities.

Furthermore it is now possible to start defining the major decisions that have to be taken within a process for it to operate well and consequently to define the information requirements of the managers and operators. This definition of the information requirements is the first step in defining the information strategies needed to support the business process.

The cost and information systems are therefore constructed to support the processes, and their component activities, which satisfy the customer. This is in contrast to many of the existing systems which were developed to serve the organisational structure; often the boundaries of these information systems coincide with the organisational boundaries and the performance parameters themselves are related to a narrow definition of departmental performance rather than measuring the behaviour which the customer perceives.

Cultural change

It is worth bearing in mind that most of the overhead function 'walks on two legs'. No matter how impressive the analysis or the systems, if the staff have the wrong attitudes or are prevented from using their ability, very little will improve. In bringing about an organisation where improvement is possible, there are two dominant principles.

The first is that the organisation should be framed so as to meet the need of the customer as opposed to any functional specialisation. The reason for this is that most problems within organisations occur at the interfaces between subdivisions. It is at these interfaces that the responsibility for actions is most ambiguous and there is often a discontinuity between information systems. Enhancing customer service requires minimising the number of interfaces that must be crossed to satisfy a customer demand and designing a 'pipeline' into which a customer demand is input and from which emerges a satisfied customer requirement.

This distinction is often expressed as a contrast between the organisation represented by the internal functional hierarchy and the organisation represented by the processes which traverse the organisation and satisfy the customers' requirements. Moving from a functional form to a process form may seem simple in principle but it does have a profound impact on the strengths and weaknesses of an organisation and the career progression of staff:

- Functional structures encourage functional excellence, whether this be in accounting, research or manufacturing. Process structures encourage co-ordination between disciplines.
- Following on from the above, staff who succeed in functional organisations are those who master their chosen specialism. On the contrary, staff who prosper in a process environment are multidisciplinary and can appreciate the operation of the overall process.

A change from a functional to a process view is therefore likely to be controversial, if the implications are fully understood.

The second dominant principle is to push responsibility down to the lowest possible level within an organisation and allow all within the organisation to use their initiative to the greatest possible extent. This is in contrast to practice earlier in this century where tasks were subdivided into small components, to the point where the individual did not have a view of how his work fitted into the overall picture and did not have any latitude to exercise initiative. This earlier system chose to maximise efficiency and reduce variation by very close definition of the task and the removal of individual discretion. This was appropriate to the era of mass production but creates difficulty where it is necessary to provide flexibility and deal with complexity.

Allowing staff to use their initiative permits them to respond flexibly to a more uncertain environment while minimising the additional overhead costs.

In the last step of the programme we discuss the difference between 'crisp' and 'fuzzy' structures and when each type is most appropriate. At this stage we simply note that the increase in complexity faced by overhead functions makes it less economic to use staff in a highly directed fashion and more economic to permit discretion. This trend has coincided with advances in technology which have made it possible for staff to have greater access to information, thereby increasing the potential for decisions being made at a lower level within the organisation.

There are also substantial cost and lead-time savings to be obtained in avoiding the continual checking and approval of decisions taken at lower levels in the organisation. Here again technology can assist by use of artificial intelligence techniques to provide expert, on-line assistance for junior staff.

Outsourcing options

'Outsourcing' refers to the subcontracting of substantial parts of overhead processes. There is nothing new about subcontracting itself: there has always been a possibility of gain if the factors in favour of subcontracting – e.g. access to economies of scale in a specialised subcontractor – exceed the factors against, such as the additional cost of managing a new supplier. Subcontracting on this local level will continue to be an option.

What is new is the willingness to subcontract whole tranches of activity, as long as they are not considered to be strategic to the business. The logic behind this move is that organisations cannot be good at everything. They should therefore focus on being good at what is essential for their success, and allow other organisations to handle the rest. Often, the major advantage of such a move is that the attention of the senior management is no longer cluttered with the minutiae of administration and therefore they can concentrate on matters of genuine importance.

The move to outsourcing has major implications for the shape and culture of the company. The company will tend to consist of a core of key staff, who call upon the services of outside companies. In some cases the outsiders are not companies but simply 'outworkers', who are not viewed as being genuinely part of the organisation.

The risks and benefits are therefore apparent. Management attention is more focused but there is a risk of loss of control over quality as the organisation becomes dependent on those it does not care for, and who do not care for it.

THE FIVE-STEP APPROACH

Project focus

It is possible to consider the task of creating new information for the control of overheads as either a specific project or as part of the ongoing tasks of a nominated department. There are several advantages in creating a formal project, which include:

- Projects have an end. Therefore there is an expectation that the improvement will be delivered by a specific date, rather than begin to appear gradually. This generally improves the probability of delivery.
- High-level backing can be given. The work will require the time and co-operation of many people, which may not be granted if the project has not been given conspicuous backing within the organisation.
- Wide involvement becomes possible. A project team can be formed which can be drawn from across the organisation. This ensures both ownership of the results and a wide contribution to the input.

Continuous improvement

If a project approach is adopted a natural question is whether it is intended to deliver a single improvement or be part of a process of continuous improvement. The answer is that these two objectives are not in any way exclusive.

Where there has been an absence of information to control an organisation effectively it is natural that there is latent potential for saving; usually it is the knowledge that this latent saving exists that is both the motivation and the justification for carrying out the programme. The justification is necessary, since the provision of better information is not without its cost and there has to be a belief that the project will 'wash its face' financially. The latent saving represents a single improvement.

During the initial project, sound information on which to base decisions will have been produced. A natural consequence of better information, especially of a sort that bridges departmental boundaries and focuses on the processes that serve customers, is that those who base decisions on the information will start to think and act in a different way. There is no better vehicle for cultural change than new information. Managers and staff attune very rapidly to the measures on which they are assessed, and act accordingly.

The programme

One approach for a book on controlling overheads would be to set down the major principles, grouped by technical area; the reader would then apply these principles to his own situation. The disadvantage to this approach is that even after reading all the text to gain a rounded view, a major hurdle would exist, namely to apply the understanding of the principles of overhead control to the planning of a set of tasks to achieve it. It is this translation from concept to practice which is usually the greatest difficulty in exercising control and achieving change, particularly in systems with a human element.

To avoid this problem, the approach put forward in this book has been arranged into a sequence of steps in a programme. In this way, the description of the concepts has been directly linked to their implementation. Five steps have been identified; at each step we identify the objectives of the phase, the deliverables and the major issues. We then describe in detail the tasks which need to be carried out and the tools to be used.

The programme is a generic one, formed from the experience of numerous projects carried out in the public and private sectors. Not every task in the programme needs to be executed but the general approach is surprisingly universal. It is equally relevant whether the project seeks short-term or long-term benefits. It applies both to projects which have simple cost reduction as their objective and to those which have wider ambitions for a major performance improvement.

We now describe the five steps and logic behind their sequence. The programme is illustrated in Figure 1.2, which also shows the main flows of information between the steps.

Outline of steps

The five subsequent chapters describe the approach in detail. Each chapter details one step. In summary, these steps comprise:

- *Step 1, External Review*. In bringing overheads under control it is essential to consider the value of activities as well as their cost. An activity's value cannot be considered in isolation: its value derives from its relevance to the business strategy and from its part in a business process, which in turn exists to satisfy a customer requirement. Therefore the first step is to understand the fundamentals of why an overhead exists, and the broad business processes which deliver satisfaction to customers.
- *Step 2, Internal Analysis*. Once the external assessment is complete, the next stage is to understand in close detail the activities which take place within the organisation. Conventionally, organisations measure and

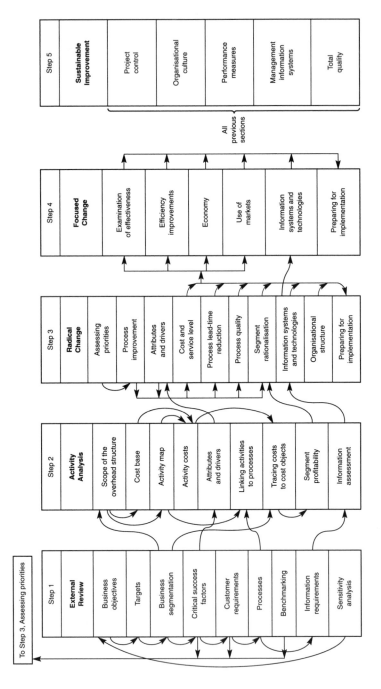

Figure 1.2   Five-step programme

describe themselves in terms of departments, but this description needs to be extended to obtaining an understanding of the actual activities which are undertaken. Acquiring an activity-based view of the corporation is absolutely necessary for rational control of overheads.

- *Step 3, Radical Change.* Following from an understanding of the external demands on an organisation and its internal activities, there will emerge options for comprehensive changes in the way whole processes are structured and the portfolio of products and services which is offered. These options need to be explored to identify benefits that accrue from a major alteration in the overhead structure.

- *Step 4, Focused Change.* Not all improvements that are available will involve widespread change. Once the overall shape of the organisation has been determined there will remain many opportunities for making gains in value for money through incremental improvements in effectiveness, efficiency and economy within particular parts of the organisation or through the use of markets.

- *Step 5, Sustainable Improvement.* Project planning is undertaken to prepare for implementation. Barriers to effective implementation are also considered, e.g. poor corporate culture or inappropriate performance measures.

While these steps form a natural sequence there are different possibilities of ordering the programme, which are discussed in the next section.

Sequence of steps

In bringing overheads under control one possible sequence is to define, *ab initio*, the objectives of the organisation, its customers, their requirements, and the business processes which must be provided to support these requirements. From this fundamental definition of the purpose of the organisation, the component activities are defined and the level of resources set and finally an organisation structure is put in place.

A less radical approach is to begin with the present organisation, make improvements in the existing arrangements and, after these have been achieved, to question whether a more radical approach is then required.

The first approach has the advantage of being the more logical and of having the potential to generate far greater savings, since there is not the danger of being heavily influenced by previous practice. The approach does however involve a greater degree of abstraction than the second approach. As a result the project team has a more difficult task in conveying its ideas to the managers of the existing organisation; in the extreme this can lead to a rejection of the proposals on the grounds they are 'too theoretical', though it would be more accurate to describe them as 'too unfamiliar'.

The second approach would appear to the organisation as more down to earth. Familiar language and departmental structures will be examined and improvements proposed. Furthermore since the proposals for change will be less radical they will be capable of implementation more quickly. The big drawback is that only incremental improvements will be forthcoming and any major gains that may have been possible through changing the basic principles of operation will go undiscovered.

The five step methodology, taken in its natural order, tends more to the first method, though seeks the best of both worlds. Immediately after taking the global view in Step 1, *External Review*, to avoid remaining too conceptual, Step 2, *Internal Analysis* involves a thorough review and costing of the organisation's activities, before any proposals for change are made. Early on in the project therefore, the project team will have acquired a great deal of information on the current organisation and this will help ensure any radical proposals are made with a full understanding of the current activities.

When proposals for change are made, Step 3, *Radical Change* should precede Step 4, *Focused Change* because some of the more radical ideas generated may make some potential local changes irrelevant. However, if a more limited exercise is appropriate to the reader's own organisation, then the initial work could lead from Step 2 to Step 4.

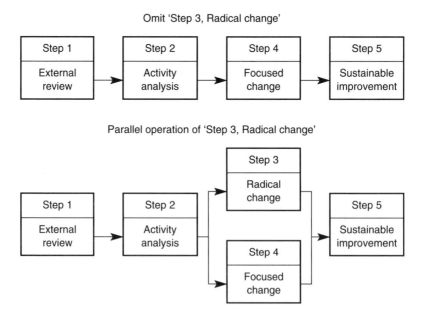

Figure 1.3 Alternative programme sequences

Alternatively, Step 3 and Step 4 could proceed in parallel. This has the advantage of providing evidence of some early benefits to justify belief in the project. The parallel operation of the two steps reduces the chance that any local improvements generated will be incompatible with the more radical proposals. The drawback is that the organisation now would have two independent initiatives taking place at the same time and there would be scope for confusion and overload of the organisations's management as a result.

The different sequences are summarised in Figure 1.3.

Programme timing

The programme usually involves around four months of intensive effort before the start of implementation; this period represents a natural balance between ensuring sufficient time for digesting the information and the risk of a loss of momentum. A typical programme phasing is shown in a bar chart in Figure 1.4, however there can be wide variation from this typical case. Below, we discuss the assumptions underlying the bar chart:

- *Step 1, External Review*. If the appropriate corporate strategy and market research work is in place, then the external review can be completed very rapidly – in a week or two – since the only task is the collation of information. If the basic information does not exist in a usable form, it will need to be collected. There is a case for this being undertaken before the launching of the full project team, since both the corporate strategy and the market research would involve lengthy analysis and the project team would have little to do while the information was being gathered.
- *Step 2, Activity Analysis*. This is a highly intensive part of the programme, during which most of the information needed to make subsequent improvements is gathered. The key to success is to gather detailed information across the breadth of the organisation and to relate it to an activity

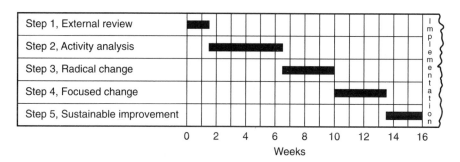

Figure 1.4 Programme timing

framework. The time taken can vary with the size of the organisation, though a duration of four to six weeks can be expected.

- *Step 3, Radical Change*. This is the first creative stage in the programme, where the external and internal views are brought together to identify where major improvements can be made. The idea generation and consultation phase is likely to take three to four weeks, before the more promising ideas are developed to the point where they can be taken over by task forces who will be responsible for implementation.
- *Step 4, Focused Change*. The ideas for improvement generated in this step will be smaller in scope but more numerous. Developing the ideas and obtaining consensus with the departmental managers of the practicality of the changes is likely to take three to four weeks.
- *Step 5, Sustainable Improvement*. This step involves agreeing the structures and systems to enable the changes identified in the earlier steps to take place and be monitored, and the project team handing over the project to the company's management. This may take two to three weeks before the team can be dissolved. The implementation follows and, depending on the changes proposed, may take months or years.

The largest effort is expended in Step 2 because this is the phase in which the organisation is analysed in detail. Thoroughness at this stage ensures proposed savings are regarded as realistic.

Sponsorship

A project to bring overheads under control is best led from outside the finance function. Since the finance function is the source of most of the current quantitative information, it may appear to be the natural choice for leadership of the programme. There are, however, disadvantages and it is often better to choose a sponsor from the marketing or operations area of the organisation, for the following reasons:

- There is likely to be dissatisfaction with the current information provided by the finance function, and this is less likely to translate into scepticism of the proposed project if the sponsor is from elsewhere.
- The finance function is often viewed as the corporate policeman, and if the project is run from this function it could be misinterpreted as an attempt to collect more information with which to criticise operational staff.
- More use is likely to be made of the information by marketing and operational managers if it is viewed as their own and this is more likely to occur if the project is led by the operational managers themselves.

However, regardless of who leads the project, the project team needs to be drawn widely, and include both operational and finance staff.

Project team

We now consider the complement of skills that need to be present in the team for it to function well. A further dimension is the role each member prefers to play in a team, for example chairman, ideas-man etc. Readers interested in this topic should refer to the 'Cultural Change' section of the last chapter.

A broad mix of skills is absolutely essential. Most of the ideas for improvement will arise because, possibly for the first time, there has been an in-depth review of all the functions of the organisation simultaneously. For the review to retain credibility the project team needs to be well versed in the major functions. This will always include the marketing function and operations.

The other necessary skill is a familiarity with the accounting systems. Not only will there be a need to manipulate a large quantity of accounting information but the results of the work will need to be fully credible with competing interests within the organisation, and the accounting systems are usually viewed as the statement of record.

The minimum complement of skills is therefore: marketing, operations and accounting. This is consistent with the minimum recommended size of a project team, namely three including the project leader. Larger organisations require larger teams, though in the author's experience, a team of more than six can become unwieldy and it may be advisable to subdivide the work. After the project and during implementation the number of staff involved in creating change may grow considerably.

It is also a great advantage if a senior person within the team can come from outside the organisation. Many of the issues that need to be addressed will have a history within the company and the presence within the team of an outsider can reassure the managers that even-handed treatment will be applied.

Impetus for change

For the implementation phase to succeed, after the programme itself has concluded, there has to be an overriding pressure to act. Sometimes this is the desire to exploit a new opportunity, more commonly it is reacting to a pressure to change and improve.

Without this impetus there is a danger that the implementation will run into the sand, regardless of the excellence of the analysis. Usually there are losers as well as winners in any change and the determination of the former may exceed that of the latter. Even if there are no serious disadvantages to any party in the proposed change, sheer inertia and preference for the familiar can obstruct any serious improvement.

Therefore, during the programme an assessment has to be made of whether the managers consider the need for change to be paramount. If this is not the case, there must be an inititative to persuade them otherwise.

Hostile environment

The question arises of whether the programme can be made to operate in a hostile environment. The answer is that it can work but the scale of the improvements is likely to be far less. Many of the improvements come about from suggestions from within the organisation itself. If managers hold back or operate according to hidden agendas, fewer benefits will arise. However, if the objectives are mainly concerned with cost reduction, it is possible to achieve useful cost reductions in the teeth of opposition.

It must be stressed that this is far from ideal, so a great effort needs to be made at the start of the project to win over the management of the company and convince them that their long-term interest is best served by co-operating.

Ancillary structures

If the project team works in isolation within the organisation, it will fail. Four types of structure need to be created during the project, the first two at the start of the project and the final two towards the end of the project. Those created at the start comprise a:

- *Control structure*. The manager of the project team needs to report either to the Chief Executive personally or to the Board of Directors. The senior level is necessary because of the significance of the changes which will be produced.
- *Steering group*. The middle management of the organisation needs to be kept informed of progress and the project team needs an independent view on the direction which they are taking. These needs are best met through a steering group, meeting perhaps every two to three weeks during the project. The steering group comprises middle managers from the major functions within the company.

While the project team will be soon become immersed in their own work and, if all goes well, become a cohesive unit, the overall success of the project depends on the receptivity of the organisation. A good reception depends on the two groups defined above being confident of the worth of the project. The implication for the project manager is clear: he must resist the temptation to become totally involved in the details of the project and devote at least half of his time to building confidence in the project within the organisation.

The two groups to be created towards the end of the project are:

- *Task forces*. The advantages of the intensive project approach have already been highlighted. The drawback is that, after the project has finished, the team is dispersed and there are no lasting benefits. The key to a successful transition is to set up groups dedicated to carrying forward specific initiatives. The task forces are formed by managers who are affected by, and can affect, the proposed transition.
- *Monitoring authority*. There is a need to monitor both the performance of the task forces as they implement the widespread changes and the departmental managers as they manage the changes within their own area. Ideally this monitoring authority is the Chief Executive.

It is generally far harder to successfully implement change than to identify the opportunities and to develop the necessary project plans. Implementation requires a far wider participation and there will inevitably be some who prefer the status quo and resist change.

A summary of the relations between the project team and the ancillary structures is shown in Figure 1.5.

Relation to business process re-engineering

This programme for controlling overheads has not been labelled a business process re-engineering approach. The programme for overhead control

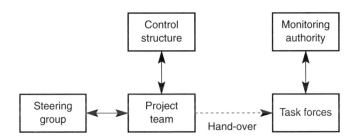

Figure 1.5 Ancillary structures

described in this book emphasises the analysis, design and control of the activities of the organisation, in the context of its selected markets.

Nonetheless for those who are committed to a business process re-engineering approach, the methods outlined in this book should prove useful. In particular:

- The activity analysis methods outlined in Step 2, *Internal Analysis*, will be useful in relating the abstract top-level processes to the real organisation, which can be a severe problem in business process re-engineering.
- The organisational analysis techniques will be useful in identifying where the opportunities for improvement lie and so avoid a 'Now a miracle happens' step in the proceedings.

Compatibility with a business process re-engineering approach is assured because the methods proposed here are based on the process view.

2

EXTERNAL REVIEW

Cast thy bread upon the waters: for thou shalt find it after many days.

ECCLESIATES 11:1

INTRODUCTION

Objectives

The overall objective of Step 1, *External Review*, is to look outside the organisation and confirm the viability of its objectives and strategies. We begin by clarifying the objectives of the organisation, hopefully drawing upon previous business strategy work, and expressing the objectives as a set of targets. Once the target markets and products have been clarified, the next objective is to define the customers, channels and products of the company. The critical success factors, upon which the ability of the organisation to fulfil its objectives depends, are then defined and quantified, as far as possible, into the level of performance in these areas required by customers.

The business processes which are to deliver the required performance are identified and a search made for examples of best practice in these business processes, often referred to as benchmarks. The decisions which have to be made within the processes are examined and these lead to a top-down review of the information needs, the currently available information systems and technologies which can assist in decision support.

Finally the sensitivity of decisions to changes in the business or technology is examined to understand the possible impact on the external review.

Deliverables

In meeting the objectives given above, the project team will have carried out a set of tasks shown in Figure 2.1 and described in subsequent sections. These tasks will generate the following information which will be used in subsequent steps:

- a set of business objectives;
- a set of business targets;
- the business segments, in terms of customers' groups, products (or services) and distribution channels;
- a statement of the business's critical success factors;
- an analysis of the customer requirements;
- a set of core business processes;
- benchmarks showing the level of performance expected in the processes;
- the information required to support the decisions to be taken within the process;
- an assessment of the effects of possible changes in business and technology.

Issues

The first part of the external review draws upon information that should have been produced by a strategic planning exercise, namely a statement of business objectives and targets, a segmentation of the business and a statement of the critical success factors. In practice, this may not have been carried out sufficiently thoroughly prior to the start of the project. If the pro-

Figure 2.1 Step 1, External Review

ject team is responsible for putting right the shortfall this will make heavy demands on the senior management within the organisation.

Analysing customers' requirements obviously requires some contact with these customers, through any market research work which may have been carried out and through discussions with major customers. This is essential, even if there is some reluctance to provide access to customers. The statement of customer requirements should be as detailed and as quantitative as possible, but the practical limitations have to be recognised; if no preliminary work has been done in this area, the team will have to settle for a brief statement of the major factors, deduced from a few interviews.

The identification of the major processes is done in conjunction with senior management, either individually or as a group. The object is to name the processes and delineate their boundaries. The collection of benchmarking information needs the involvement of the senior management, both to agree on the form of the exercise and to enter into agreement with the benchmarking partners. If this has not been started before the start of the programme, it is unlikely to be practical to complete the exercise in the available time.

The identification of the major decision-making areas and their information requirements follow. It might be thought that considering the information requirements of the company before even learning of its detailed activities in Step 2, *Internal Analysis*, is premature. There are however four advantages of obtaining an early top-down view:

- The practicality of the proposed definition of processes can be confirmed. By examining the necessary decisions to support the processes and their information needs, any ambiguity or overlap will be exposed.
- The project team can form an assessment of the information that is ideally required independently of current practice.
- For many processes there are systems commercially available to provide support. These systems provide a view on outside best practice and are a source of ideas with which to challenge the current views of the organisation.
- The state of relevant information technologies can be understood. These could have a dramatic effect on the design of the processes and awareness of these developments may change the emphasis of the internal analysis.

For example, a process may benefit from the use of forecasting. Currently, the company may make little use of forecasting, and in the absence of this information, the advantages are not understood. If the external review showed that trends in technology were permitting better and cheaper forecasting, perhaps through the use of knowledge-based systems, then forecasting would be an issue to be explored during the internal analysis. At this stage, however, we are only seeking an overview and the detailed analysis of information requirements is to be carried out in Step 2.

Finally, the purpose of the sensitivity analysis is to ensure that any proposed organisational or systems solution is relatively robust to future changes.

BUSINESS OBJECTIVES

Required objectives

Before the overhead structure can be put in place, it is necessary to ask 'What is the organisation here for?'. It is a question that is relevant to both the private and the public sector.

In the private sector the answer is usually delivered after a strategic planning exercise involving an examination of the market. In the public sector, the objective is usually provided when the organisation is created. Whatever the source, the stated objectives must not be so platitudinous that they are useless for guiding decisions on the organisation's future. To avoid this, the objectives must:

- be measurable, otherwise it will not be apparent if they have been achieved;
- provide guidance and place constraints on decisions which are faced by managers, otherwise the objectives are redundant.

An indication of the usefulness of the objectives that are eventually adopted is the extent to which they enable decisions on alternative courses of action to be made. If when considering alternatives, it is found that both would allow the business objectives to be met, it may well be that the objectives are too imprecise.

It is unlikely that an organisation's business objectives can be expressed in a single sentence; on the other hand too many subsidiary objectives will blur the clarity of the statement. A statement of the business objectives should include:

- the targets on which the organisation is to be assessed;
- a statement on any constraints faced by the company, e.g. employee and social policies;
- the markets and customers the organisation will serve and the market share or coverage which is desired;
- the products and services which will be delivered to these markets and customers.

While these objectives have been framed in the language of the private sector, all are applicable to the public sector: 'customers' translate directly into 'clients'; while there may not be 'competitors', there will be agencies offering similar services which should not be duplicated and the term 'share-holders' is widened to include all those who have an interest in the organisation, i.e. 'stakeholders'.

If the business objectives have not been refined to thi; degree then this needs to be done prior to the start of the exercise. For public sector organisa-tions this will involve a process of self-examination of what the organisation can best achieve given the needs of its prospective clients and the facilities offered by other agencies. For the private sector, the emphasis is on seeking a viable competitive position. This is not a trivial task and for those starting from scratch, this topic could easily be the subject of a separate book.

However, in the next section we provide a brief overview of the factors to be considered in defining a set of objectives for a private sector organisation, to allow the reader to check the thoroughness of the process by which the organisation's objectives have been derived, and to make enhancements wherever possible.

Defining objectives

The starting point for determining a viable competitive position is defining the market the company intends to operate in. Even the step of actually iden-tifying the market can be difficult, with the danger that the company defines its market in the narrow terms of the product being offered (i.e. the means to an end) while customers take a wider view, including the use of radically different means to obtain the desired result. Sometimes this widening of per-ception can be used by the company itself, e.g. ferry operators facing competition from a high-speed rail link seeking to position their service as the first stage in the holiday experience, as opposed to simple transportation.

Once the market itself has been defined the next step is to clarify its struc-ture. One accepted format for this analysis has been provided in *Competitive Strategy* (Porter, 1980), in which he saw an industry influenced by five sets of forces:

- the power of suppliers, bargaining for the highest prices of the factors of production;
- the power of customers, attempting to minimise the costs of goods and services produced;
- the threat from new entrants to the industry;
- the threat from substitutes for the products and services;
- the pressure that exists in the intensity with which the members of an industry compete.

Overlaying this analysis of competitive forces is the operation of the regula-tory and legal structure and less formal social pressures, which can sometimes be the dominant short-term influence on an industry, whether through manipulation of tariff barriers, employee legislation, anti-monopoly actions, environmental legislation or simply disdain for certain types of goods.

These factors affect the conditions of supply and demand within the industry and ultimately determine the rates of return on capital that are possible. Using these factors a 'snapshot' can be taken, and from this projections made of the:

- changes in the size of the demand from the markets in which the company operates, both as a result of changes in buyer behaviour and the economic cycle;
- productive capacity capable of supplying to the market, including the effect of new competitors or substitute products;
- opportunities and threats presented by takeovers, particularly through integration and the removal of intermediaries;
- implications of new technology. Part of this will be the concerned with the appearance of more advanced or substitute products, or advances in information technology.

The preceding analysis is concerned with the external environment. To complete the exercise it is useful to consider the internal strengths and weakness-

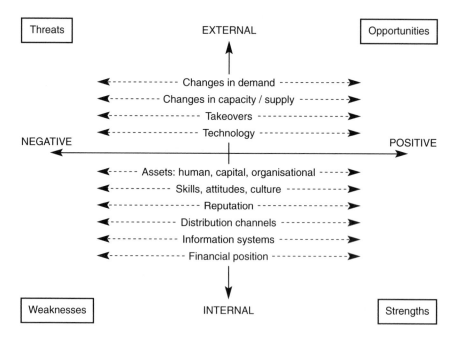

Figure 2.2 SWOT analysis

ess of the organisation. This entails considering the stock of human, capital and organisational assets the organisation possesses, and those assets it is lacking. The scope of this stocktaking is as wide as the organisation itself, but as a minimum would include: key skills, staff attitudes and culture, presence and reputation in markets, distribution channels, information systems and financial position.

All this analysis can then be summarised in the form of a Strengths/Weaknesses/Opportunities/Threats (SWOT) analysis shown in Figure 2.2, to provide an understanding of how the organisation stands in its environment. From this analysis and an appreciation of the constraints of the organisation, business plans can be developed which will influence the statement of objectives in the areas given above.

Agreeing this statement of objectives has to be carried out at the highest level within the organisation and gaining agreement can be difficult. Ideally the organisation will have already carried out a strategic planning exercise and any changes needed will simply be an amplification of detail.

Impact of information systems and technology

One tenet of the proposed programme is that the organisational issues should be considered in tandem with the information issues for the effective design of overhead structures. This is opposed to the typical arrangement where they are considered separately.

The consideration of the information issues begins at the very start of the programme, namely the clarification of the business objectives. The impact of information systems and technology on the competitive position of the company can be assessed using Porter's five-force model as a basis. This was explored in 'Using IS/IT to Gain Competitive Advantage' (Peppard, 1993). If this format is employed, the issues can be summarised as:

- *Suppliers*. Information technology enables a wider and more rapid evaluation to be made of alternative suppliers. Once a supplier is selected, it permits a tighter integration of both the design and operating functions by increasing the volume and celerity of information transfer, thereby enabling new alliances to operate.
- *Customers*. The investment in electronic links can be a double-edged sword; it also has the effect of 'locking in' suppliers to their customers. Therefore it can be an advantage for a company to approach its customers and offer to invest in electronic data interchange so as to increase the switching costs and impede effective competition.

- *New entrants*. If a company wishes to deter new entrants to the market then raising the expectations of customers in terms of cost, time and quality through a large investment in information systems and technology can be effective.
- *Substitute products*. The ability of information technology to accelerate the design process increases the risk of substitute products appearing. Conversely the investment in computer aided design facilities allows a company the option of entering other markets.
- *Competitive rivalry*. Greater access to information and the ability to make a greater number of contacts increase the rivalry which may exist within a given market.

Information technology and systems therefore affect all the influences on competitive position. It is therefore necessary that it is considered when strategy is being formulated.

A second advantage of considering information strategy at this early stage is that it encourages the project team to consider both the systems and the technology as a vehicle for radical change and source of advantage. By searching for potential uses for information system and technology at this early stage, the chance of genuinely radical ideas for the better control of the overhead structure is increased. Any such chance needs to be exploited, because once the programme is under way, the opportunities for minor improvements to the current arrangements usually abound but the ideas for major improvements are less numerous.

TARGETS

Type of target

The question of targets needs elaboration, not least because the nature of the targets and the timescales attached to them will affect the conduct of the proposed programme.

Most organisations face targets expressed in terms of:

- *Profit, earnings per share or dividend payment*. This is the most common situation for a profit centre or for a company where the owners have expectations of sufficient earnings to guarantee a dividend payment. This provides a sharp short-term pressure to increase revenue, or where this is not possible, to reduce costs.
- *Margin or added value*. This measure is common in retail operations, where the merit of the operations is taken as the value added to the inputs expressed as a proportion of revenue.

- *Return on capital or residual income*. These targets seek to capture the efficiency with which capital is utilised. Return on capital is the more common measure, though it is criticised for discouraging capital investment by penalising investment in both the numerator (profit is lessened by depreciation) and the denominator (the capital employed rises). Residual income encourages investment where the increase in profit from an investment is sufficient to counter-act the capital charge.
- *Market share*. These targets apply where the emphasis is on obtaining a position in the market, with a view to the long term. The drawback is of course the lack of recognition of profit. While this target is rarely applied formally outside the sales function, proxies for revenue are often informal targets, where the leaders of an organisation view 'size', expressed as turnover or other unit of throughput, as a virtue in itself.
- *Annual cost*. This particularly applies to cost centres within private organisations and to public organisations, where revenue is difficult to identify. A variation on this is cost per unit of output which seeks to place a target on operational efficiency.

Despite the diversity of targets available, in practice the first three have common implications for the purposes of overhead control. Margin is simply profit expressed as a proportion of revenue. Investment may not be a major issue in overhead control, when compared to the quantities of investment committed elsewhere in the organisation; therefore the capital-related targets have a similar impact to the profit-related targets. The fourth target, market share, is quite different, but when minds are focused, costs are not ignored and the concern returns to profit.

In practice therefore we usually see two basic approaches to overhead control:

- those (such as the first four above) which recognise the value of services to a customer and seek to balance cost against revenue;
- those (such as the fifth listed above) which deal in cost alone and aim for a cost reduction target.

The former assumption clearly leads to a better future, however, unfortunately the regressive second course is the more common! A very typical situation occurs when the managing and finance directors of a company realise halfway through the year that they will not achieve planned earnings, or be able to pay planned dividends, and search for a means to make substantial reductions to the cost base. The assumption is that, for the relevant timescales, revenue cannot be improved upon and therefore the only course is to cut costs by a specified amount.

Whatever the targets used in the organisation, it is essential they are uppermost in the mind of the project team. Not only must the project team deliver a solution that meets the target as far as possible, the changes implied by the solution need to be incorporated into the organisation's operating plans for the purpose of monitoring achievement.

Timing of targets

The timescales associated with the targets are crucial. Targets requiring savings and improvements to occur in the near future place a far greater pressure on the project team to deliver hard proposals, since there is no intervening period for 'development' of the ideas by the local management. This can be a two-edged sword, particularly where cost reduction is involved. On the one hand, the short time available to deliver provides impetus to provide real results, but on the other it can destroy any prospect of co-operation within the company, if managers feel their interests will suffer as a result of this exercise.

Often managers within the organisation are keen to acknowledge savings in the distant future, but not in the nearer term; this should not be encouraged. A saving or an improvement achieved early is far more useful than one achieved later. This is not only the case because the net present value of the cash flows is greater but, more to the point, savings and improvements which are projected to occur in the distant future usually do not happen. There will often be an intervening reorganisation or staff change which will destroy accountability for achieving the improvements.

During the work, the project team must always be mindful of the required timing. There is little point developing grandiose plans for long-term improvements when the expectation is for action in the short term.

Announcement of the project

When the project is announced to the organisation, the announcement should include a statement to the management involved in the study on the objectives of the project. This statement should link the project objectives to the attainment of specific corporate targets. In this way the management can place the project in the context of the business plans which the organisation is working to achieve.

BUSINESS SEGMENTATION

Principles

Dividing the business into segments is essential for proper control of its overheads, with the exception of small homogeneous companies. If this is not done, information on parts of the business with different characteristics will be mixed and the quality of the information will be impaired.

Since we have stated that the basic purpose of the project is to control overheads by obtaining the information necessary for rational decision making, the rigour of the whole exercise depends on finding the right basis for division. The information produced during the project will be aggregated into these segments to support major decisions; not only must the segments form sensible groupings, but it is also important to avoid being swamped by detail by the use of too fine a level of subdivisions.

The first step in the segmentation is to identify the major groupings which are relevant to the external view of the business, often in terms of:

- *Markets and customers*. Where there are a few large customers these are also identified individually; smaller customers are grouped into market segments.
- *Distribution channels*. If the same markets and customers use different distribution channels, these need to be identified. In cases when a given customer or market uses only one distribution channel, these segments fuse into those defining markets and customers.
- *Products or services*. The broad product and service ranges need to be identified.

This identification should not be difficult because these parameters were defined in the statement of business objectives. The aim should be to restrict the number of segments to no more than thirty. If there are far more than this then the procedure for tracing costs to the objects becomes too complex and the resultant information becomes too detailed to be useful.

We now outline the factors which need to be considered when defining the segments.

Markets and customers

In aggregating customers and markets the intention is to group together different types of customer, according to:

- any special activities or demands which they impose on the overhead structure, i.e. special cost behaviour;
- any special values they place on goods and services, i.e. special revenue behaviour.

If no groups of customers or markets pose specific demands there is no need for this dimension to the analysis, since the profitability of each individual customer is simply determined by the cost of its product mix and its revenue.

It is unusual, however, for affairs to be so simple, because:

- large customers are in a position to impose their own conditions on suppliers and these will involve particular costs and pricing structures;

- different markets, e.g. inland or export, will almost always involve different activities.

The key to dividing the customers into profiles is to identify groups of customers who place similar demands on the organisation; some of these groups may represent a large proportion of the revenue of the organisation. This is not a problem as long as the groups are genuinely homogeneous.

When grouping customers in this way it is essential that the groups are compatible with the market segments which the organisation recognises in its management of the marketing department, since the marketing expenditure, which can often be a considerable cost, will already have been allocated to existing segments. If the project team uses segments compatible with existing classifications then the cost allocation and hence the calculation of segment profitability becomes straightforward. Compatibility between the proposed and existing classification does not imply that they are the same, only that one classification can be easily mapped onto the other.

Distribution channels

Often the distribution channels of an organisation are customer or market specific, but it may be the case that particular customers or markets receive goods through more than one distribution channel. Where these channels have different revenue and cost characteristics it is necessary to recognise these, so later, the parts of the business which support these channels can be examined separately.

The classification of these segments is usually quite straightforward, since the number of different types of channels is frequently quite small. Examples for a retail business might include:

- the customer collects;
- delivery to the customer's distribution depots;
- delivery to the customer's retail outlets.

These might multiply however if distribution revenue or costs depend on a geographic zone. In this case it is necessary to segment the customer base into zones depending on the distance of delivery and the charges made.

Products and services

Many, often most, overhead activities can be related to particular product or service ranges, as opposed to customers. The broad product or service ranges need to be identified. The principles in defining the ranges are similar to those defined for customers:

- to consider whether a particular group of products or services places a different demand on the overhead activities than another type;
- whether there is a need to calculate product or service profitability for a particular range, perhaps to review pricing policy, i.e. the customers consider this range to have individual characteristics.

In practice, there is usually little difficulty in drawing up the list of main product ranges to be analysed for manufacturing and most service companies. However, there are some organisations that do not think in terms of either products or services; such a case would be a retail organisation selling one product, e.g. petrol stations. The response is simply not to define any product or service cost objects but to concentrate the analysis in other areas, e.g. distribution channels.

Other types of segments

Other types of division can be created; an example would be different suppliers to an organisation. If the overhead activities to support different suppliers varied dramatically, then it would be necessary to analyse this in order to control the overhead activities and costs. To do this would require the major supplier groups to be identified as business segments so costs could be traced separately.

Later in this chapter we will also discuss another major type of classification – the business process. When tracing revenues and costs to business processes this is done independently of the allocations to the business segments, i.e., the whole of the revenue and costs amount is allocated to business processes in a second and independent exercise.

CRITICAL SUCCESS FACTORS

Competitive position

The critical success factors are simply a catalogue of what the organisation must deliver if it is to meet its objectives. Most of these factors will refer to the customers' requirements. In the private sector this will in turn relate to buyer behaviour.

While the term 'critical success factor' may be unfamiliar to some readers, the concept is almost certainly not. It has occurred in many different forms, as illustrated by the classifications given below:

- *Cost, time and quality.* In project-related environments this is a common division. Different customers will have a different balance of expectations; e.g. 'a man on the moon by the end of the decade' was a case of absolute priority to time and quality at the expense of cost. In other cases a customer may need something on time and to budget, but is prepared to compromise on quality. In delivering a specific product or service, it is essential to understand the customer's own priorities in these terms; if this is not done, the final result may be judged a failure, simply because there was the wrong emphasis.

- *Price, position, product, promotion/packaging.* Since most success factors are linked to customer satisfaction it is not surprising that the 'Four Ps' of the marketing mix, concerned with influencing buyer behaviour, can be used as a framework for analysis. Indeed, the four Ps are re-expressions of the cost, time, quality formula in corresponding order, with the last term 'quality' covering both 'product' and 'promotion/packaging' categories in the marketing mix. A further restatement of the same concept is given in the third classification below.
- *Cost, delivery and specification/quality.* This classification, which uses the language of supply chain performance, is similar to the previous two. Converting from the marketing mix terminology, 'price' and 'cost' are linked, as are 'position' and 'delivery' and, finally, 'product' and 'promotion/packaging' are equivalent to 'specification/quality'. This classification also reflects a division of the expectations of customers at the end of the supply chain, so a customer may accept poor delivery arrangements for low cost but expect a high-quality product, e.g. driving to a discount warehouse to buy a consumer durable, or alternatively accepting poor quality in return for rapid delivery, e.g. visiting a fast-food bar in preference to waiting in a restaurant.

The classifications used are a matter of convenience only, but adopting a classification that is familiar to the managers within the organisation and its

COST	TIME	QUALITY
Initial purchase cost	Quotation lead time	Closeness of fit of specification to need
Life-cycle cost	Design lead time	Conformance to specification
Recurring/Non-recurring cost	Delivery lead time	Reliability of product
	Support response time	Delivery reliability
		Promotion and packaging
		Product/service support

Figure 2.3 Critical success factors

customers helps gain acceptance for the concept of critical success factors. To assist in this discussion we will now give some practical examples of critical success factors. They have been divided into the categories of cost, time and quality. The factors are summarised in Figure 2.3.

Cost factors

There may be a few customers for whom cost is no object but most are concerned with value for money. The numerator, value, is concerned with both timeliness and quality, which are discussed below. The denominator, cost, seems straightforward but has many aspects to it. The relevant cost will depend on the product or service being purchased and the sophistication of the buyer:

- *Initial purchase cost.* For consumer goods this is the salient cost. When this is understood by manufacturers and retailers, the response is often to lower initial purchase prices and raise support costs! The most extreme example is a major film manufacturer which sold cameras at cost so as to increase the subsequent sales of film.
- *Life-cycle costs.* To avoid the ploy described above the more sophisticated buyer will estimate the total cost involved in retaining a product for a period, accounting for support costs, resale value and so forth.
- *Recurring and non-recurring costs.* Where the volume of future purchases is uncertain, then the fixed and variable elements can be separated. This distinction becomes important when potential buyers have very different volume requirements, so a company's cost structure may appear competitive to one customer but not so to another.

We will discuss the subject of overhead cost extensively in subsequent chapters as a means to reducing the eventual cost to customers. However before reducing costs it is necessary to understand which costs are important to the customer. Otherwise there is the risk of minimising the wrong type of cost.

Timeliness factors

The importance of responsiveness in competition is now being fully recognised. Timeliness can be critical all the way through the life-cycle of a product or a service, from quotation, to design, to manufacture and finally to aftersales service:

- *Quotations lead-time.* In the financial services sector, in particular, the ability to offer a rapid quotation, perhaps a property mortgage to a customer in a race to exchange contracts on the property, has become a key competitive parameter. Providing a quotation can be far from simple, e.g. for computer vendors when the configuration of a working system for a particular requirement is not a trivial task.

- *Design lead-time.* For manufacturing companies this can be the most important timeliness parameter of all. The ability to introduce new products consistently more quickly than the competition is a massive advantage. The company which can develop and deliver products more quickly will succeed even where its prices are not the lowest; they provide high value-added products which command high margins, which are reinvested in yet more superior products.
- *Delivery lead-time.* This is a well-recognised performance parameter. The speed of delivery of a standard product, though not a service, can be improved by holding inventory at considerable cost; however, a better approach is to redesign the supply chain processes.
- *Support response time.* The quality of after-sales support will affect a rebuy particularly for capital items or consumer durables. The most crucial service is usually repair and maintainance and naturally the timeliness with which this is provided is of prime importance.

Since timeliness is one of the key factors in becoming and remaining competitive, it is an area on which performance measures should be focused. In a later chapter we explore the whole topic of performance measures, including those concerned with lead-time.

Quality factors

Quality is an elusive element of any product or service. The value attached to 'quality' cannot be disputed but it is often unlinked to the specification of the product itself, residing instead in the perception of the product, the outlets through which it is distributed, or the way it is packaged. The critical success factors in this area are therefore varied. They include:

- *Closeness of fit between the product and the customer's need.* The alignment between product and need is important than generally superior technical performance. One method that has been used to align the technical design of a product and service with the customer's needs is Quality Function Deployment, which will be discussed later, since it is as relevant to process design as to product design.
- *Conformance to specification.* This is applicable where a formal specification has been drafted. Where this is the case, conformance is essential. The reason is that many customers, in a desire to control their own overheads, wish to avoid incoming part inspection so look to their suppliers to provide conforming parts. Failure to do so can be dire, since a concomi-

tant change is usually to reduce the number of suppliers, and those who cannot supply conforming parts are the first to go. The preferred method of ensuring close conformance to specification is to rely on tight control of the processes leading to delivery, rather than on repeated inspection.

- *Reliability of the product.* Where a physical product is delivered, then reliability is usually a factor which influences customer satisfaction. One method which is used to analyse and improve this performance is Failure Mode Effect Analysis, which rigorously catalogues the possible failures, their likelihood and their effect.
- *Delivery reliability.* The ability to stick to delivery schedules or delivery promises clearly is a buying point in many industries. To achieve it, the first step is to ensure that the original schedule or promise is realistic, rather than that necessary to gain the order. Once this is assured, the task then becomes one of control of the underlying processes.
- *Promotion and packaging.* For many goods, consideration of the specification of the product is irrelevant. The purchase, and hence the success of the company, depends on the perception presented by the promotion and the packaging.
- *Product/service support.* Finally, a customer will often not view the purchase of a product or a service as an isolated transaction. There is an expectation of subsequent support. This is particularly the case in the purchase of large equipment. Succeeding in this area is not only a matter of performance but also of perception. Improving the way the customer views the quality of support is a matter for 'customer care' programmes.

The customer's expectation of product or service performance is central to the rational control of overhead because these expectations, and the subsequent design of product or service itself, are the main determinants of the overhead activities necessary to support production and delivery. Mismeasurement of customers' expectations in this area can lead to the operation of an overhead structure that is uncompetitive compared to a rival which has understood the customers' requirements correctly.

Treatment of different markets

An important point in considering each of the three elements of an organisation's success factors is that, even for the same product or service, the factors will differ between markets. For example, a car when sold to the consumer market may be evaluated on initial cost but a leasing company will calculate the life-cycle cost; taking delivery, the leasing company buyer may place great store on reliability of delivery, whereas the consumer market may be more interested in delivery timing.

While a fresh set of factors should not be needed for each market or customer, the potential for different requirements needs to be recognised and accounted for in the analysis. This point is explored further in the final case study.

CUSTOMER REQUIREMENTS

Introduction

Once the critical success factors have been identified, the next stage is to translate them into specific customer requirements. To do this requires an understanding of the buying behaviour of the customers in each of the markets served by the organisation.

The only way to understand buying behaviour is to talk to customers; this can be done informally or through market research programmes. To the traditional mind, the use of market research to control overheads would seem bizarre, but of course once overheads are accepted as potentially adding value then the first step must be to find out what, in particular, the customer finds valuable.

This is best illustrated by the parallel with 'value engineering'. Some years ago the author was commissioned to carry out a value engineering exercise on a large piece of capital machinery. Large amounts of cost had been added to the design to create various advanced features, not least a large free-standing control console, which was viewed as a major step forward. While this was the pride of the design department, no feedback had been obtained from customers on the worth of these additions, despite the fact that there were several local customers who were willing to give a few hours of their time. The results of the discussions with the customers were startling. Many of the expensive 'advanced features' were irrelevent and the free-standing control console, in particular was viewed as a positive nuisance because it blocked the factory aisles! The lesson was simple: a few hours in the company of the customer is time well spent.

There are two stages to analysing customer requirements:

- the first is to translate, if necessary, the success factors into qualities recognised by the customer and to add sufficient detail to allow the customer to state his preferences unambiguously;
- the second is to measure the importance the customer attaches to the different requirements.

After outlining the theory of buyer behaviour, we describe these two steps: namely the identification of the requirements and then their quantification. We then outline a specialised measurement technique, which may be of use for some readers.

Buyer behaviour

This section considers the theoretical foundation for the analysis of buyer behaviour and customer requirements. It is not essential to understand the material to conduct the overhead control programme, however it should be enlightening for those readers who wish to understand the basic principles behind setting customer service levels.

There are different approaches to the analysis of buyer behaviour. Some are concerned with psychological and social motivations. However, to examine customer preferences on overheads, we are concerned with economic motivation. The framework for this examination is provided by 'utility theory', which is a major element of economic theory.

The 'utility' of an item refers to its usefulness, or value, expressed in monetary terms. Curiously, despite the heavy use of the term 'value', its measurement, in terms of utility, is rarely considered. The simplest arrangement assumes that the value of some goods is proportional to the quantity possessed, i.e. the relation between utility and quantity is linear. For most goods this is not the case: the amount paid for, and hence the value of, the thousandth item would be less than for the first. Therefore, for this case, the marginal utility decreases with the quantity consumed.

In economics, this is referred to as 'The Law of Diminishing Marginal Utility'. Unlike the laws of physics, however, the laws of economics can be broken! A minor exception concerns necessities, which have an infinite marginal utility for the necessary quantity; for example, as Mark Twain observed 'Each person is born to one possession which outvalues all others – his last

Figure 2.4 Utility model

breath'. The second exception concerns small initial quantities of an item which is not a necessity. It is possible that small quantities are viewed as not worth having, so have a small marginal utility, while moderate quantities have a larger marginal utility.

We now have a basis for evaluating the performance of the organisation in the eyes of its customers, which is shown in Figure 2.4. For a given parameter, e.g. lead time, there will be:

- a minimum level of performance, below which the customer will not buy, i.e. for performance below this level there is zero marginal utility;
- a range of performance, in which increasing performance leads to increasing value, i.e. there is positive marginal utility;
- a high level of performance, beyond which performance has no value, i.e. there is a zero marginal utility.

The ideal situation is, for each element of performance, to be able to identify the high and low breakpoints and the value the customer attaches to increasing performance in the range between the breakpoints.

Identification of customer requirements

The critical success factors are a statement of what the business must achieve if it is to meet its objectives. This is one step away from a statement of customer requirements, which is more detailed. So, for example, if 'prompt delivery' is a critical success factor, this needs amplification to show how rapid delivery should be.

The next step is to ask the customer to value the different requirements. The simplest method is to ask the customer to rank their requirements in order of importance, e.g. particular product features, levels of delivery performance, etc. This can be quite useful in clarifying customer needs. This in turn can show the necessary emphasis of the overhead activities required to meet these needs and the level of performance that is required. However, the method is rather coarse.

An obvious refinement is for the customer to quantify his expectations of performance. So, for example:

- cost expectations need to be quantified, either in terms of an absolute level of cost or as a maximum permissible uplift on the minimum available price, e.g. a customer could conceive paying up to 120 per cent of the minimum available if other conditions were right;
- timeliness needs to be broken down into bands. For example, delivery time may be important, but it is necessary to ascertain the proportion of

the customers who require same day delivery, next day delivery or delivery within the week. When analysing the expectations on product introduction, there needs to be a view on the frequency of new product introduction that is preferred;
- the quality requirements need to be expressed in terms of the degree and frequency of deviation that is permissible.

As discussed in the previous section, this quantification will have two aspects, namely the minimum level of performance, below which the customer will not purchase, and the level of performance beyond which no additional value is perceived.

This then allows the organisation to set minimum levels of performance, and also to understand the level beyond which it is not worthwhile to improve. For most organisations, achieving this much would be a major advance on their current state of knowledge and is sufficient for an initial programme to control overheads.

It is possible however to take the understanding of customer requirements further: there is still not enough information for the organisation to optimise the customer service levels, in the sense of providing best value for money. To do this requires a knowledge of how much more a customer would pay if the product specification or delivery were improved by a particular amount. In this way the service levels within a particular parameter can be adjusted for maximum profitability, by identifying the service level which provides the largest difference between revenue and cost.

The technique, which is called conjoint analysis, is discussed in the next section. It has been used extensively in product design and is equally applicable to process design.

Conjoint analysis

It is certainly not essential for the success of this programme to use conjoint analysis. The overview of the technique is included to show how to calculate information on customer requirements that is often sought but rarely available, namely how much a customer will pay for some element of service.

In an ideal world customers would be able to place a value on each of their requirements. So if they claimed to prefer shorter delivery lead time, then the value of each degree of reduction could be given, up to the level when any further reduction would not be useful. In practice customers are not able to do this: the question is too abstract. In response to this difficulty, conjoint analysis has been developed; it infers the values which customers place on different requirements from their response to a series of questions.

The first step is to identify the set of customer requirements to be valued. If there has already been an exercise to rank or score customer requirements then this information will be available, otherwise it will have to be collected. This must be the subject of some preliminary market research. The main danger is that a requirement is not included in the analysis, because this will not become apparent subsequently. The inclusion of a superfluous customer requirement is less serious, though it does unnecessarily complicate the analysis.

A series of questions is then formed: different combinations of the stated requirements (usually termed attributes) are grouped and the customer is asked to choose between the combinations. The groups of attributes are chosen so that the relative merits, in the eyes of the customer, of each of the attributes within the group can be evaluated. For example, the relative merits of particular specifications, or delivery options are ranked against each other.

When financial parameters are introduced into the analysis it becomes possible to quantify the value the customer places on particular attributes and then compare this with the cost of providing these attributes. This is illustrated in Figure 2.5 and discussed further in the last case-study.

PROCESSES

Introduction

We have said that this programme uses a process approach. By this we mean that the method is primarily concerned with processes and activities. The former represent a top-level view of how to satisfy the customers' requirements and the latter an analysis of what actually occurs in the organisation in order to meet those requirements.

Figure 2.5 Striking a cost versus service level trade-off

Now that the needs of the customer have been clarified we can propose a set of processes which serve them. We first define a process and then give examples of some typical processes. Of course, not all the processes listed will be applicable to any one organisation, indeed many of the sample processes represent different ways of slicing the same cake.

Definition

At a simplified level, a process is a co-ordinated set of activities which meets a customer requirement. This simple definition captures the essence of a process, namely:

- It is the means by which a customer is satisfied, which has been the subject of our discussions so far.
- A process consists of component activities, which require co-ordination and control. For a process to function well not only must the component activities be functioning well, but they must also be linked and co-ordinated smoothly.

Following the logic of this approach, a process will only have been identified if it fulfils an external requirement. As a first assumption this has much to commend it, because it encourages an outward-facing view. Nonetheless the question arises whether there are processes, or individual activities, which do not work towards satisfying a customer requirement. There are, for example:

- External bodies, who are not customers in the common sense of the word, but whose requirements need to be satisfied, e.g. there may be some activities which are involved with supply of shareholders' information. There are also other interested parties, e.g. the workforce, the local community, who are generally referred to as stakeholders.
- Groups of activities which are necessary for the growth of the organisation, but which do not have an immediate customer. Examples would include developing new products or services, and customers and markets.
- The operation of internal systems for the eventual benefit of a customer, e.g. the financial management function or the information technology systems.

In summary therefore, our definition of a process given above has to include stakeholders as well as customers in the literal sense, future customers as well as present customers and the maintenance of a business infrastructure which permits customer requirements to be satisfied. Notwithstanding this caveat, however, the emphasis within the organisation should always be towards the satisfaction of genuine customers who exist today.

Process identification

The next step is to identify the key processes within the organisation. This has to be done in the context of a particular organisation. However, we now discuss some sample processes which will serve to get the ball rolling when trying to identify processes which are specific to an organisation.

The question arises whether it is realistic to even consider processes for a general organisation, or if processes need to be specific to an industry. The answer depends on the level of detail into which processes delve. We envisage between five and twenty processes being identified; the lower figure represents a fairly superficial top-down view of the organisation and the higher figure a relatively detailed top-down view. Nonetheless even with the higher figure, we are only considering very broad processes, many of which will apply to different corporations.

It must be stressed that the general processes given below are only a guide; not all will be relevant to any one organisation and there will be some processes which are relevant to a company but which are not covered in the sample given below. For convenience, we group them into broad categories:

- *supply chain management*, namely the co-ordination of the activities which take a customer order and fulfil it;
- *customer development*, which spans obtaining customers, understanding their requirements and maintaining contact after the sale has been completed;
- *business development*, which covers developing markets and products within the organisation;
- *business maintenance*, which includes the processes concerned with keeping the organisation intact.

These divisions are appropriate to many, but not all, industry sectors. In the retail sector, for example, it is likely that the process names and divisions would reflect the traditional distinctions between merchandising, distribution and store management.

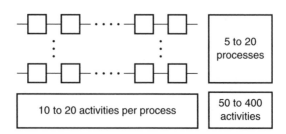

Figure 2.6 Number of processes and activities

The identification of the processes relevant to the particular corporation is only the first stage in the analysis of the processes. During Step 2, Internal Analysis, we examine the activities of the company in detail; we identify between fifty and four hundred individual activities, depending on the level of detail adopted, and link these to the five to twenty processes. In doing so we break down each top-down process into between ten and twenty activities, analysed from the bottom up. This synthesis is illustrated in Figure 2.6.

Supply chain management

These processes refer to the fundamental operations of most businesses namely taking an order and meeting it. It would be possible to have a single process spanning the whole company, from sales order entry to dispatch; this would be appropriate if the logistics task was relatively simple, perhaps the dispatch of an order from stock from a single location. However, for a more complex supply chain, a more detailed approach would be necessary. The processes might include:

- *Define customers' product or service requirements.* This is appropriate where the contents of an order need careful definition, especially where there are many different options which are available and there must be consistency with existing equipment.
- *Agree delivery and schedule operations.* This is one of the more complex processes which involves agreeing the delivery timings with the customer and scheduling the operations to ensure they are met. Unfortunately management control of this process can often be split, with the sales function agreeing delivery and the production function scheduling the operations.
- *Manage operations capacity.* This refers to the management, as opposed to the scheduling, of the operations, e.g. a production plant. This can be considered as a self-contained process, whereby orders up to a certain level are placed on the plant, and it is then the responsibility of the plant management to deliver.
- *Procure material.* This is similar in principle to 'manage operations capacity': a requirement for material is identified and then it is a separate responsibility to ensure that the material is available at the required time at the best price.
- *Supervise inventory.* Once the inventory levels at the different points in the supply chain have been set, there remains the task of supervising the storage locations and the movement of material between them. If this is a minor part of the business the process can be subsumed into 'manage operations capacity'.

When dividing up the supply chain into individual processes, it is worth considering who is responsible for key parameters in the business, assuming that managerial responsibility is also divided along process lines. In the previous example, responsibility for the levels of inventory would be held within the 'agree delivery and schedule operations' process; the holder of the responsibility would have discretion over the trade-offs between inventory holding and levels of customer service, choosing perhaps to increase the availability of products by increasing the levels of inventory which are held. The organisation may choose to limit this discretion by placing bounds on either the maximum level of inventory held or on minimum levels of customer service; probably constraints will be placed on both, though the conflicting constraints must be compatible and realistic.

Remaining with the division of processes given above, it is less obvious who is responsible for bought-in material costs, which may well amount to over half the costs of the company! While the manager of 'procure material' obviously holds some responsibility, the price obtained for a given material will depend on the delivery requirements; if the supply chain is arranged so that material has to be obtained at short notice, then prices will rise.

It should be emphasised that the processes given above are merely examples of a possible division of the organisation and others are possible. For example, for organisations for whom out-sourcing is only a minor facet of their business, a single process 'procure material' would suffice. Where, however, procurement is a substantial part of the overall organisation then the management of suppliers needs to be resolved in greater detail; processes such as 'identify suppliers' and 'manage suppliers' would be used.

Customer development

Although most processes are concerned with satisfying requirements of existing customers, some are specifically concerned with developing the customer base. We include here those processes which work to satisfy a customer, other than through the operation of the supply chain:

- *Acquire customers.* Once decisions have been taken on the markets in which the company is to operate and the products which it is to offer, there remains the critical process of acquiring new customers. The input to the process can be considered as a number of defined market segments and a given product or service range; the output is a series of new customers. The activities undertaken will vary and will often include the activities of the field sales force.
- *Identify customers' requirements.* This process exists in organisations where the onus is on the supplier to identify the customers' needs, as

opposed to simply match a portfolio of products to needs which have already been identified. This is not common since in most industries this diagnostic phase is the responsibility of the potential customer; it is not always the case though, e.g. in the professional services sector where a key winning factor is to identify the problem.

- *Customer support.* This is sometimes part of the ongoing relationship a salesman forms with his customer; in other cases the after-sales support is relatively technical, e.g. as with computer hardware and software sales. Sometimes this takes on more of the characteristics of a logistics exercise and can be termed 'logistics support', e.g. the support of heavy construction equipment in the field.

There are also important questions regarding the division of responsibility between these processes. One question is the degree of responsibility the 'acquire customers' process should have for general marketing. Where the link between acquiring particular customers and eventual sales is weak, e.g. for a manufacturer or supplier of branded retail goods, whose eventual sales depend on the number of purchases by consumers, the emphasis is upon brand management and the control of marketing expenditure should reside there. However, where, sales are made to individual customers there is an advantage in a division of authority which separates the product portfolio planning and the actual implementation of the marketing and sales programmes. In this case, much of the marketing budget will then be controlled within the 'acquire customers' process.

A second question is whether sales order entry should fall within 'acquire customers' or within the supply chain management processes. The author's view is that sales order entry has more in common with the logistics processes than with the sales function. Furthermore, for the managers of the logistics processes to have a span of control which matches their responsibilities, they should have control of order entry, since:

- They will be responsible for meeting lead time promises, and therefore the time it takes an order to clear the sales office is an important part of this total time.
- Poor quality of sales order entry is a common problem of faults occurring 'downstream' in the supply chain and therefore it is advantageous if the activity is controlled by those who will be most affected by the poor quality.

There is frequently reluctance, however, in assigning responsibility for order entry to the logistics functions. One reason for this is that the sales function is measured on the value of orders taken and may wish to retain the ability to make any promise on specification, delivery or price necessary to obtain an order. The subsequent problems are clear enough.

Business development

There are some processes which are concerned with the development of the future business, in terms of products and markets. These processes cannot be related to current customers but nonetheless they are necessary. In many organisations the responsibilities for these processes are diffused across the organisation and consequently they are not carried out well. The first step to remedying this situation is to recognise the key business development processes, which may include:

- *Product planning*. The product and service origination process spans market research and selection, concept generation, specification and setting up of distribution networks where necessary. It also includes product abandonment, an important decision which unfortunately is frequently carried out by default. It would usually be impractical to remedy this by creating a product planning department or directorate because the task is inherently multidisciplinary, especially in linking strategies for marketing, products and manufacturing. However, the process of managing the product portfolio can be recognised, and responsibility assigned for its management, even though the participants in the process will have other responsibilities.
- *Brand management*. For branded goods much of the product planning and marketing referred to above is, of course, centred around the brands, and brand management becomes a process in its own right. This would usually encompass the product planning described above, as well as responsibility for accepting the design of products and packaging, pricing policy and the choice of distribution outlets.
- *Product development*. The importance of product development in both manufacturing and service companies is seldom disputed. The potential for high margins for advanced products is well recognised. Furthermore product development is crucial in the control of future cost. It has been estimated for manufacturing companies that some 80 per cent of a product's manufacturing cost is committed once the design is completed. It is important to recognise that while management responsibility for the whole process must be clear, the process itself needs to be multi-disciplinary and that product or service design carried out in isolation will have poor results.

These processes pose special problems in the costing of the products or services. If a cost is being incurred for the benefit of a future product or service, there is no logical way to relate this to the present product ranges. Therefore any allocation of development cost is bound to be arbitrary. If it is necessary to properly allocate development costs to individual products then a form of life-cycle costing is required.

Business maintenance

There are a few processes which must be undertaken for the organisation to continue; a difficult balance has to be struck. On the one hand these groups of activities do not add value directly, but on the other hand, if they were not carried out at all, customers would not be served. The main processes include:

- *Human resource management.* Little mention has yet been made of the stuff of which processes are made, namely people. A decision needs to be made on whether the organisation adopts a development standpoint, whereby individuals are carefully recruited and then developed, or if it adopts a more *laissez-faire* attitude. If the former course is selected, then human resource development is an important process. While it might seem the former type of company enjoys a natural advantage, it often seems that the disadvantages of inbreeding implied by concentrated internal development more than outweighs the benefits.
- *Financial management.* The financial management function usually appears self-contained within and organisation, often called simply 'the accounts department'. Most of this function falls naturally within the financial management process, but not all. For example, the debt collection activity can be viewed as the final stage of the supply chain management process; this is appropriate where the most effective debt collector is often the person who delivered the service. The importance of financial management is rarely disputed, especially since many view it as a source of profit equal to operations management. The only danger is that financial management can be too dominant and detached from the day-to-day operations of the organisation. If this happens, the organisation begins to be run by proxy, substituting financial measures for those which measure the parameters which matter to the customer.
- *Infrastructure maintainance.* There will always be a need to maintain a physical and information infrastructure to allow for the co-ordination of the business; this corresponds to the traditional view of 'overhead'. When comparative studies are made it is startling how wide the variation can be between different organisations carrying out identical tasks.

It is in this area that the traditional view of overhead control is most appropriate. If business maintenance costs do not add value to the customer directly, even though they support other processes which do, the organisation should minimise these costs without compromising the level of customer service.

Summary

We have outlined the principle of processes and provided some examples. The actual processes chosen for a particular organisation will depend on its basis of competition and need to be tailored to the organisation. An important consideration to be borne in mind when devising processes is to understand in which process the responsibility for certain parameters resides, e.g. the responsibility for inventory levels, bought-in prices and delivery reliability.

Typically, between five and twenty major processes will be used to encompass the activities of the organisation.

BENCHMARKING

Benefits

The new interest in benchmarking arises from a need to inform managers whether they are the best in the world in particular processes and if not, the usual case, to determine who is better and by what margin. For those organisations which do not have to compete for their existence, the reward for the exercise is simply the knowledge that the organisation is fulfilling its role in the best way possible. However for most private sector organisations, the benefit is less high minded – it is the survival of the organisation itself.

The threat to survival has grown with the advent of global competition: when companies only had to compete with those in their vicinity, i.e. they supplied a local market, the managers of the company were generally aware of how good their own operations were compared to a competitor. If a more distant company operated more efficiently it would not be a matter of immediate concern, since the distant competitor could not threaten sales to local customers. This has now changed with the lowering of trade barriers and improvement in communications, with the result that companies now compete with organisations in parts of the world of which they know nothing. This may be apparent to companies who already supply to the international market, but it is equally applicable to those who supply a local market because there is nothing to prevent their customers from sourcing components from international competition.

In these circumstances there is naturally a need for management to find out how good they really are, not just compared to the competitor in the same region or nation, but the world. This is the rationale behind benchmarking.

Before we discuss how to do this we first outline the different types of benchmark available.

Benchmark types

Benchmarks differ in the extent of the comparison undertaken. We now outline the different types of benchmark available and it will become apparent that much old wine is in new bottles. We can categorise benchmarks, beginning with those with relatively narrow horizons and finishing with those which take a broad view:

- *Ideal benchmarks*. As a desktop exercise, it can be worth considering what the absolutely ideal level of performance could be, assuming all the constraints are removed. This is frequently done in work study, where the ideal throughput of a function or a machine is calculated, assuming no breakdowns or interruptions. This ideal standard is then adjusted to allow for a certain amount of lost time that will always occur in practice, in order to set the real target. Carrying this out for a whole process, requires more imagination, but can point the way for future development. For example, some years ago it generally took six weeks to offer a mortgage loan on a property; now it can it can done within the day, assuming all the documentation is in order. Setting an ideal benchmark of same day service would have seemed absurd in the past, but this level of performance has actually been achieved.
- *Internal benchmarks*. These are comparisons between different parts of the same company. Such exercises are well established and have the advantage that the management of the company have the knowledge to make meaningful comparisons, without being misled by anomalies. This last point touches an oft-repeated adage in benchmarking, namely that 'You cannot separate the numbers from the people'. The disadvantage of internal benchmarks is, of course, there is little understanding of what is being achieved elsewhere in the world. If the company is genuinely amongst the best in the world in certain functions, then suitable comparisons exist within the organisation; for the vast majority of organisations, however, internal benchmarks are insufficient.
- *Best practice surveys*. In a similar way to that in which organisations rank potential suppliers, according to their adoption of contemporary best practice, it is possible for companies to participate in surveys on their

own initiative, often through the use of a trade association. The drawback is that the results do not focus on actual performance, i.e. the output, but only on the input. To overcome this, comparisons of performance are also sought, sometimes in ratio form.

- *Ratio and performance comparisons.* This is not a new idea: many companies have long subscribed, through the medium of a third party, to reports on comparative business ratios and other performance indicators. Under this arrangement, companies transform financial information into ratio form and report on other parameters by completing a questionnaire. They then submit the information to a third party, which publishes the information in anonymous form. Each participant can then compare its own performance with that of others, but is unaware of the actual identity of each comparative organisation.

- *Industry benchmarks.* These involve the comparison of an organisation with others in the same industry or service sector. On the positive side, interesting comparisons can be drawn between organisations, because on the whole they undertake broadly similar activities. On the negative side, there is only the opportunity to define the level of performance that is 'good enough', i.e. as good as any current competitor; benchmarking within a sector does not help define the level of performance which is best practice for a given process, across all industries. Furthermore there are problems in sharing confidential information with competitors, although this can be ameliorated through the use of third parties. Active third party involvement is essential to overcome the confidentiality issue, which would otherwise frustrate the exercise. This is because when creating benchmarks it is necessary to separate out the differences in cost which are controllable and those which reflect historical factors, e.g. in comparing the costs between organisations where one is using fully depreciated equipment while the other is not. To separate the controllable and non-controllable differences between organisations involves working at a close level of detail and this is likely to involve a sharing of information that would prove unacceptable for competitors, unless a third party carried out the analysis.

- *Process benchmarks.* It is in this area that most of the latest interest in benchmarking has arisen. The basic change in thinking is that once a corporation is defined from a process viewpoint, it is then possible to compare the performance in those processes not only with those in the same industry, but also in other industries. The steps in doing so are to identify the key processes of the organisation, research the best performers in the world, regardless of industry, contact them and arrange visits by a benchmarking team. Benchmarking in this way has the dual advantages of avoiding the situation where competitors are expected to divulge confidential information and allowing a comparison to be made with the best performer across all industries, thereby offering the prospect for the company to move ahead of its own competition as opposed to drawing level with it. The only difficulty is in selecting the right processes and comparator organisations; this is discussed in the next section.

Only the last item, the concept of benchmarking processes against the 'world-class' standards is genuinely novel, however, all are useful. We confine the subsequent discussion to process benchmarking, since the other types will already be familiar.

Selection of processes

It is impractical to benchmark every process of an organisation and therefore one or more must be selected for the procedure. We now discuss the criteria for selection.

Perhaps the most important criterion is that the process outputs must be relevant to the critical success factors of the organisation. An analysis has already been made of the factors on which the organisation competes and if a particular process affects several of these factors in a major manner, then it is a candidate for a benchmarking.

Beyond this, there is an issue of the general level of resource consumed. For example, some processes may be critical but satisfactory results can be achieved by committing additional resource, while the cost of the process remains within reasonable bounds. In such a case, benchmarking would not be worthwhile and instead attention would turn to those processes which consumed a large amount of human or capital resource and where increases in productivity would substantially improve performance.

The final point, which may smack of appeasement, is that the exercise should begin as a process where the people concerned view it positively. If benchmarking is a new departure within the organisation, perhaps one which has not been outward looking in the past, then the first exercise must be a success. This will not happen where those involved in the process are likely to be resistant to change and to regard a comparison with outside practice as either threatening or irrelevant. The first benchmarking assignment must therefore concentrate on a process where the participants are eager to change and prove themselves. If none of the key processes in the organisation are operated by such people the prospective benchmarking enthusiast should rapidly find another job!

Selection of comparator organisations

Once the processes which are candidates for benchmarking have been identified, the next step is to identify comparator organisations. There are two major criteria:

- They are good performers in their own business, which may be very specialised.
- Their success depends on competence in the process of interest.

To illustrate with a practical example from the author's own experience: where would a benchmarking company be found for the efficient design, in terms of space and power, of electric motors? Thinking laterally, compactness and efficiency (which is tantamount to coolness) is of central importance to dental drills, where a dentist judges a design on the convenience and comfort of the drill. Sure enough, a visit to the one of the world's leading manufacturers of such equipment proved an education to a motor designer (who would have considered himself an expert within his own country) on the degrees of compactness and efficiency that were possible; the potential for improvement was believed because of the evidence seen with his own eyes.

Within this anecdote, there are lessons:

- Seek out international comparison. Within national boundaries, tales of good practice will already have travelled thorough movement of employees or professional associations.
- Seeing is believing. Whereas reported comment on best practice elsewhere can be counter-productive, if employees are taken to see what is possible from people such as themselves, with the opportunity for discussion, then the results are likely to be more encouraging.

The search for comparator organisations can be conducted by trawling through press cuttings, industry statistics or membership of various trade and industry associations. The problem with this approach is that the end of the search there has to be a 'cold call', which may be treated with suspicion and result in rebuff. Not surprisingly, the most fruitful groups are forums of companies which have declared an interest in benchmarking from the outset.

Before approaching a prospective benchmarking partner, it pays to anticipate the question 'What's in it for me?'. There has to be benefit on both sides. This could encompass the exchange of best practice across different processes, which in turn is likely to be more applicable where there is a general similarity between the organisations. If all else fails appeal to the prospect of publicity! Apart from the vanity of those who would be involved in the project, the appearance at various conferences generally provides a level of publicity, and credibility, that would cost a fortune if it were paid for through advertising.

Comparison issues

The benchmarking exercise should be concerned with measuring the aspects of each activity which contribute to satisfying the requirements of the customer in terms of time, cost and quality. This has to be done at the detailed level, since it is at this level that most improvements become apparent.

The fact that comparison is to be made at a detailed level tends to make general guidelines of limited use. However, there are three main issues which are always of interest:

- *Product or service structure.* Many differences in performance can be traced directly back to the structure of the product or service that is be delivered. This fact is probably less of a surprise than the degree of influence that the original design of the product or service actually holds: we have already remarked that some 80 per cent of the operating cost of the organisation can be pre-determined or committed once the product or service design is complete.
- *Process structure.* The same product or service can be produced and supported by differing overhead processes. Some of the variation in overhead processes will arise from differing characteristics of the products or services being delivered. However there may be other factors, such as an overhead structure that was designed to support a greater or lesser scale of activity than that which occurs at present. Another problem can be processes which are more appropriate to a differing variety of product or service than occurs at present. This often happens where there has been a proliferation in product or service range without a commensurate increase in volume. This leads to inefficiencies if there is a lengthy preparatory set-up period for the support of each product or service.
- *Human and capital resources.* This comparison has to be made in the context of differing product and process structures remarked on previously. In practice it is very difficult to disentangle the differences in resources from structural differences and the effects of scale and mix etc. One technique which is proposed later is the use of activity-based costing to disaggregate processes into their component parts so as to examine such effects in detail.

These three factors are concerned with the objective and the quantifiable factors which affect a process. This is only part of the story. The other part of the story is concerned with the behaviour and attitudes of the people within the organisation. This would include factors such as: motivation, the ability of individuals to work with each other, the sense of competition that exists between the different parts of the organisation and between the organisation and outside.

It is important to take note of both the objective and the more subjective factors. The latter can differ considerably for no reason other than history; this was brought home to the author in a comparative analysis of three electricity utilities. The functions of each electricity utility were identical and their structures were similar, but the attitudes which prevailed were very different. In one, a 'let's get down to do it' culture prevailed with the emphasis being placed on results; in a second, a sense of formality and procedures prevailed, with the head of the organisation being addressed in formal terms; in the third, there was a sense of informality but one that was not associated with an impetus for change. None of these differences had a logical cause, nor could they be easily 'proved', but their existence was not in doubt and was a major contributor to the differences between the companies.

Practical matters

Even when suitable comparator organisations have been found and they agree to co-operate, there remains the question of how to conduct the benchmarking exercise. The subsequent description assumes that a decision has been made to visit the comparator, as opposed to working through questionnaires. There is no doubt that personal visits are the more useful route.

The first point is that it is worthwhile to visit more than one comparator company so as to avoid being misled by idiosyncrasies within one organisation. There is no maximum number but obviously a law of diminishing returns begins to operate. Two comparators can be considered to be the bare minimum, though more than four is unlikely to be economic.

Prior organisation is essential; the benchmarking delegation cannot simply arrive and wander around. To achieve this it is best that a preliminary assessment is made by a senior manager, who will draft out a programme in conjunction with the benchmarking company. This needs to cover what should be included as well as an understanding of areas which are off-limits. Once this brief has been drafted, it should then be passed to the benchmarking team who can elaborate on the areas they wish to examine and draft a request for information which can be sent ahead. This may seem a tall order, particularly where there is a limited understanding of the processes which actually exist at the comparator, but it makes the time spent at the comparator company (which must necessarily be kept short) far more productive.

The team itself should be drawn from middle management, supervisors and experienced operators. The inclusion of relatively junior staff is essential if the exercise is to produce real change within the company. If too senior a team is used there may well be a reaction against the exercise back at the company with it being viewed as a stick to be used against the work-force.

During the visit it is essential that attention does not wander away from the nominated areas. Observations need to be documented and a period allocated to this. The duration of the visits will of course vary, though a period of one or two intensive days is usually sufficient.

After the visit it is essential to summarise the findings and report back. A dual reporting line is useful; one to senior management on the main findings, so they are reassured about the value of the visit, and a second report to those involved in the operation of the processes so as to spread best practice. The latter is best done verbally to the group involved in the operation; this assumes that there are such groups in place who meet to sponsor continual improvement within the organisation; if not, then one should be set up and made operational prior to the benchmarking visits, otherwise the usefulness of the exercise will be limited.

Relevance of activity-based costing

On encountering the comparator organisation, the first observation is bound to be the difficulty in comparing like with like. Departments and responsibilities are likely to differ from the familiar and these differences have to be teased out before valid comparisons can be made; so for example a comparison between two purchasing departments is likely to founder on the fact that they undertake different activities, e.g. one organisation may spend time vetting vendors while another does not.

It is therefore necessary to consider the activities, and their costs, taking place within the areas under review. In the next chapters we outline in detail an activity-based costing approach, which is far more involved than would be necessary for calculating benchmarks. Here we simply note the advantages that activity-based costing provides. It gives:

- A common language for comparison across different organisations. It is activities which form the basic units of an organisation and as long as there are clear definitions of activities at a sufficiently close level of detail, it is possible to apply these common definitions in different organisations and arrive at valid comparisons of resource cost and process structure.
- A method for analysing the effects of experience curves. Experience curves apply at the activity, not product or service, level. Quite often the question of experience curves enter into benchmarking and it is necessary to resolve these issues at the level of particular activities.

- A way of understanding the different emphasis that an organisation places within a given function, e.g. does a company spend a great deal of its time expediting deliveries from suppliers, or alternatively, concentrate on educating suppliers to deliver product or services on time.

The principles and techniques of activity-based costing will form a major part of subsequent chapters, where it will become apparent that the topic is not only of use in explaining differences between organisations, but also in improving the performance of a given organisation in detail.

INFORMATION REQUIREMENTS

Need for information

The final step of the programme involves the setting up of a sustainable system for the control of overheads This, of course, requires the systematic generation of information to support decisions within each process. Now that business processes have been defined for the organisation, it becomes possible to understand the types of decisions which have to be undertaken within each process and consequently the type of information required for the processes to function properly. Employing the classification of processes used previously, we now discuss:

- the types of decision which need to be made within each process and a top-down view of the type of information required to support those decisions;
- the performance measures which need to be generated to enable effective management.

Once the information and performance measure needs have been understood an assessment can be made of the readily available systems which might support the management of the process.

Identifying the relevant information systems is the first stage in defining an information systems strategy and an information technology strategy for the organisation, which are necessary to avoid duplication and incompatibility. It is however only a preliminary stage; the detailed assessment of information requirements takes place in Step 2.

Supply chain management

The supply chain is usually the most information- and decision-intensive part of the business, demanding information on capacity planning, resource scheduling and sometimes, inventory levels. The sample processes given earlier were:

Define customers' product or service requirements

The decision is to choose which of the company's products or services will meet the customers' needs. This requires information on both the product and its relevance to the customer. The demands on the company's information systems are not great but the work can be complex and mistakes very costly. The information systems required by the process are concerned with:

- the specification of the product and, where appropriate, configuration control;
- composition of a quotation or sales order.

The main performance measures required for the management of the process relate to the cost of quality associated with:

- specifying products which are either not compatible with the installed base or are not fit for purpose;
- incorrect composition of the order.

This area can be a problem in manufacturing companies, where a complex product offering may need to be configured for a particular circumstance.

Agree delivery and schedule operations

The decisions in this area are particularly complex, involving a decision on when the company can commit to delivery, and the deployment of capacity so as to best meet the various commitments.

Unsurprisingly, this is a very information-intensive process. For produce-to-order operations, in both the manufacturing and service sectors, setting a delivery date requires knowledge of resource and equipment availability; once a feasible date has been given for delivery, the order has to be incorporated into a master schedule for the operating units. For produce-to-stock operations and wholesale or retail businesses, agreeing delivery requires knowledge of stock levels and future commitments. In many companies the information systems are already well developed. The most developed systems occur in manufacturing, in the form of Manufacturing Resource Planning systems, which provide:

- master scheduling, which is the compiling of what the organisation intends to produce;
- capacity planning, which confirms the master schedule is compatible with the available capacity;
- material resource planning, which computes the material requirements needed to fulfil the master schedule. A closely related system is stock

control, which can be used to supplement or substitute for material resource planning;

- capacity requirements planning, which computes a detailed consumption of resource by work centre;
- operations scheduling, which produces 'work-to' lists for each operating unit.

These subsystems, with the exception of material requirements planning, are fully applicable to the white-collar functions of service companies.

The performance parameters for this operation are concerned with:

- the reliability of delivery promises. It is necessary to separate the effects of unrealistic promises and poor co-ordination from the failure of the operational capacity to deliver;
- the response times offered to customers, given the level of inventory held, if this is relevant.

In the past great importance was also placed on the level of utilisation of the operations capacity, i.e. the schedules should not over-utilise (through the use of overtime) or under-utilise the available operational capacity. This is now given a lower priority and the emphasis has shifted to being flexible to the customer's needs.

Manage operations capacity

The decisions in this area are concerned with tracking the physical operations and controlling them to ensure that actual performance complies to the schedule. While the process is certainly information intensive there are fundamental differences in approach to the control of this process. One approach favours a top-down directive approach and requires work-in-progress tracking and the continual updating of the work priorities for each work centre. However this can become too cumbersome and an alternative is for information to flow 'horizontally' between operators and for working priorities to be developed at the operating level.

Interestingly, Japanese manufacturing companies put greater emphasis on the use of simple visual systems for the day-to-day control of operations as opposed to reliance on direction by computer systems. Nonetheless there has to be some method of transferring the top-level master schedules to the operating level. One method is to use 'pull' systems, whereby customer demands are declared at the final operational stage and these are fed backwards through the supply chain with each stage making demands on its predecessor. These are described when 'Just in Time' is discussed in Step 3, *Radical Change.* Assuming a top-down approach is adopted, the information systems necessary to control the operations will include:

- tracking systems to identify the state and location of work-in-progress;
- measurement systems to collect information on the resources consumed in the work;
- comparison systems to compare the actual and scheduled work and to highlight backlogs.

In the past performance measurement has concentrated on:

- overall conformance to agreed delivery schedule, i.e. the proportion of orders which are completed on time;
- the backlog of overdue orders;
- the actual consumption of resource, compared to standard.

Now it is recognised that the major influence on performance is the level of quality problems which are occurring. The focus of the performance measurement is shifting from an overriding concern with cost to timeliness and quality.

Procure material

The decisions to be taken in this process revolve around the management of the purchasing cycle (which is fully detailed in Step 4, *Focused Change*). The cycle comprises research, specification, supplier selection, ordering, monitoring, acceptance and ensuring payment.

The research phase needs to be supported by stand-alone systems to provide:

- market intelligence, including the monitoring of market conditions, especially movements in cost indices for monitoring buyer performance and assisting in price negotiations;
- the status of the supplier qualification programme, which should be dynamic and include the monitoring of supplier performance and reliability.

For the remaining phases in manufacturing industry the process makes use of the following systems:

- Material requirements planning, which specifies the items to be purchased and the due date. The preferred supplier is also held within the system, typically in the item master file.
- Purchase order.
- Goods received.
- Purchase ledger.

For service companies, the material requirements and goods received systems will be much simplified, but nonetheless there is still the need to identify what services are required when and to take note of their delivery.

The management of the function requires similar information to the previous process, namely conformance to agreed delivery schedule, backlog of overdue orders and the difference between actual expenditure and targeted expenditure.

Supervise inventory

The decisions in this process involve the movement from one location to another, to ensure inventory is being held where it is required and expected. The information systems needed to support the process are those covered by Distribution Resource Planning systems, which cover:

- stock recording systems, to record the current status of the inventory;
- distribution planning systems, to plan the deployment and distribution resource;
- systems, using forecasting or ordering information, to indicate the inventory requirements in each location.

The success of the inventory management is measured in terms of:

- the non-availability of items;
- accuracy of stock records;
- the degree of unnecessary distribution cost.

A further measure is, of course, the level of waste in the inventory, though a distinction has to be made between inventory becoming obsolescent, and the deterioration of inventory.

Customer development

The customer development processes, with the exception of after-sales support, tend to be less demanding on the organisation's core information systems. Where systems support is required, it can be developed separately.

The investment in these systems is worthwhile, for three reasons:

- They increase the productivity of the sales force, which will either lead to an increase in sales or to a reduction in this expensive resource.
- They lessen the dependence on individual sales people.
- They benefit the business by providing advance warnings of trading conditions. This can be invaluable, since otherwise the limit of the horizon is the forward order book. In industries where there is a long time between an expression of interest and the fruition of an order, the feedback from the sales force can provide a useful indication of future volumes, which could influence investment and recruitment plans.

We now describe the information requirements of the three processes defined earlier:

Acquire customers

The decisions in this process are mainly concerned with the directing of resource, but the direction is very dependent on market intelligence, including:

- the market's composition, in terms of customers and their characteristics, location and the purchasing authorities;
- signals which indicate the intention to buy.

Once the market intelligence is understood, the remaining need is for information to match the resource to the opportunities through a measurement of availability and suitability of each salesman to the task at hand. This is usually relatively simple.

The measurement of the performance of a sales force requires systems to report on:

- a series of ratios, showing the rate of conversion achieved in the sales process, e.g. customer population to number of enquiries, the number of enquiries to the number of quotations, the number of quotations to the number of sales etc.
- the net effect of the conversion process, i.e. the numbers and value of sales closed, split by product or geographic area and salesman.

The most difficult task is to separate the proactive sales, created by the efforts of the salesmen, and the reactive portion, where the customer takes the initiative.

Identify customer requirement

The decisions in this process can be highly judgemental, especially given the limited access to information on the potential customer's full situation. In this case, there can be no general statement of the information necessary to effectively manage the process; instead there is a dialogue with the customers to develop a full understanding of their needs. This dialogue is also an opportunity to develop the relationship between company and its customers.

It is also a difficult to measure performance. Assuming potential customers are fair judges of the competence with which their requirements have been identified, two possible measures of success are:

- the strike rate of proposals produced following the investigation into requirements;
- the time and expense involved in the process.

For businesses where there is an expectation that a potential supplier will research the customer's needs, this process will usually be the largest source of activities which do not earn revenue. Effective control is paramount, both to ensure a stream of future business and to avoid the wasting resource;

After-sales support

The decisions in this area can vary from reacting to the customers' needs for support, to a proactive sales role. Assuming the former case, the decisions require knowledge of the products or services that have been delivered. This history can be very complex, particularly where issues of configuration control are involved and there has been a long sequence of updates and changes. Quite often the bulk of the cost of ownership of an item can occur during the support phase; this has prompted interest in Computer-Aided Acquisition and Logistics Support systems to pull together a consistent set of data from the inception of the project.

Performance measurement of the function requires information on the satisfaction of customers; where delivery of physical components is involved the supply chain performance measures become relevant, e.g. availability of items, timeliness of delivery.

Business development

The business development processes usually do not rely on the collection of large volumes of information, though information may be collected from a wide variety of sources. Instead the decisions depend on the manipulation of data and the drawing of inferences.

Consider the processes highlighted earlier:

Product planning

The decisions within this processes concern the management of the product life cycle, from inception and development to abandonment. This management of the product portfolio requires information, for each product, on the size and growth in market share and the product profitability or cash flow in order to funnel development expenditure into promising products. The assumptions on sales growth and development expenditure then need to be modelled for their business implications.

This process is fundamental to the future business and, consequently, many of the relevant performance measures are at the corporate level, e.g. growth, market share. These are not useful for monitoring process performance because they can be affected by many other factors. In some cases it is possible to measure the lead or lag the company has compared to its direct competitors, in months or years. This allows a clearer view of the competence of the product planning process.

Brand/product management

The decisions in this process seek to maximise the value of the brand, which in turn depends on maximising profitability. The main variable elements are, of course, revenue and the distribution and promotion costs, the product cost itself usually being fixed. Maximising the profitability needs information to deduce the incremental revenue and costs arising from any prospective action. This process requires diverse information on:

- the environment into which products are being sold, in terms of changes in demography, preferences and regulations;
- the markets themselves, in terms of size, growth and competitor products;
- the supply chain, including the availability of goods and the performance of the distribution channels;
- access to new concepts from which to make proposals for new product development;
- feedback on the actual product performance compared to planned, broken down into relevant categories, e.g. market, distribution channel, geographic area.

The basic measures of performance are the value and profitability of the brand as alluded to previously. As with corporate profitability however, an eye has to be kept on future as well as current profitability.

Product development

'Decision making' understates what is required in product development, which is an inherently creative process. However, this does not apply to the actual management of the process; nonetheless even the process management is difficult and to make it simpler each development project is usually decomposed into a hierarchy of small projects, each having its own input information, its own plan and a set of conditions for defining when the process is complete.

Particularly for engineering companies this process can be highly information-intensive and demand the use of computer-aided design systems to manage the information and to reduce the design lead times. Whatever the systems used, the basic information requirements are:

- The product specification, which the design must meet.
- The process targets and constraints, e.g. timescales and resources.
- An understanding of available technologies and components, which may of course involve years of training.
- A comprehensive definition of the current design, in terms of material, geometry etc., and access to definitions of past designs. This last point is important for the whole enterprise; by building up a stock of 'retained design', not only is design productivity increased, but also the learning and complexity costs are reduced outside the design department.
- An assessment of the degree of completion of the design. This is not always straightforward; input measures, e.g. money spent, time taken, are very poor surrogates. The assessment is much easier if the design has been broken down into small tasks, because it is at least possible to identify if a subsidiary task has been finished.

Measurement of performance is in terms of cost, time and quality, with the first of these three factors usually being the least important. The costs associated with late or bad design usually far outweigh the additional costs of getting it right.

Business maintenance

We have noted that the process view does relatively little to reform the business maintenance functions, since there are no clear definitions and ends or even identifiable customers. However they do require information with which to operate. The information requirements of the process responsible for human resources, finance and infrastructure will be identical to those of current personnel, accounting and administration departments. For completeness, we describe these because they will have a bearing on the information strategy of the organisation.

The three business maintenance processes highlighted earlier are:

Human resource management

The decisions taken within this process vary according to the division between staff and line functions. The minimum information requirement needs systems to report on:

- the current workforce, their grade, pay, age etc.;
- manpower requirements to drive the recruitment process;
- appraisal and training needs;
- prevailing rates of pay for the various grades of staff;
- legislation governing employment law.

There is a second type of information, which is less commonly collected; this is on the attitudes and behaviour within the organisation. This information can either be collected by occasional surveys or by use of the appraisal system and by 'exit interviews' with departing personnel.

Financial management

In nearly all organisations, the financial management systems are well developed, because these systems are the mainstay of decision making throughout the organisation, not just within the finance function. The systems provide for:

- Planning, ideally with the top level strategic plan cascading down into a series of lower level short- and long-term plans. In this way the organisation can work in unison and confirm that all the proposed actions are affordable.
- Monitoring of actual performance against that planned and ensuring there is clear accountability.
- Enabling competent financial management of the organisation.

The core of these systems are the general or nominal ledgers, connected to which are the sales and purchase ledgers. Ideally, although it is not essential, other systems, e.g. asset registers and budgeting and forecasting systems, should be consistent and integrated with the ledger systems.

The performance of the three functions is measured by the degree of coordination achieved, the integrity of the information and the financing charges;

Infrastructure maintenance

The decisions involved with providing the general administration and information systems are varied, but their underlying principle is an understanding of the requirements of the business, the current state of the infrastructure and a viable path to meet those needs from the present position. The basic information requirements are therefore:

- a statement of the needs of the organisation, derived from an exercise such as this;

- a compilation of the current systems and assets;
- the opportunities presented by current technology and the constraints faced in the development.

The performance of this function is difficult to measure, since shortcomings will be felt by a general lowering of efficiency throughout the organisation. Even if there are no serious complaints, this does not mean that opportunities have not been missed or that the same result could be achieved at lower cost. Nonetheless, the only feasible measures relate to the degree of satisfaction amongst the users of the various services provided.

Survey of available systems and technologies

We have discussed at length the type of decisions to be made in each process and the types of information required to support these decisions. This enables a survey to be made of the market to understand the relevant:

- Types of system that are available to assist in the management of the process. While it might be thought that this risks prejudging the eventual systems solution, most types of system are available on a variety of platforms (that is, hardware plus operating system), so it is unlikely that any constraints on a future system will be introduced.
- Technologies which are available. These are not confined to data processing or storage, but include input/output technologies and communication.

It can be useful to be aware of this before Step 2 is undertaken, since they can then be discussed during the interview programme. Becoming aware of the wider possibilities early on in the process increases the likelihood of innovative solutions, before thinking has been conditioned by current practice.

SENSITIVITY ANALYSIS

Finally, thought needs to be given to the sensitivity of the results of the external review to change. There is little point in conducting a thorough review based on current information, if the changes in the offing are likely to alter the conclusions beyond recognition.

We do not propose a sophisticated methodology for this assessment. It is important, though, to review the conclusions at the end of this step and understand the salient factors which influenced them. The permanence of each factor can then be considered. If change is likely then the consequence of change is analysed.

In practice the main changes are likely to be in the area of corporate strategy and technology. A decision to vertically integrate, the entry or exit of a competitor from the market or a decision to adopt widespread out-sourcing of internal activities could well affect the conclusions on customer requirements, key processes or information requirements; in a similar way major advances in technology can create new opportunities and threats.

BENCHMARKING CASE STUDY

Background

The company is engaged in the generation of electricity, mostly from coal power stations of similar design. The generation operations as a whole employ over ten thousand people, of whom the vast majority work in power stations.

The stations themselves are widely distributed throughout the country and the local management has to be largely autonomous. As a result of this autonomy and the relatively small size of the central staff, each power station has tended to follow its own course.

Objectives

A large cost reduction target has been imposed on the generating function, to be implemented over several years. The chief concern of management is that in enforcing cost reductions, the temptation will be for local management to choose the easy short-term options. This is a major hazard because a key function of the management is the stewardship of the capital assets: if the assets begin to be neglected, to achieve short-term cost savings, this would not be detected until the damage has been caused and the cost to retrieve the situation would be enormous.

The objective is therefore to seek ways of ensuring that dispersed and autonomous local management adopt the proposed cost savings and do so in a way that does not jeopardise the capital base of the company.

Approach

The first step is to extract from the company's general ledger systems the costs incurred and the number of people employed in each cost centre (unusually this information is held on the ledger systems). The cost centre structure is not uniform across all the power stations, as a result of the local autonomy, but the cost centres have been resolved down to a fine level of detail and have clearly descriptive titles.

Operations	Maintenance	Administration

• OA Operate Power Station
  * OA1 Production Planning and General Management
  * OA2 Shift Management and Training
  * OA3 Technical and Chemical Services
  * OA4 Fuel Operations
  * OA5 Waste Operations
  * OA6 Coolant Operations
  * OA7 Cleaning
  * OA8 Miscellaneous
 	
• OB Monitor Performance
  * OB1 Monitor Performance
  * OB2 Enhance Performance
  * OB3 Staff Safety
 	
• OC Sell Electricity
  * OC1 Sell Electricity
	• MA General
	  * MA1 Headquarters Maintenance
	  * MA2 Power Station General Maintenance
	  * MA3 Power Station Inspection and Testing
	  * MA4 Projects
	  * MA5 Training
	
	• MB Control and Instrumentation
	  * MB1 Control and Instrumentation Maintenance
	  * MB2 Protection and Measurement Maintenance
	
	• MC Mechanical
	  * MC1 Mechanical
	  * MC2 Corrosion Protection
	  * MC3 Welding
	  * MC4 Workshop and Outside Plant
	
	• MD Electrical
	  * MD1 Electrical
	  * MD2 Workshop and Outside Plant
	
	• ME Chemical/Civil
	  * ME1 Chemical
	  * ME2 Civil
	
	• MF Extension of Plant
	  * MF1 Plant Life
	  * MF2 Power Station Projects
	
	• MG Dismantle Plant
	  * MG1 Dismantle Plant
	
	• MH Materials Management
	  * MH1 Contracts
	  * MH2 Purchasing
	  * MH3 Inventory Management
		• AA Human Resources
		  * AA1 Management Planning and Development
		  * AA2 Training
		  * AA3 Employee Relations
		  * AA4 Employee Benefits
		  * AA5 Safety Risk Management
		
		• AB Finance
		  * AB1 Mangement
		  * AB2 Finance
		  * AB3 Systems
		  * AB4 General
		
		• AC Administration
		  * AC1 General and Management
		  * AC2 Office Services
		  * AC3 Communications
		  * AC4 Document Management
		  * AC5 Security
		  * AC6 Transport
		  * AC7 Horticulture
		  * AC8 Plant and Technical Support
		  * AC9 Commerical Mangement

12 activities	21 activities	18 activities

Figure 2.7 Sample activity library

It is essential to have a uniform system of cost analysis and therefore we define the broad activities required to run a power station. This is done in conjunction with the staff of one of the power stations. The ledger systems divide the costs into operations, maintenance and administration and the activities maintain this distinction. The activities defined for each category are shown in Figure 2.7. Once the broad activities are clear, the next stage is, for each power station, to map the detailed cost centres onto the activities; this is done with the assistance of the staff of each power station, mostly by means of conversations over the telephone.

We now turn our attention to the cost information itself. It is held down to a very fine level of detail and it would be overwhelming to extract it without significant aggregation. Therefore the information is aggregated into broad categories prior to extraction from the system. These are: staff cost, materials, expenses, and contracts. The detailed cost lines are then aggregated into these broad categories. In doing so, the balance sheet items, the revenue items and the finance charges, which are also held within the ledger systems, are dropped from the analysis.

Programming

The aggregation of the raw ledger data, from individual cost lines into cost elements and from detailed cost centres into activities requires some programming.

Aggregating cost lines into cost elements is carried out in the ledger systems. The code each of the individual cost lines is allocated to a particular cost element and a programme run to sum the ledger costs of each line. Fortunately in this case, the detailed lines were already arranged in a sequence that bears a strong resemblance to the cost elements which were to be used in the analysis. The programme therefore is not particularly complex and comprises a series of 'If' statements to identify if the ledger code of a particular cost line is in a relevant range.

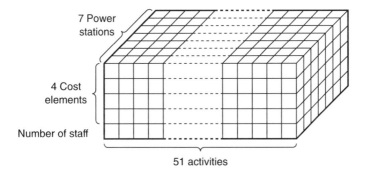

Figure 2.8 Activity analysis

The second task is carried out after transfer of the aggregated data to a PC database application. A mapping is established for each power station, which relates each cost centre (whose costs have now been aggregated into broad cost elements) to a particular activity.

The manpower figures are treated in a very similar way. The headcount, split by grade, is recorded by cost centre in the ledger systems and is also passed over to the PC database application. The application aggregates the manpower figures into manning levels by activity.

At the end of these exercises, the company now has, for the first time, an ability to compare the costs and manning levels in a uniform way across all the power stations. The form of the analysis is shown in Figure 2.8.

Internal benchmarks

With a common classification of costs and manpower, it is now possible to form internal benchmarks; the comparison is restricted to power stations of similar design. The comparison can be carried out at the activity level, using either costs or manpower. For brevity, we consider the manpower comparisons only. Figure 2.9 shows the comparison in manning levels between almost identical power stations. The first conclusion is that the differences in manning are surprisingly large and merit further investigation. Figure 2.9, also groups the activities into three categories, namely:

- operations, which are concerned with the running of the power station;
- maintenance, concerned with protecting the asset base;
- administration, containing support and policy activities;

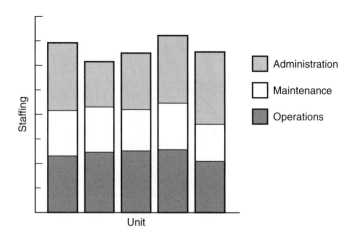

Figure 2.9 Comparison of power station staffing

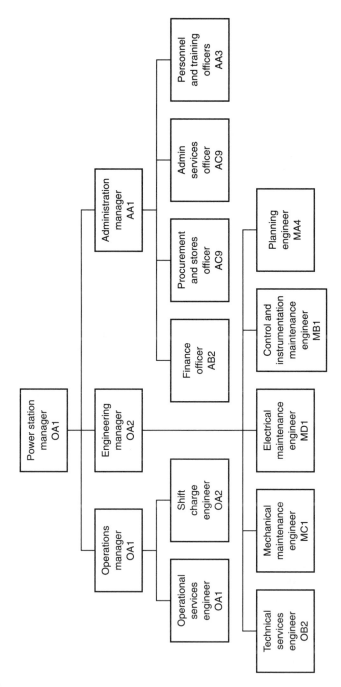

Figure 2.10 Power station model

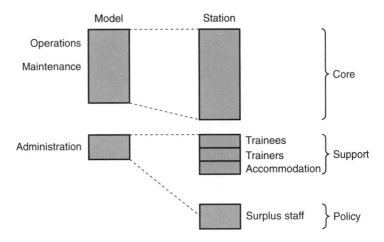

Figure 2.11 Comparison of model with actual

The first conclusion is that the major differences in manpower occur in the area of administration activities. This highlights the consequences of total devolution of management to individual power station managers. The managers are taking their own views on retention of surplus staff, the appropriate level of training required and the need for support activities.

Analysis of the operations and maintenance activities requires further work. The approach is to seek a world-class benchmark, as well as to provide an indication of the appropriate level of administration expenditure to set targets for these activities.

World-class benchmarks

An engineering manager of many years' experience of operating coal power stations is asked to define an ideal organisational structure, with the only constraint being the physical design of the power station. This definition includes every single employee required to operate the station, the top level is shown in Figure 2.10. The structure is very different from that currently in place within the company, though the structures in individual power stations also differ between themselves.

This would ordinarily create a problem for comparison, however since the activity library has now been defined, it is a simple matter to map the world-class organisation on the activity structure giving a set of world-class activity benchmarks.

A comparison is then made with the manning levels for the activities in a typical power station, as shown in Figure 2.11. The world class benchmark suggests significant reductions in manning are possible overall but, more usefully, the company can see which of its activities are overmanned and also which are undermanned. The latter include some maintenance activities, where there is a danger that the capital base of the company could be endangered if the level of maintenance is not improved.

Conclusion

The management is left with two key conclusions:

- there is a need to set firm policy guidelines for managers, which determine the boundaries on the discretion they are able to exercise;
- the staffing of some activities is out of balance with the world-class ideal and, after allowing for specific local conditions, the levels need adjustment.

Furthermore, these conclusions have had to be formed as a result of a one-off exercise. There is a need in future to adopt an activity-based budgeting approach, where the cost centres refer to a specific activity. In this way not only will the comparisons between power stations become far easier but also a comparison can be made continually between each power station and the world-class benchmark.

3

ACTIVITY ANALYSIS

The thing that hath been, it is that that shall be; and that which is done is that which shall be done: and there is no new thing under the sun.

ECCLESIATES 1:9

INTRODUCTION

Objectives

The basic purpose of this step is very simple: we want to find out what is being done within the organisation, why, how well and for what cost. While organisational structures can vary widely, in a potentially distracting way, the basic activities of companies in the same industry are largely the same and, subject to technological advance, will remain so.

We must first define the boundaries of our study and then define the costs which are being incurred within this boundary. These costs are referred to as the cost base. We then research, by means of interview, the activities which cause these costs to be incurred. Once this is done we can then relate the two and calculate the activity costs of the organisation, allowing managers a view for the first time of what is being done and how much it is costing.

However, the calculation of activity costs is only the start. It is also possible to trace these costs to customers, products or the other segments of the organisation defined earlier. The project team can calculate product and customer profitability to a higher degree of accuracy than has been done before. In fact, this is usually one of the key deliverables of the project.

A further enhancement is to consider, for each activity, its:

- attributes, which are simply features of an activity which can be recorded for subsequent analysis;
- cost drivers, namely the factors within the company which influence the level of cost.

A further objective is to link the top-down process view to the detailed bottom-up activity analysis. Once this is done the project team will be in a unique position, to:

- combine the breadth of understanding only available to senior management with the knowledge of detail available to departmental managers;
- relate the activities carried out within the organisation to the satisfaction of the needs of customers.

We then analyse the company's information requirements, its current systems, its data, and data processing requirements. Although we considered the decision-making and process information requirements in Step 1, *External Review*, this was only at a very superficial level. The detailed analysis of the information systems will be carried out in this step.

It will become apparent that the data storage and data processing requirements of the project team itself are far from trivial. We will discuss, therefore, the use of PC support tools to facilitate the process.

Deliverables

During this step, illustrated in Figure 3.1, the project team will define the following information:

- the departments which fall within the scope of the exercise;
- the cost base of the overhead structure;
- an activity map of the overhead structure;
- the activity costs;
- the attributes and drivers of the activities;
- the links between activities and their associated processes defined in Step 1;
- the costs of each cost object, i.e. customer, distribution channel or product family;
- the segment profitabilities;
- the requirements for information systems and technologies;
- a database of costs and other information.

Issues

The framework for reporting the deliverables listed above is the activity map of the corporation. By building this map and using it to analyse all the costs, performance and information issues of the organisation, the project team will form a consistent view of the whole company. This view, though broad, can focus down on the basic unit of the operation of the company: the activity.

There is also a great emphasis on building a cost model of the company. Unless the costs of each activity are properly understood, and these costs

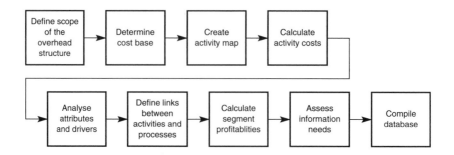

Figure 3.1 Activity analysis

used to calculate the profitability of the products, customers or distribution channels, good decisions on changing the overhead structure cannot be made. However after the cost model has been built, the influences on the cost and performance can be understood and overheads can be controlled without resorting to crude across-the-board cuts or simply demanding higher performance for the same resource consumption.

The outcome of the reporting of the activity-based costs for the first time usually prompts many changes in priority within the organisation. Prior to their calculation, managers have a view limited to their own horizons.

Before beginning the description of the actions to be taken in Step 2, Activity Analysis, it is useful, but not essential, to consider the nature of 'cost'; below, we discuss the ways in which it has been measured in the past, namely full-absorption costing and marginal costing, and how it is to be measured in the future using activity-based costing.

The nature of cost

Much of the subsequent analysis will be concerned with the subject of costs, which is a concept more subtle than is often imagined. The apparent precision with which costs are calculated suggests to many that they are accurate and 'true'. In fact this is not the case, for two reasons:

- The method of calculation does not usually reflect how costs are caused by the activities of the company. This can be tackled by adopting better methods for the calculation of costs, and we later advocate the use of activity-based costing for this purpose.
- More fundamentally, there is no such thing as a single 'true cost'. This goes to the very heart of what constitutes a cost.

A cost is a number which is used to support a decision. How that number is calculated depends on the decision which is to be taken; in other words when asked 'What is the cost of this ?' the first response must be 'What do you want to know for ?'.

Usually the cost will be to support a decision to be taken on whether to adopt two different courses of action. The cost which is calculated represents the difference in expenditure between these two different courses. This cost is often called a 'differential cost'. This is closely related to the concept of 'marginal cost', which is the difference between the costs involved in maintaining the status quo and adopting a new course of action.

In the language of economics, we are searching for the 'long-run marginal cost' between the different courses of action. However for the economist, the cost is the 'opportunity cost', or the value forgone of the benefits of the best alternative use of resources. This view of costs cannot be faulted in principle, though accountants tend to feel uneasy about such definitions because of the lack of documentary evidence for adopting a particular figure as the 'cost'. Furthermore economists are quick to point out that when calculating costs to support future decisions, historical expenditure should be ignored: only future costs and benefits are relevant. To illustrate, a reliable (but unconfirmed) anecdote reports that at one time the first essay for first year students at the London School of Economics was 'Deidre, you must marry me. I have spent three hundred pounds courting you. Discuss'. The theme of the essay was that historical costs are 'sunk', cannot be recovered, and therefore should not affect future investment of expenditure.

The arcane differences between accountants and economists need not trouble us. For practical purposes, when calculating costs it is necessary to:

- Regard the cost of a resource as the price paid for it, except where issues of obsolescence are involved.
- Examine historical expenditure to understand which relate to the normal activity and which should now be written off as no longer relevant. The former needs to be considered even if it refers to assets or material which have no alternative use, since it represents costs which must be recovered if production is to continue in the future, e.g. to allow for the purchase of new machinery or material once the current stock is exhausted.
- Carefully define the decision which is to be made on the basis of the cost calculation.

On the last point, in many cases the decision to be made is implicit rather than explicit. For example, when calculating a 'product cost' the implicit decision is usually to determine the minimum selling price for the item; if, however, the purpose was to consider deleting the product, care would have to be taken to differentiate between those costs which would disappear if a certain product were deleted and those that would remain.

In the subsequent discussion of product cost we will assume, however, that the purpose of the objective is to trace all the costs of the company to the products, customers or distribution channels in a way which reflects why costs were actually incurred.

We now discuss the two bases on which costs are usually calculated, namely the full-absorption basis and the marginal basis. Neither is satisfactory, for different reasons, and we then introduce a third method which is finding increasing favour, namely activity-based costing.

Full-absorption costing and its problems

Full-absorption costing separates costs into direct costs and indirect costs.

Direct costs

These are allocated to a product individually. Significant direct costs include materials and direct labour. Allocating direct costs to products is of course the general aim in any costing system, i.e. to relate a cost being incurred with a particular product or service; when direct costs formed the major proportion of total costs, then there was little to discuss about costing systems – the task was simple.

Indirect costs

Costs are indirect when it is uneconomic or impracticable to relate a cost to a particular product or service. Under full-absorption costing the response is to use a two-step process whereby:

- Particular types of cost, e.g. heating or rent, are allocated or apportioned to various 'cost centres', typically either production departments or service departments. In the case of service departments, costs are subsequently further allocated or apportioned to the production departments. If costs need to be apportioned, this is done on a representative base, e.g. rent and heating costs are typically apportioned on the basis of floor area.
- The allocated and apportioned costs are then 'absorbed' from a production-related cost centre into the product cost, on the basis of a parameter such as direct labour hours, machine labour hours, or direct labour costs.

The problem arises from the relative sizes of the absorbed cost in a modern business. To illustrate, when direct labour cost is used for absorption purposes, the indirect costs are typically 350 per cent the magnitude of the base used for the absorption!

The absorption of indirect costs into product costs can be highly misleading. This is not just because the indirect cost is far in excess of the cost on which the absorption was based, but also because the indirect costs do not vary in the same fashion as the base on which they are being apportioned. The bases used nearly all vary with the volume of goods being produced (for example, the number of direct labour or machine hours). However, many indirect costs do not vary in linear proportion to volume, but instead vary in proportion to the rate of clerical transactions, e.g. these costs would vary only slightly if it was decided to double the production volume of a single product, but may well double if it was decided to add a second product range.

Producing misleading information in this way can have a dramatic effect on long-term overhead costs. Taking an example from manufacturing industry, the costing system will suggest to the product designers that in order to minimise product cost, they must reduce the number of direct labour and machine hours and so reduce both the direct and the absorbed costs. In fact decreasing the former could well increase the latter; such an event could arise if the designer chose to:

- specify an externally manufactured component, which had no in-house manufacturing associated with it, but which involved considerable procurement effort;
- reduce the direct labour, but in a way that resulted in a large increase in the number of parts, which is a major influence on the level of indirect cost.

Even if the designer ignores the costing system and follows his instinct, the resulting product will be overcosted and may fail if the minimum selling price is set on the basis of the outputs of the cost system, due to inadequate sales and volume being achieved.

The previous example explored the damage a full-absorption costing system can do when it is used for the purpose for which it was intended, namely product costing. More dangers appear if the costing systems is used as a source of general performance measures. This usually happens in the case when the organisation is driven by the need to perform well in periodic financial reporting, as is the case for most publicly quoted companies.

Continuing to use examples drawn from manufacturing industry, because it tends to be a very demanding environment for costing systems, the potential problems may include:

- The temptation to produce for stock, even where there is no clear demand, so as to enhance overhead recovery in the production facility. As a result of the accounting standards for the valuation of stock, overheads involved in production are considered 'absorbed' into units produced as opposed to being fully written off in the relevant period; this even applies to timebased overheads which would have occurred at the same rate regardless of production. Because under-utilisation of the production facility will lead to lower profitability, there is a temptation to keep the facility fully occupied even if there is no immediate market for the goods. Many an inventory reduction programme has foundered on the needs to maintain factory utilisation in a quiet period.

- The need to maximise the standard hours of production in a period can lead to a preference for large batch sizes so as to reduce set-up times as a proportion of total hours. Apart from leading to excess inventory, this can reduce their responsiveness to customers in a make-to-order environment.
- The use of the cost information for decisions on operating procedure. A classic misuse of the costs is by operations staff seeking to minimise the cost of each item and selecting process route with the lowest cost. This will normally result in the use of old fully depreciated equipment and lead to the paradoxical result that the best equipment is the least utilised.

To summarise, full-absorption systems provide a rich seam of misinformation, which is misleading even when used for its main purpose of product costing and capable of further damage if it is applied to create performance measures.

The fundamental shortcoming of these systems is that they do not recognise causality: i.e. the principles of their calculation do not recognise why costs are incurred.

Marginal costing and its problems

Given such vagaries, many companies choose to adopt a 'marginal costing' system. Under this system costs are classified as either 'fixed' or 'variable'. Fixed costs are those which are deemed not to vary with the volume of production, while variable costs do. To a first approximation, direct costs can be considered variable, and indirect costs can be considered fixed. The company then seeks to maximise the 'contribution' towards fixed costs, where contribution is defined as the difference between revenue and variable cost. While this certainly circumvents the problem of dealing with indirect costs, it hardly solves it. It has the major disadvantage that much of the overhead cost, including overhead labour cost, is now classified as fixed, and therefore excluded from the analysis. This rather misses the point that many of the labour elements of indirect cost are far from fixed: not only are they controllable, they are variable, but in proportion to parameters other than volume.

Moving back to the language of the economist, if the objective is to calculate the long-run marginal or differential cost between two different courses of action, this will not be achieved if costs which are variable in the long run are mistakenly classified as fixed. Doing so will favour the course of action which gives a lower short-run variable cost (which is simple to identify) even though it has high long-run variable costs, because the latter will have been classified as fixed and therefore irrelevant to the decision. The classic case where this occurs is in the addition of new products or services to an organisation's portfolio. The short-term cost may appear small compared to the increased revenue, but the long-term variable costs of supporting systems to deal with the increased complexity go unrecognised.

As with full-absorption costing, many of the problems of marginal costing occur when the information is misused. For marginal costing the most common error is when marginal costing is transformed into marginal pricing. Marginal pricing is the temptation of organisations operating at under-capacity: where there is the prospect of time-related overhead costs being incurred but not recovered there is the option to fill empty capacity with orders which show a positive contribution, but whose prices do not allow for covering fixed costs.

The danger is that, if this is repeated, the organisation will never recover its fixed costs. The main obstacle of marginal pricing is that news travels fast and if an organisation has supplied a product or a service at a price just above marginal cost to one customer, a customer paying full price will demand similar treatment. The response is usually to invent a string of conditions for the lower price to apply, to deny the lower price to full-paying customers. Airline and railway companies are skilled practitioners of this art.

For others the irony is that marginal pricing is only wise where an organisation is working at overcapacity and the fixed costs are already covered. A common reason for doing this is where the leading supplier in the market wants to move into a monopolistic position; by attacking competitors with prices to which they cannot respond, there is the prospect of driving them out of the market, or perhaps lowering the value of the business for an eventual take-over. This highly rewarding anti-competitive practice is given the unflattering soubriquet of 'dumping'.

Activity-based costing

We have discussed the difficulties in measuring costs and how the methods used in the past have had their limitations, both in their principles of calculation and in the ways the information has been used. The dissatisfaction with traditional approaches to calculating costs spurred a drive to develop new costing methods; much of this work has been sponsored by those outside the finance function, i.e. the people responsible for the operations of companies have been demanding better cost information. The movement has been successful and the results of the exercise have gained popularity under the title activity-based costing. The standard reference work on this topic is *Activity Accounting* (Brimson, 1991), which describes and develops the work carried out under the auspices of the Computer-Aided Manufacture – International (CAM – I) task force.

The activity-based costing methods outlined below are based on the CAM – I approach. The other influence is the use of a series of structured interviews to gather data with the maximum of efficiency, which is a method that has been proven on many assignments. The structural interview method was summarised in 'Cost Leadership and Activity Analysis' (Booth, 1992).

Activity-based costing starts with the premise that activity causes cost and activities occur for a reason, namely to provide, or to support the provision, of a product or service. Therefore in calculating a product cost, for example, it is necessary to link the performance of an activity with the creation of the product. In forming this link, 'tracing factors' are used. Most tracing factors are not connected with the volume of goods produced but instead to the number of particular transactions, e.g. sales orders, purchase orders.

Activity-based costing resolves costs into three categories:

- *volume-dependent costs*, which equate to the traditional direct labour category;
- *fixed costs*, which are genuinely of a fixed nature over a short period of time, such as rents and rates;
- *transaction-dependent costs*, which cover the bulk of indirect labour activities.

It is the last category which is the focus of attention in activity-based costing. Whereas in the past this category was relatively insignificant, its size now merits a proper analytical approach. We now outline such an approach, which is a major part of Step 2.

THE SCOPE OF THE OVERHEAD STRUCTURE

Identifying the boundaries

During Step 1 some definition of the organisation's boundaries must have been formed, as a necessary step to understanding both the customers of the organisation and their requirements. Nonetheless, there could still be some ambiguity on the precise scope of the work because the analysis so far has been process based, and processes can cross organisational boundaries. In fact, these interfaces are of crucial importance because they usually represent the main source of poor control. If there is any choice in the matter, the scope of the work should, wherever possible, encompass complete processes. If only fragments of most of the key business processes lie within the boundary the result will be that the project will optimise parts of the process, perhaps to the detriment of the process as a whole.

Furthermore, there is little point in conducting a project on controlling overheads on a structure over which the sponsors of the team have little control. The control need not be absolute but it must be substantial. It is possible to bring suppliers within the boundary if there is a close relationship with the supplier, e.g. a partnership sourcing type of arrangement.

Of course, these two requirements may be incompatible, i.e. those sponsoring the work only have substantial control over fragments of the processes. In this case the question must be asked whether the project is best conducted at a higher level within the organisation or even whether the organisation boundaries are appropriate in the first place.

For many readers the previous discussion will not apply, because it will be quite clear where the boundaries of the corporation lie. We now consider identifying the departmental units that lie within the boundaries of the study.

Defining the enclosed structure

The proposed method for calculating activity costs makes heavy use of interviews and discussions with the line managers of the organisation. It is therefore essential to define who should be interviewed and on what topic. In so doing we are, in fact, creating an internal structure within the boundaries; this structure consists of a series of centres, termed 'activity centres', which are closely related to the cost centres.

The activity centres should be consistent with the departmental and budgetary framework of the organisation, if at all possible. There is no doubt that this makes the ensuing interviews far simpler, because the interviewees are being asked to:

- comment on the activities which they are responsible for supervising;
- allocate a set of costs with which they are familiar.

There will be greater accuracy, accountability and ownership of the eventual results if there is a clear relation between the activity centres used in the analysis and the familiar structures of the organisation.

Sometimes the costs which are allocated to an activity centre do not match those reported for the constituent cost centres. This can happen if all the costs which fall within a manager's area are not all reported upon, perhaps because the costs are outside his control, e.g. depreciation. This can be tackled by including the additional costs in separate categories and explaining that these costs are relevant to the operations of his department but are not normally apparent in the usual statements.

Usually cost centres have to be combined, because there are too many centres for the purposes of the analysis; we explain in the following section that this is tackled by aggregating the cost centres and involving all the relevant managers in group interviews; this does not generally present a problem. More difficulty arises where cost centres need to be split, perhaps because the cost centre is too large and contains too many dissimilar activities. If cost centres are split the computational effort and the potential for confusion is considerable. The preferred route is therefore to aggregate existing cost centres where necessary and to avoid splitting of centres.

Distribution of activity centres

We have discussed creating a series of activity centres and, if necessary, aggregating cost centres in cases where the existing ones represented too fine a level of detail. This begs the question of what is the appropriate level of detail at which to conduct the data collection.

For the smaller organisation, the number of activity centres will approximate to the number of managers, though sometimes managers may be considered to be in charge of more than one activity centre, if they control two distinct sets of activities. For example finance and administration could be considered as separate activity centres, even if they reported to the same manager.

The number of activity centres does not, however, increase in direct proportion to the number of employees within the organisation: there is a natural limit, beyond which the exercise becomes unwieldy. Most exercises are conducted with between ten and forty activity centres and this gives a satisfactory compromise between sufficient detail and prohibitive complexity.

Apart from deciding upon the number of activity centres, decisions have to be taken on their distribution. Activity centres should be created where there is:

- either, a significant amount of overhead cost incurred;
- or, there are several key activities undertaken, i.e. there is significant complexity.

Applying these guidelines will result in the costs of the different activity centres being broadly similar, except where:

- A large amount of cost is incurred in a single homogeneous area. In this case the activity centre would be large because it would not make sense to divide the area. This situation most usually occurs where there is a white-collar production-type function, involved in the processing of large amounts of information in a repetitive way.
- Several distinct activities are taking place in a particular area of the firm. This would justify the creation of an 'undersized' activity centre.

Where there are multiple sites carrying out similar activities, these sites should have the same activity centre structure to permit a comparison across sites. Where there are a large number of sites it may be necessary to select a few as models for the rest. This should be viewed as a last resort, because it is difficult to make suggestions for improvement at a location which has not even been visited.

To summarise, in creating the activity structure we are seeking to identify between ten and forty activity centres, which account for significant areas of cost or complexity and which will usually contain between five and ten activities. The number of activities can therefore vary between fifty, for a simple analysis and four hundred for a detailed study. This is illustrated in Figure 3.2.

THE COST BASE

The scope of the cost base

The next step, and one that is frustratingly difficult, is to establish the 'cost base' of the organisation, namely how much cost is being incurred during a period within the declared boundary. As well as establishing how much is being spent, it is also useful to understand what type of resource is being purchased, e.g. labour, materials.

Figure 3.2 Activity centres and activities

Although we are primarily interested in overhead costs, at this stage there are many advantages in understanding the total cost base of the organisation since:

- It allows a view to be taken of the relative significance of the overhead cost, compared to other types of cost.
- There is often not a clear distinction between what can be regarded as overhead, and that which is direct labour. For example, there is little difference for the purposes of cost control between the cost of an operator of a machine-paced work centre and the cost of a clerk who schedules work for the centre.
- It is far easier to exclude costs from specific analyses than to add back costs not included in the original analysis, which always carries the risk of double-counting.

It is straightforward to create categories for direct costs as well as the traditional overhead costs to permit the two categories to be kept apart. Even when a decision is made to examine the total cost in establishing the cost base, there still seems to be room for endless debate on whether it makes sense to include some items, particularly in the area of finance charges. The author's preference is to include these, and to allocate the finance charges on the basis of the capital requirements.

The ideal situation is to be able to reconcile the cost base used in the analysis with that formally reported in the periodic financial statements; this applies equally to private and public sector organisations. If this is achieved not only is the credibility of the subsequent analysis improved, i.e. there is recognition of the 'official' figures, but also in calculating activity costs there is reassurance that nothing has been missed. We now discuss which of the various periodic financial statements provides the best source of information.

Period of analysis

A decision has to be taken on the period over which the cost information and the non-financial information, which is used to support the tracing of costs, is collected. The most difficult part of the data collection is usually the gathering of the non-financial information needed to trace the activity costs. This has a bearing on the choice of period. There is little point in selecting a period in which to analyse costs if there is no non-financial information which has been kept for that period, or if it cannot be estimated.

Other considerations apply where the company is undergoing change. Where there is a seasonal cycle to the business, the period chosen has to include a whole number of seasons; e.g. if there were three seasons per year, then the period could either cover four months, eight or a whole year. If this is not done, any extrapolation will be misleading both in terms of product mix and total volume.

Where there has been a number of exceptional events in the past, e.g. unusual orders, product deletions, a period has to be selected which is representative of the future. If there is a general volatility in either volume or mix then taking a relatively long period of time allows these variations to be smoothed out. However, if there are underlying trends then too long a period could obscure these by including too great an amount of outdated information.

Finally, given the need to reconcile the cost base with the reported financial statements, if there is a recognised period for the preparation of financial reports, it is useful to arrange for the period for the collection of cost information to coincide. In this way, any queries on the overall sum of costs used can be answered by reference to an accepted document.

Sources of information

Mention was made in the previous paragraph of the need to reconcile the cost base to the periodic financial statements. The reason for this is that it is likely that the results of the activity analysis exercise will be controversial; if they are not, it is questionable whether the exercise was worthwhile. It is natural that those who feel that their interests will be damaged by the new information will seek to discredit it. One approach is to question the competence of the method which produced the results. However if the process described in this chapter is followed, there should be little problem in explaining and defending it.

A second approach is to challenge the validity of the input data, and care has to be taken in ensuring that all the data used have an authoritative and traceable origin. Obtaining authoritative non-financial information, which is used to trace costs, can be difficult, because it is typically collected and stored less thoroughly. In practice the non-financial information is derived from a variety of systems and it is the responsibility of the project team to keep track of the managers who supplied it and to ensure that it is consistent. If the cost base is to be based on a future estimate of costs, e.g. the forthcoming budget, then this requires obtaining the forecasts of the *future* non-financial information on which the budget was based, e.g. production volume, number of orders.

Turning our attention to the financial information, this is not usually gathered individually. Instead the task is to identify the most appropriate source documents. There are two common sources:

- *The general ledger*. This is the main document of record of money spent within an organisation, and hence it cannot be challenged numerically. Furthermore it is usually kept to a fine level of detail, and consequently it is often straightforward to aggregate these detailed categories into larger categories needed for the analysis. Its disadvantage is that it is a historical document, and if the organisation is in a state of flux, the cost behaviour of the past may not resemble that of the future.
- *The budget*. This offers the advantage of being based on estimates of future costs, rather than being a historical record; however, it is often not compiled to such a close level of detail. A further disadvantage is that it is sometimes not accepted within the organisation as an accurate picture of future costs. While this would be a sad comment on the competence of the budgeting processes, it is something which is worth considering before adopting the budget as the source of information.

In the subsequent discussion we will assume that it is the general ledger that is used as the source of financial information.

It is usually the case that information is modified after extraction from the source document. Reasons for this may include the need to negate the effect of cross-charging that can occur within a general ledger and obscure the level of costs which actually occur within a given costs centre, or a belief that the ledger costs are not appropriate. We now consider these adjustments to the source data.

Adjustments to the source data

Ideally, once the source of the cost information has been settled, it could be used within the analysis without further ado. This is rarely the case and it is usual to have to manipulate the cost information. This manipulation will not usually affect the overall total cost; if this is not the case, then reconciliation procedures need to be set up to ensure any additional cost being added or subtracted to the cost base is understood and can be verified.

Taking the case where the total of the cost base does not change, there are two common types of adjustment:

- *Removing cross-charges*. It is frequently the case that cross-charges have been made in the source data that will obscure the actual costs of particular activity centres. For example, the charges for information technology may have been apportioned across many departments, obscuring the total cost of the function. In these cases the cross-charges need to be reversed.
- *Apportionment of resource costs*. Sometimes particular resource costs will not have been allocated to activity centres, e.g. telephone charges, leasing

charges; instead they remain in the source data as resource costs. Since we wish to trace the activity centre costs to activities, these resource costs need to be apportioned to the activity centres. The only exception would be where a particular cost was not to be allocated to the general activities, but preserved in total, for direct allocation to cost objects. This can be done by keeping the cost in a dummy activity for subsequent allocation.

These adjustments are illustrated in Figure 3.3.

Other types of adjustments to the cost base affect the overall total. The two most common reasons are:

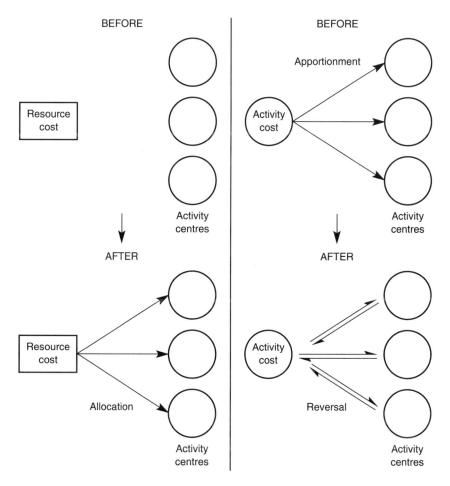

Figure 3.3 Adjustment of allocations

- Substitution of a particular cost for a more relevant parameter. For example, it may be felt that the inclusion of depreciation would give a misleading view on the future costs of certain overhead activities, because the relevant equipment was fully depreciated and would soon need replacement. In which case, the depreciation figure would be replaced with a charge reflecting the replacement cost of the equipment.
- Avoiding arbitrary cost apportionment. In many cases the boundary of the study will have been drawn along familiar financial reporting boundaries, which cut through departments or indeed individuals; when this happens the department or individual concerned has its cost apportioned accordingly, usually in quite an approximate manner. Either these apportionments can be taken at face value, or the gross costs can be included in the analysis and the activity analysis used to examine whether the existing apportionments are, in fact, accurate.

The necessary adjustments of the source data are usually carried out in a spreadsheet as a preliminary to the main analysis. Needless to say, if changes are made, reconciliation procedures need to be undertaken to check that the total costs have not been accidentally inflated or reduced.

Aggregating cost centres into activity centres

So far we have explained how to define the scope of the cost base, collect information on it and make any necessary adjustments. The next step is to transform the cost base from a statement of cost by cost centre into a more summarised form, of a statement of cost grouped into between ten and forty activity centres.

We have already discussed the principles behind identifying activity centres. There now remains the detailed computational task of transforming the source data, which is in cost centre form, into activity centre form. If the activity centres are simply aggregated cost centres, this is not too difficult. Where cost centres have to be split the task is more difficult. This summary is illustrated in Figure 3.4.

Aggregating cost lines into cost elements

After the scope of the cost base has been defined, the next step is to determine the types of cost which will be used in the analysis; in the argot of activity costing, these different types of cost are referred to as 'cost elements'.

Before we discuss the various categories which are available, it is worth considering why different categories are needed at all. The reason is that

Figure 3.4 Forming activity centres

different types of cost within a cost centre may need to be traced to different activities in different proportions. For example, it is conceivable that within one activity centre, most of the labour cost will be allocated to one activity, most of the travel expenses to another activity and most of the depreciation charge to a third. In such cases having more than one cost element is essential, if costs are to be traced accurately. However, the message here is 'keep it simple', since the complexity of the analysis rises in proportion to the number of types used. Indeed in cases where the vast majority of cost is employment cost and the remaining costs are generally concerned with employee support, e.g. the costs of premises, stationery etc., it is possible to work with a single cost element.

We now give examples of cost elements which can be used in the analysis of the cost base. Following on from the earlier comments, we include categories that can be used to analyse the whole of the cost base, not just the overhead portion. Though once the non-overhead portion has been categorised separately, it may be subsequently excluded from the analysis, if desired.

Not all the cost elements in the following list need be used and conversely there may well be some which are not included below which would need to be used in a particular organisation. Whatever the choice of cost elements, the computational process is to take the source data, which consists of details of cost lines grouped by activity centre, and allocate each cost line to the most relevant cost element. The cost lines are then added together to arrive at a summary of the costs within each activity centre, stated in cost element form. Possible cost elements include:

- *Direct labour.* The term is usually applied to the employment costs, including non-cash benefits, e.g. pensions and insurance, of staff who are directly associated with the operations; their time input is recorded by the booking of time or the use of standard times. In the past this has tended to be mostly manual operators, and the term is often equated to 'manual labour'. This can be misleading since it is quite possible for the time of designers to be directly booked to a particular product or service, especially when a job or project costing system is in operation; on the other hand some manual labour may not be associated with particular products or services, such as machine maintenance. For our purposes direct labour is labour which can be related to a particular product or service by means of a standard time. If this relation exists it is possible to link the costs directly to the products, and hence calculate profitability, without the intermediate step of activity analysis (the standard times are themselves a form of activity analysis). Nonetheless this is not always done, either because the standard times are not trusted or because they do not account for issues such as setup time.
- *Indirect labour.* This refers to the cost of employees who are engaged in activities traditionally described as 'overheads'. Identification of indirect labour is simple once the definition of direct labour is settled: it is simply the remainder of the labour charge which is not deemed to be direct! The question sometimes arises whether indirect labour involved in production should be classified separately to that involved in sales, administration and distribution. There is no doubt that it is often useful to distinguish between the two. This can be done either by the costs being classified as different cost elements or by means of the attributes described later.
- *Materials and consumables.* Material costs are those which can be directly related to a unit of output. Consumable costs refer to items 'consumed' during operations, but whose relation to units of output is indirect. Consumable costs are usually small, so they are categorised with materials, however a separate classification is possible.
- *Expenses.* These comprise charges for administrative support services or facilities. Some expenses represent bought-in services which may otherwise be carried out by indirect labour; others are charges for facilities. There may be merit in separating production expenses from those incurred by sales, administration and distribution..
- *Travel and accommodation.* Where certain activities incur specialist travel costs for a company, perhaps related to selling or, alternatively, to

the buying of particular materials, it is worthwhile to treat these expenses as a separate cost element so as to allocate them to these activities.

- *Depreciation.* When machinery or buildings are purchased their costs are accounted for through a depreciation charge which appears in the financial accounts. This is usually treated as a separate cost element. An alternative course is to employ a capital charge proportional to the cost of replacing the asset to avoid being misled by the use of fully depreciated equipment or by a depreciation policy designed for tax purposes.
- *Other charges.* There is usually a category required for miscellaneous charges which fall within the cost base. One example is the cost of servicing any debt, or other finance charges, that fall within the cost base; another example would be the cost of offering discounts. In many cases the costs in these categories would be allocated to special dummy activities, rather than the general activities, and then allocated to products or customers directly.

For example, the finance charges are linked to the capital requirements of the business and are best traced directly to products or customers via a dummy 'finance charge' activity. The tracing of these costs should reflect the different capital requirements of the products and customers. We now consider how to analyse these capital requirements.

Capital requirements

In the control of overhead costs, most attention will be paid to the operating costs of the organisation, i.e. 'revenue costs' which are deducted from income in order to calculate earnings before interest and tax (EBIT). However, the interest payments, or finance charges, are also overhead costs, which are dependent on the capital requirements of the organisation; these cannot be ignored, especially since they are controllable.

To assist in this control, the intention is to trace the finance charges of the company to its products and customers in a way that reflects the need for capital. The various categories of asset used in the analysis and the methods used to trace the costs are:

- *Fixed assets.* This refers to machinery or buildings which have been purchased to support the operation. One measure for the recognition of the contribution of fixed assets towards the finance charge is the 'gross book value', namely the amount of money originally paid for an asset, which is the amount of money committed and which cannot be used for alternative purposes. Sometimes it is not possible to use the gross book value for tracing purposes. An alternative though not ideal, is to use the depreciation charge which is proportional to net book value; this is obtained by setting all the cost elements in the model, apart from depreciation, to zero and observing the depreciation cost allocated to each product and customer;

- *Working capital charges.* The three components of working capital (inventory, debtors and creditors) are traced to either products or customers, as follows:

    - the amount of inventory by product range is estimated;
    - creditors are traced in a similar way to inventory, namely an estimate is made of the creditors associated with each product range and credit given accordingly;
    - the debtors are of course related to customer groups and it is relatively simple to estimate the average time it takes a particular customer group to pay, and hence the capital tied up in this group for a given turnover.

The capital requirements of each individual product and customer are then estimated and used to trace the finance charge. In a similar way other activity costs will be traced later in the programme.

An alternative to tracing the actual finance charge is to apply a nominal capital charge, calculated as a percentage of the capital requirements. This has the disadvantage of losing the reconciliation with the cost base, though makes the application of the capital charge independent of the debt/equity position adopted by the company; it would be particularly appropriate where the finance charge was in fact a credit item or was subsidised by the holding company. The most appropriate method is that which produces product and customer costs which reflect the different uses of capital.

Figure 3.5 Formation of cost base

Conclusion

In this section we have outlined the preliminary steps needed to produce a well-conditioned set of cost information. It began with specifying the boundaries of the cost base, selecting the appropriate period for the analysis and identifying a reliable source of cost information.

Once this was done, the next step was to specify the structure into which the cost information would be summarised and then to rearrange it in that form. The process is illustrated in Figure 3.5.

THE ACTIVITY MAP

General

'Building an activity map' is a phrase often heard during an activity analysis exercise. It is a graphic phrase and quite a good one. Most 'maps' of organisations are organisation charts or organograms, showing how line management responsibilities are defined. While purporting to show everything, they in fact show very little. They do not show what is done, nor how the different activities link together to form the processes which satisfy a customer's requirement. Moreover it is not apparent that different activities may be duplicated in several departments, or that the fulfilment of a simple process will require numerous interfaces between departments.

An activity map is the first step in overcoming these shortcomings. It shows the activities that take place within the company, and their location. It is the basis for much of the subsequent analysis. We now outline how an activity map is constructed.

The first interview

To build the activity map will require the participation of a large number of people, between ten and forty. To limit the drain on their time and to make the task of the project team manageable, it is essential to adopt a formalised approach to the gathering of the information.

The best approach is to prepare an information pack and questionnaire which can be sent to all the interviewees for completion prior to the interview, so that the interview itself is confined to answering specific questions and exploring the meaning of the answers given. The pack can be sent in the internal mail, though it will often appear formidable, so a short pre-meeting to talk the manager through the material can be useful.

To set the scene the information pack must begin by briefly describing the exercise and why it is being undertaken. This formality may seem excessive for smaller organisations, but nonetheless it is surprising how even among a small group of people misunderstandings can arise. The most frequent misunderstanding is that the exercise is the precursor to declaring redundancies when in fact there is nothing of the sort in mind.

There should follow a description of the task immediately at hand, and how it fits into the overall scheme, i.e. this is the first interview which will determine the activities which take place in a particular department, and a subsequent interview will be used to trace costs to these activities and to label the activities with various attributes.

In assisting the manager in his task of identifying the activities of his department, there is an advantage if the manager is supplied with an initial list of activities and is then asked to add and delete activities from this list. We now discuss the use of these activity libraries.

Activity libraries

An activity library is a standard model of an organisation, sometimes referred to as an 'enterprise model'. Models can be built for different industries, e.g. banks, public utilities of different sorts and various manufacturing industries. The implication is that the activities for organisations in a particular field are not organisation-dependent, but are largely standard. This is the case if the industry is defined closely enough, e.g. is not sufficient to have a single manufacturing industry model, there needs to be individual models for various industries, e.g. aerospace, automotive, batch manufacture, process manufacture, textiles.

If a standard model can be used, it offers many advantages which include:

- *Transfer of experience*. If an organisation in a particular sector has been examined previously, there is a great economy of effort involved in retaining this analysis. The list of activities will have been tried and tested. Where there are differences between the organisations this itself is a topic for examination.
- *Explanation*. When a manager receives the information pack for the first interview it may appear daunting. If there is a list of activities which can be expected to occur in his department this gives the request for information a tangible foundation. It demonstrates that some thought has been given to the manager's own area.
- *Standardisation*. This is the largest benefit of all. There is a danger that during the discussions with different managers the same activity can be called by two different names, and the same names can be given to two different activities. This will invalidate the work and must be avoided. By

starting the discussions with a list of activities and their descriptions the risk of this taking place is minimised.

There are also two disadvantages:

- there is a danger that genuinely unique features of the organisation will be ignored as an attempt is made to fit all activities into the standard mould;
- it reduces the need for managers to think about the activities which take place in their department.

In the author's view the use of libraries does provide a net benefit, as long as the drawbacks are borne in mind during the interview.

Interview conduct

The information pack needs to be sent out a few days before the interview takes place. The interview itself is best kept to an hour's duration, with the possibility of a follow-up if necessary. Longer interviews can lose direction and become too discursive, and place an unacceptable load on both the project team and on the interviewee.

After answering preliminary questions it is necessary to confirm with the manager the activity centres for which he is responsible. Once this is understood the conversation can then move on to the specific activities within each activity centre which the manager has identified as under his control. Usually there will be between five and ten such activities; a greater number than this should be avoided because subsequently costs will have to be apportioned between activities, and this can be difficult if there are a large number of them.

There should be some degree of commonality between the manager's view of the activities under his control and the initial list supplied from the activity library. If this is the case, the discussion can then concentrate on the additions and deletions. These need to be discussed carefully, since, after all, they are the first input the manager has made to the project. They are also a sign of operations being carried out in a different way to that which was expected, and this may either show an advancement on previous practice or scope for improvement.

In considering additions to the list it is important that the new activities have a clear purpose; to illustrate, it would be unwise to add activities such as 'answering the phone' or 'attending meetings'. Instead the team would want to identify why these events took place.

The interviews have to strike a balance between the gathering of information and obtaining a wider view. Too mechanistic an approach will deny the background information that will prove invaluable for identifying opportunities for improvement, but a too discursive approach should not be adopted.

Collation

At the end of the first interview round, the project team will have identified a list of activities which are taking place in each activity centre. In some cases an activity will be unique, though in other cases it will be seen that an activity is being undertaken across the organisation. The information needs to be collated and checked for consistency. If similar functions take place on different sites but they report very different activities, this needs to be investigated.

The finalised activity map needs to be entered into a software support tool, which is used for the storage of information. We describe the uses of such a tool at the end of this chapter.

ACTIVITY COSTS

Introduction

The identification of all the activities within a company is the first step in controlling them. However it is not sufficient simply to identify what activities take place, there must be some indication of their significance. Significance can be measured in different ways. One way is by counting the number of people engaged on the activity. This headcount measure is popular because of its tangibility, though it does suffer from two disadvantages:

- It makes no allowance for different grades of people engaged on an activity. Very expensive and very cheap people appear as the same resource.
- It does not allow for different practices in buying in external services, e.g. it is possible to appear more efficient on a headcount measure simply by subcontracting out services.

For this reason, cost is the preferred parameter for gauging the size of activities.

The second interview

The second interview is a far more formidable affair than the first, both for the project team and for managers being interviewed. It is also far more likely to create defensive reactions from the managers being interviewed. In the first interview, we were asking 'What do you do?', which is relatively non-threatening; now we are asking 'How exactly do you spend your budget?'.

Before the second round of interviews can begin the project team needs to have calculated the costs within each activity centre, split into cost elements. The principles behind this have already been described. The actual calculation would usually be undertaken in parallel with the building of the activity map.

For each interviewee a documentation pack needs to be prepared giving a brief summary of the purpose of the interview, namely to link costs to activities, followed by:

- A reminder of the activities the manager has identified as occurring in the activity centre.
- A statement of the costs for which the manager is responsible, broken down for each cost element. If it is the intention that the manager verify these costs, it will also be necessary to show how the cost elements have been built up from the individual ledger lines.

The task is to take each cost element and to apportion it across each activity. This is a formidable task, and in most cases the best approach is to start with the labour cost element and take each employee in turn and allocate their time to each activity, perhaps using time-sheet information. In this case, it would be useful to provide the manager with:

- a list of employees in each activity centre;
- a matrix which can be filled in to allocate each employee's time between the identified activities.

If the rate of pay of employees differs widely in an activity centre this has to be accounted for by obtaining salary information.

Once the labour cost element has been dealt with, the non-labour cost elements must be allocated. In some cases, these cost elements are traced to activities in the same proportion as employee cost. This is certainly not always the case, e.g. some activities may:

- use a wide area and incur a disproportionate amount of building-related expenses;
- incur large travel expenses;
- use capital machinery and so incur depreciation.

The parameters used to trace costs (e.g. employee hours, area, net book value) are called tracing factors.

The interview documentation has to convey these principles so the manager can begin to think how to allocate costs from activity centre to activity. While it is possible to post the documentation pack to the manager, its complexity is likely to confound. Therefore it is best to talk the manager through the allocation process when handing over the pack and to return in a few days.

Interview conduct

Hopefully, there will need to be little discussion over the costs and activities for which a manager is responsible, but if there are queries, these need to be dealt with straightaway. Once the cost and activities have been agreed, the meeting can move on to examining the tracing of costs to activities. It is necessary to review the assumptions to check if the most reliable method of relating costs to activities has been found. If the meeting is going well, this discussion on the nature of each activity and their cost behaviour is a useful start to discussing attributes and cost drivers which are the subject of the next section.

ATTRIBUTES AND DRIVERS

Use of attributes

We have already stressed that controlling overhead activities does not just equate to the monitoring and control of cost. The implication is that any theoretical framework to be used for overhead control must embrace parameters other than cost, and it is to these that we now return our attention.

We first introduce the concept of an 'attribute' which is the accepted term but which makes the concept sound more complicated than it is. An attribute is simply a characteristic of an activity. This wide definition results in a very diverse choice of attributes, and we discuss some of these below. The common theme however is that attributes are ways of collecting information in a structured way on the activities of an organisation. Given the analytical effort which is involved in the interview process, it would be a waste to stop at calculating the activity costs. There are many other characteristics of activities, knowledge of which would illuminate decisions on alternative ways of organising the company or on improving the quality of service provided to customers.

Attribute types

We have already introduced the concept of an attribute. We now give examples of types of attributes, and in doing so their usefulness will become apparent.

Class of activity

Classifications of activity by type vary. Some classifications are binary, the most common being 'value-added' and 'non-value added', or 'primary' and 'secondary'. The author's own experience of such classification is that they lead to fruitless arguments with individuals who are responsible for activities in the less glamorous category. With this in mind, ternary classifications are sometimes adopted; a common version is to split activities between 'core', 'support' and 'other' where core activities are involved in directly serving customers and support activities are those which allow core activities to take place. This can work well but in the author's view a quadripartite classification is ideal; the core and support activities are retained, but the 'other' category is split between:

- 'policy' expenditure, which refers to costs where the level of cost is set by management, e.g. research and development;
- 'waste', which refers to activities undertaken to correct mistakes, e.g. answering customer complaints.

Once it has been agreed whether to use a binary, ternary or quadripartite classification, it is straightforward to go through the activities and allocate each one to a category.

Critical success factors

Some activities are more likely to have an impact on the critical success of the organisation than others. Each of the critical success factors can be set up as an attribute and the impact on each activity recorded.

Timing

One use of the activity map will be to relate the demands of an organisation's customers to the internal processes, or sequences of activities, which satisfy them. Invariably the time to deliver a product or service is a key part of this analysis. The raw data can easily be collected during the interview when activity costs are being discussed. One parameter of interest is the time to complete an activity, if appropriate. This can be expanded to include the 'setup' time, i.e. the time needed to start carrying out the activity on a new range of items. Another parameter is the typical queuing time for which an item must wait before it is worked upon. A large amount of information can be collected on timing, and the decision on how much to collect depends on how much emphasis needs to be placed on lead-time reduction;

Quality

Obtaining a view on the cost of poor quality is often a key part in reducing overhead costs. The cost of quality is conventionally split between appraisal, prevention, internal failure and external failure. It is possible to record using attributes whether the activity is affected by any of these categories, or even estimate the proportion of activity cost falling in each of the four categories. This will allow the total cost of quality to be estimated and identify where it is being incurred. This is certainly a worthwhile start, though the real objective is to find out where the costs are being caused, as opposed to where they are being felt. We will outline how to do this in Step 3, *Radical Change*.

Cost behaviour

The cost collection exercise represents a snapshot of costs at a particular time. It is useful to understand how the costs may vary in future. It is possible to use attributes to record whether costs are fixed in the short term, represent past decisions (e.g. depreciation charges), vary with the volume of production, or vary with the complexity of production. This is particularly useful when considering the effect of volume changes, perhaps arising from product deletions.

Make versus buy

In organising overhead activities a recurrent question is whether a particular activity is best carried out internally, or whether it is better subcontracted; during the analysis it is useful to record whether it is practical for the activity to be subcontracted. This will be discussed in more detail in Step 4, *Focused change*.

Life-cycle costing

Each activity can be tagged as being relevant to a certain phase in the product life cycle, or none. The build-up of life-cycle cost can then be examined and contrasted to when cost is committed.

In practice it is unlikely that attributes will be used to analyse all the above parameters, and of course there will some issues which are particular to an organisation which will give rise to specialised attributes. The range of possible attributes is endless. The use of attributes for identifying opportunities for improvement is considered in Step 3.

Types of driver

One of the most heavily used terms in the lexicon of activity-based costing is that of 'cost driver'. Unfortunately it has taken on several meanings, the most common of which are:

- A general factor which causes cost to occur for a particular activity. One technique in the control of overheads is to identify drivers which have an influence on a large number of activities and to control these. Within this programme, this is the meaning given to cost driver.
- A specific factor which causes cost to occur for a particular activity. These factors are not likely to be common across a large number of activities, but are very specific to a particular activity, e.g. the number of lines on a sales order. These factors are very useful when matching resources to workload, and will be referred to as 'activity drivers' although this terminology is not universal.
- A factor which is of use in allocating costs from an activity centre to an activity, or from an activity to a cost object, such as a product or customer. We have already used the term 'tracing factor' for this concept. Of course, in many cases the tracing factors will also be activity drivers.

Each of these terms, cost driver, activity driver and tracing factor will recur as we discuss how to exercise rational control over overheads.

Examples of cost drivers

We have defined a cost driver as a general influence on cost. The purpose of collecting information on cost drivers is to see if there are common factors across the organisation which influence the level of cost. If there are such factors and they are under the control of the organisation, then they represent an option for cost reduction.

Typical cost drivers, and responses available to management may include:

- *Number of special orders*. In both manufacturing and service industries it is often the atypical which occupies a disproportionate amount of time. If this is the case, then realistic surcharges for special requirements could be imposed.
- *Number of customers*. If there is a substantial overhead in maintaining a particular account, e.g. if customer liaison is a major cost, then it brings into question the value in continuing with smaller customers. Either such customers could be discontinued or a discount structure can be adopted which rewards customers who place large amounts of business.
- *Number of orders*. There is often a fixed cost associated with processing an order, because of the documentation that has to be generated. If this is a major factor for an organisation, then a minimum order level is called for.
- *Number of parts*. For those engaged in manufacturing, the costs associated with maintaining records and inventory on a large number of parts are probably all too familiar. However a similar concept applies to service

industries, where a diverse product range can increase support costs because of the consequent complexity of internal systems, training requirements etc. The solution is range rationalisation; however, to carry this out requires good product profitability information, which is one of the key outputs of activity analysis.

Other possible cost drivers are less specific. There may be a general feeling of dissatisfaction with the information systems of the company. Alternatively managers may report their time is wasted by the number of meetings they are required to attend, or the time spent briefing senior managers. It is worthwhile recording these vaguer causes of cost by noting them as a cost driver. These cost drivers are then used in Step 3 to identify opportunities for improvement across the organisation.

Activity drivers

The primary use of activity drivers is to match resources to workload. When an activity driver has been identified, it is often worth considering whether it represents an input to the activity or an output. To illustrate, a customer enquiry centre could either consider the activity driver to be the number of enquiries received or the number of instructions issued. The latter has the advantage that the driver accounts more closely for the actual amount of work involved in each enquiry, but has the disadvantage that if it is used for workload modelling, staff can create workload and hence additional resource for themselves by 'keeping busy' through being overzealous in their response to enquiries.

In practice there is rarely the luxury of choice between the use of a driver related to input or output; usually the availability of information dictates which is to be used. In Step 4 we will discuss ways in which the workload driver, once identified, can be used to allocate resources to activities in a rational way.

Information collection and storage

The collection of data on drivers and attributes is best done in discussion with the managers concerned; classifications by the project team acting in isolation are unlikely to be accepted. The storage of the information is best done with a PC support tool, since it then becomes possible to search for patterns in the drivers across the organisation. The use of these tools is described later in this chapter.

LINKING ACTIVITIES TO PROCESSES

Background

In Step 1, *External Review*, the main business processes were defined; the starting point for this definition was the identification of the customers and their requirements. In this step we have taken a very different view and examined the internal activities of the corporation. It is now necessary to link these two perspectives.

Establishing this linkage is vital. One of the obstacles experienced by practitioners of business process re-engineering is the gulf between the top-level redesigned processes and the current practice of the corporation. If this gulf cannot be bridged, then not only is there no clue as to the practicality of the top-level processes, but also those involved in the current corporation, who must eventually accept the new thinking, are likely not to understand, and therefore deride, the team's proposals.

These problems can be avoided by being able to express the top-level processes in terms of the recognised activities. If subsequently in Step 3, *Radical Change*, changes are to the processes proposed, there may be:

- some new activities in the proposed processes, for which there is no counterpart in the existing organisation;
- some existing activities which are no longer considered necessary.

These can be dealt with as they arise. However it is unlikely there will be many cases. The reason is that the corporation will be remaining in the same business and the activities necessary to undertake this business are likely to remain the same, even if they are undertaken in a radically different way.

Process modelling

So far, we have defined the organisation's processes and the customer needs they are intended to satisfy, along with their information requirements. We now need to define the:

- links between activities and processes;
- inputs and outputs of each activity;
- resources consumed by each activity and the controls or constraints that operate on them;
- relations between the activities within a process, namely their order of execution and which are in parallel and which in series.

This type of information is best represented in graphical form, since it allows the relationships between all the activities in a process to be taken in at once and is relatively concise.

There are generally no shortages of such techniques available, some of which are paper-based while others are supported by software tools. We describe the type of tools that can be used and conclude with a preferred option:

Critical path networks

Project management is the field where the use of graphical modelling to represent the links between activities necessary to meet a final goal is most established. The method is known as critical path analysis and several individual network techniques have been developed. They include:

- Activity-on-arrow networks, in which the intermediate states of the system are represented by nodes. Activities cause movement between the states and are represented by arrows.
- Activity on node networks, where the nodes represent the activities themselves and the arrows show the links between the activities.
- PERT charts, a more comprehensive form of modelling which can be used to show the effect on the overall programme of the statistical variation in execution times of individual activities.

Flow-charting techniques

The use of flow charts to understand processes, particularly information-related processes and computer applications, is well-established. These general flow-charting techniques can also be used to represent processes and highlight decision-making points.

Simulation packages

These software packages carry the simple representation of a system a stage further to the modelling of the dynamic operation of the system. Even if this step was not required, the advantage the packages hold for process modelling is that to carry out the simulation requires a very close definition of the properties of the activities and the relations between them.

Decomposition methods

These techniques choose to model a system by successively decomposing a high-level summary into a lower level description. One such technique is called $IDEF_0$; IDEF stands for ICAM Definition, where ICAM was the United States Air Force's programme for Integrated Computer-Aided

Manufacture. The subscript zero indicates that this is the function model, as opposed to $IDEF_1$, which models information flows and $IDEF_2$ which is the outline of a dynamic simulation model. Of these it is $IDEF_0$ which has been most widely adopted.

$IDEF_0$ is now widely used to describe systems containing a mixture of hardware, software and people; its use is no longer confined to the manufacturing area. The method begins with the highest level, 'Level 0', which for our purposes would be the process name and would show the input to and output of the process. The next level, 'Level 1', would show the principle activities within the process; the $IDEF_0$ format prefers between three and six activities per level. Each activity has a name, which is a verb, and is assigned a box. There are four parameters linked to each activity which are assigned arrows:

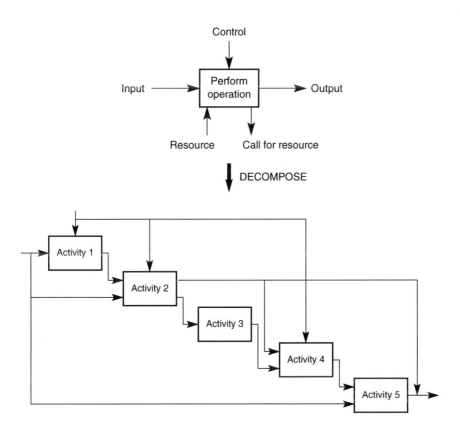

Figure 3.6 Sample IDEF$_0$ diagram

- an input to the activity, from another activity, drawn as an arrow entering the left of the box;
- an output from the activity, leading to a subsequent activity, drawn as arrow leaving the right of the box;
- a resource consumed by the activity, drawn as an arrow entering the bottom of the box;
- a control on the activity drawn as an arrow entering the top of the box.

The activities are then annotated with a code and any other information that is desired, such as cost, lead time or other non-financial attributes. Once the first level has been defined, the modelling is extended down to subsequent levels, according to the level of detail required. An example of an $IDEF_0$ diagram is given in Figure 3.6.

The chief benefit of $IDEF_0$ is its use as a communication tool. There may be several different perceptions of how a process actually operates and to resolve these requires a succinct means of describing a process; $IDEF_0$ meets this need. However, it needs to be understood that two different people will define the details of the same process in different ways, so although $IDEF_0$ is a means of sharing an understanding and obtaining an agreement of principles, it does not force a convergence in the detailed representation of that process.

While it may appear that $IDEF_0$ is a very precise method in fact the method does not comprehensively define a business process, e.g. the conditional paths a process may take. This imprec-ision is a double-edged sword; it can assist the team by allowing them to concentrate only on those parts of process modelling that are of relevance to the case at hand. However, it can result in endless *ad hoc* annotations to the process model.

The benefits of process modelling come from the benefits of a concise representation, universally understood. With this foundation it becomes possible to share ideas on the improvement of a process. In Step 3 we explore ways in which these processes can be improved. We first, however, outline the method by which activities are linked to processes.

The third interview

We have described the use of face-to-face meetings to collect information on activities and their costs. This will now be continued with a further round of interviews with the same set of individuals. The purpose of these interviews is to:

- link activities to processes;
- trace the costs to the processes;
- where possible show the relationships between activities within the process, in the form of $IDEF_0$ diagrams.

A documentation pack should be produced and circulated prior to the meeting, explaining the task at hand. It will contain:

- a list of activities and their costs;
- a list of the business processes;
- an explanation of the tracing procedures to be used and the principles behind representing processes graphically.

In some cases, the linking of an activity to a process and the tracing of cost will be straightforward: it will be clear that a particular activity belongs to a particular process and its cost can be allocated in its entirety. However, there can be complications.

The first complication is that an activity is part of more than one process. To resolve this problem requires the identification of a tracing factor, to trace the cost. Tracing factors have already been introduced, they are quantitative bases which are used to allocate costs. For example, an activity 'administer market research' may form part of a process called 'acquire new customers' and a second called 'design new products'. The activity will consist mostly of staff costs, which could be traced using time-sheet data or by estimating the time spent on specific research projects. A second activity 'commission agency', consisting of agency fees, may exist and these costs will be analysed using the value of invoices received, and how they are split between the two processes. There would be a problem however if there was a single activity 'market research' consisting of both types of cost, because the proportion of staff costs and agency fees spent on the two different processes may differ. If such an activity has been created, it is probably worthwhile to go back and split the activity.

The second complication is where an activity does not appear to form part of any identified process. This can occur because, the list of processes was derived using a top-down approach which considered the organisation's ideal activities. The list of activities was compiled using a bottom-up procedure, which sought out what was actually taking place within the organisation. Approaches vary to dealing with the gap between the two visions, namely the activities which belong to no process.

One school of thought is that it is not necessary to trace all the activities and their costs to the processes, since the intention is simply to find the costs of the processes which have been identified. The author's view is that this is hazardous, since it can easily lead to processes being undercosted and a false impression given of value for money. It is more likely that the full cost of processes will be recognised if it is the rule that all costs will be traced either to a process or a 'remainder' category which will be closely examined afterwards for value for money. This has the great advantage of providing an arithmetic check on the tracing of costs, since the sum of all the process costs and the remainder category must equal the sum of all the activity costs, which in turn must equal the cost base.

Interview conduct

The first step is to review the allocation of activities to processes. This generally does not cause a problem as long as the nature of the processes has been understood. If all the activity relates to a single process, the allocation of cost is also simple. Where an activity is split between processes, then there is a need to review the manager's choice of tracing factor.

The most interactive part of the interview is the construction of the $IDEF_0$ diagrams. The best approach to this to take a pencil and paper, discuss how the activities interact and start drawing. After the interview the end result can be entered into a PC tool, if one is available.

TRACING COSTS TO COST OBJECTS

Cost objects

During Step1, *External Review*, the business was divided into segments. One of the criteria for the recognition of a segment was unique cost behaviour, e.g. special product support requirements, special customer terms.

The segments live on, but in this step they are termed 'cost objects'. A cost object is the eventual destination of the various cost allocations which are employed: first, the cost base is allocated to activity centres, then to activities and finally to cost objects, e.g. products or services, customers or distribution channels. The term will be used extensively in the description of the cost modelling given below.

This is the final stage of the activity analysis and the one that delivers the most prized information, that is the costs incurred by products or services, customers, and distribution channels. The tracing of costs to cost objects is invariably more difficult than to processes because very few activities are carried out for a single cost object and an extensive search for suitable tracing factors is needed.

Single or multiple tracing

At this stage the question arises whether the cost base should be traced in its entirety only once, or repeatedly to each cost object. To illustrate, assuming only product and customer costs were being considered, it would be possible to either trace all the activity costs to products and then trace all the activity costs again to customers or, trace all the cost to either a product (if the activities were product dependent) or to a customer (if the activities were customer dependent).

The author's preference is to adopt a single tracing of costs to different types of cost elements. This appears more logical to the company's managers who are being asked to trace product-related costs to products and customer-related costs to customers; asking the managers to relate a product-related cost to a customer would invite disbelief! Most of the overhead activities supporting the early part of the supply chain, apart from order entry, tend to be product dependent while those near the latter end tend to be customer dependent.

A single allocation of costs does, however, require the subsequent reallocation, by the project team, of the product-related costs to customers, and vice-versa. The means of doing this is explained later.

Problems occur with single allocation where there are substantial activity costs which are dependent on more than one cost object simultaneously. In this case it is best to redefine the activity to separate out as far as possible the different components e.g. product and customer specific ports.

We will assume the latter course is taken and there is a single allocation of the cost base. Given this, the next step is to identify the type of cost object to which each activity cost will be allocated. Typically, activity costs will be traced to:

- product ranges, if they are product dependent, e.g. purchasing, design, product operations;
- customer and market groups, if they are customer dependent, e.g. customer service, most returns processing (excluding warranty returns);
- distribution channels, if they are channel dependent, e.g. dispatch costs.

There will be many activities which appear to relate to none of these. In this case, the default is to consider the activities as product dependent as it simplifies the subsequent consolidation of costs.

Tracing costs

In an ideal case, each cost object would have a Bill of Activity relating the consumption of overhead activities to the cost object, in the same way a Bill of Labour or Bill of Material can be defined. If this were the case there would be no limit to the number of individual cost objects that could be analysed: for example, the product costs could be calculated by summing the consumption of each activity by the product, multiplied by the unit cost of the activity. We can consider this as a 'bottom-up' calculation of the allocation of costs to cost objects.

If this were possible, the indirect cost could be computed in the same way that direct costs have been traditionally calculated. Unfortunately, this is rarely possible, because associating the consumption of indirect activity to each cost object is impractical.

For this reason it is necessary to allocate activity costs to product groups from the 'top-down', i.e. start with an activity cost and allocate it to a cost object on the basis of a tracing factor. The challenge is to find suitable tracing factors. Tracing factors which the author has used in the past include:

Tracing factor	*Application*
Number of:	
Customers	Customer service costs
Customer orders	Order processing
Shipments	Distribution expenses
Returns	Return processing
Brands	Brand management
Product families	Product monitoring
Purchase orders	Buying department
Production faults	Fault rectification
Production orders	Production scheduling
Batches	Production set-up costs

The tracing process is illustrated in Figure 3.7. For a tracing factor to be viable, it must be a number which can be broken down by cost object, e.g. the number of purchase orders would not be suitable for analysing purchase costs for each product range, if it was not possible to identify how many purchase orders related to each range.

Often there has to be recourse to the subjective allocation of activity cost between cost objects. It is possible for this to be rigorous where the activities have been recorded on time sheets and properly coded. Usually this is not the case, and as a last resort the manager judges that particular product range, customer or distribution channel takes up a certain proportion of the activity. This subjective process has two consequences:

- it is difficult to obtain repeatability of the process;
- it places an upper limit on the number of cost objects that can be analysed, to perhaps ten products and customers respectively, otherwise it becomes impossible to allocate subjectively.

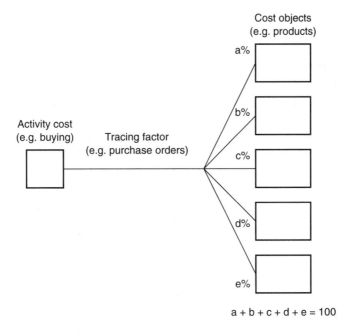

Figure 3.7 Tracing process

At the end of the interview the project team will have sufficient information to trace costs to the relevant cost objects. These costs need a further stage of consolidation before they can be used for calculating product profitability.

Consolidation of costs

The cost base has been allocated to different cost objects, according to which is the most relevant. To calculate the profitability associated with each cost object it is necessary to reallocate the costs so the entire cost base is finally allocated to each one. For example, to calculate the customer profitability it is necessary not only to know the customer-related costs by customer, but also the product-related costs by customer, which depends on product mix. This is illustrated in Figure 3.8.

In general, it is relatively easy to reallocate product-related costs to other cost objects. It is done on the basis of product mix (e.g. number of units per customer group) and as long as the mix of product groups by customer and distribution channel is known, the rest is down to arithmetic.

Allocating customer or distribution costs back to product is less simple. For example, allocating activities which were originally traced by the number of customer orders back to products using the number of units

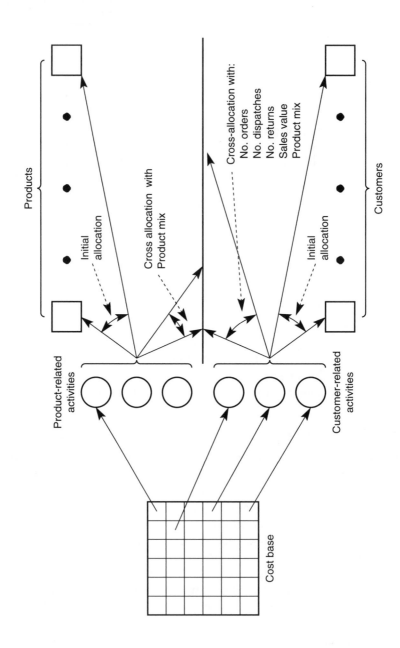

Figure 3.8 Cross-allocation of costs between products and customers

would be misleading; it is necessary to know the number of orders by product group. We have, in effect, a limited number of factors on which to reallocate costs back to product groups:

- number of units, i.e. the product mix;
- number of orders;
- number of dispatches;
- number of returns;
- value of the sales.

The procedure for reallocation is to select the most appropriate factor for a given activity and break down the total for the chosen factor by product group. This breakdown is then used to reallocate the activity cost back to products.

SEGMENT PROFITABILITY

Method of calculation

The calculation of segment profitability is not a complex task. Once the company's costs have been fully allocated within each of the cost objects, each of which represents a segment, for example, a product, customer or channel, then the remaining step is to allocate the revenue to each segment. Taking product ranges as an example, the costs associated with each range will have been calculated and once the revenue associated with each product range is also known, then calculating the product profitability is simply a matter of subtracting cost from revenue. Customer and channel profitability can be calculated in a similar way.

We now discuss the typical results of calculating segment profitability and how these can be used to ensure better control of overheads.

Product profitability

The chief benefit arising from the calculation of product profitability along activity lines is that the impact of the cost of complexity is fully understood. Typically, when costs have been absorbed on the basis of labour or machine hours, the high volume/low variety products have been penalised at the expense of the low volume/high variety products, since it is the former type which involve the use of a large number of direct hours but with relatively straightforward scheduling and tracking. In contrast, low volume/high variety products incur relatively few labour and machine hours (because of their low volume) but a large amount of effort is involved in the overhead functions to deal with the high variety. This can be a recipe for disaster: competitors offering only the high volume/low variety items are more than able to compete on price when these items have a minimum selling price based on costs. The company's market share and volume inevitably shrink, provoking a vicious circle of diseconomies of scale and yet higher prices. Eventually the company has to retreat into an array of peripheral products, and this defeat is rationalised as a victory for niche marketing!

Less typically, additional variety may involve additional direct labour or machine hours but minimal administrative effort. An example would be a manually intensive customisation at the end of the production process; this could have a minimal effect on the overhead functions, with the additional cost being confined to the cost of the operators and their immediate support functions, e.g. personnel. In this case, if the company used costs to set minimum selling prices, the result would be that such attempts to adapt to the requirements of individual customers would be prohibitively expensive.

In both cases the competitiveness of the company is handicapped by a lack of knowledge of the costs of the underlying activities required to provide a product or service. Inevitably, this affects pricing decisions and can lead to the company becoming uncompetitive and eventually failing.

Customer profitability

Many companies do not produce customer profitability information. Often the only customer-specific information that is available relates to the discounts provided to each customer. There is therefore a lack of vision on the demands particular customers or markets make on a company, either through making particular demands on the company or through necessitating particular levels of sales and marketing expenditure.

The absence of this information creates two damaging blind spots:

- There is a lack of the basic information needed for customer negotiations. For example, if an influential customer is seeking a discount, without the customer profitability information there is no way to determine if it should be granted to retain the business.
- There is an inability to construct a rational marketing strategy. For example, for most companies it is far from clear whether the small customers, who are relatively complex to service but less able to extract discounts, are more or less profitable than large customers, who demand discounts and delivery to be made in a particular form. Without profitability information, it is not possible to direct the business into the most profitable sectors.

The creation of customer profitability information enables the company to plan and negotiate far more rationally.

Channel profitability

Channel profitability information is very similar to that calculated for customers. It would only be necessary to deal with the two segments separately if the same customer received goods though more than one channel.

Distribution costs form a large part of the cost base for many companies and in the past have been apportioned on the basis of revenue, as part of the appropriately named 'SAD' category (Sales, Administration and Distribution). In fact distribution expenses are channel specific, and tracing these costs to different channels allows decisions to be made on the future distribution strategy.

INFORMATION ASSESSMENT

Introduction

A decision needs to be taken on the emphasis given to the information systems and technology part of this programme. There is no doubt that it must form some part, since the provision of good information in a systematic way is a key part of overhead control. Beyond this minimum, however, there is a choice between emphasising the organisational aspects of a programme and emphasising the systems aspect. It is assumed here that the former takes precedence and this has influenced the amount of work proposed; for example, when discussing the data used within the organisation we have not suggested defining the relationships between data entities (the items on which data is maintained, e.g. products, customers), which would be a natural step in a full-scale systems design. If the reader is considering developing an information systems and technology strategy as a preliminary stage to the complete redesign of the company's systems, rather than to make general improvements to the current systems, it would be best to take recourse to a specialist text.

Having said this, the level of examination of the information systems and technology proposed in this programme as a bare minimum goes far beyond that which is often undertaken when overhead control is discussed. Too often, there is a belief in 'more from less' with no real idea of how savings are to be made. In practice, most of the savings will come through more effective and efficient manipulation of information (though individual investments may do little towards this end); the information aspect is therefore vital.

Level of detail

During this step the team has defined between 50 and 400 activities, i.e. a geometric mean of around 150. This is generally quite adequate for examining the organisational characteristics of a company and its cost behaviour. It may not be adequate, however, for examining the information requirements, where a finer level of detail could be required.

The solution is to permit an extra level of subdivision if necessary. If it is found that within an activity there are different types of work which require different information, it is possible to define subsidiary tasks. For example for cost modelling purposes, it may be sufficient to define an activity 'issue purchase order', but for information modelling three subsidiary tasks could be identified: 'identify supplier', 'define purchase order lines', and 'issue order/update systems'.

It may be necessary to define up to five tasks per activity. This gives a maximum number of two thousand tasks within the organisation, which should be adequate for most purposes.

Timing of the assessment

The project team has three options for the timing of the information assessment. The team can carry out the assessment during:

- The first or third interviews. This has much to recommend it. These interviews are generally fairly easy to conduct and there is a natural affinity between asking a manager about the activities undertaken in his area, or the association of these activities, with processes, and assessing the information systems which support those activities and processes.
- The second or fourth interviews. This is less desirable, since the second and fourth interviews are usually difficult to complete, because of the detailed tracing of costs to be undertaken.
- A separate fifth interview. This is possible, though it does have the disadvantage of a further series of meeting arrangements and the placing of an additional burden on management time.

It will be assumed below that the first route was taken, and the gathering of details on the information requirements and systems is combined with the collection of details on the activities or their association with processes. While the two tasks may be performed in tandem, it is important that the activities are clarified first, before the information issues are discussed, otherwise the framework on which to consider the information issues will not be in place.

Structure of assessment

The first stage is to determine the information required by managers for each activity or task; this was briefly considered in the previous step. Then, the purpose was to broaden the horizons of the project team as regards the type of information which may be available. Now, the task is to ask the managers the information they require, using the previous understanding as a foil.

Once the information requirements have been understood at a detailed level, the next step is catalogue the information which is actually available and the level of satisfaction, in terms of its accuracy, timeliness and relevance to the activities and tasks at hand. The information is the output from the systems, produced by the processing of data, and the team also needs to record the databases which are maintained within each activity centre.

The systems which convert the input data into the output information consist of applications, i.e. the information conversion processes and technologies, of which the most important elements are the platforms on which the applications operate, i.e. the hardware and operating systems. The project team also records the applications and technologies in use in each activity centre.

The intention is to investigate each of the items discussed above, during the interviews. Over the past decade this approach has become an accepted way to analyse information systems and technologies and propose new strategies. Another example of a planning methodology is given in a paper, 'Strategic IS/IT Planning' (Hickey 1993); here too, one of the steps is the building of 'IDATO' architectures, where IDATO stands for information, data, applications, technology and organisation of the IT resource.

At the end of the assessment the project team will be in a position to identify weaknesses in the systems. These weaknesses will refer not only to the ability of the systems to support the current operations, but the prospective weaknesses as the organisation changes to meet its longer term goals. There follows the task of synthesising a strategy which will tackle these weaknesses while protecting the existing and future investment in systems.

Information – required and available

The procedure for gaining an understanding of the information requirements is quite simple. The manager is asked to state his views on the information needed for each activity, and if necessary each subsidiary task and the answers must however be judged critically.

Where a manager declares a need for information it is important to relate this to a decision which falls within the responsibilities of the manager; the effects of a declared absence of information can also be discussed. It is more difficult to identify where there is a lack of necessary information which may go unrecognised by the manager. However during Step 1, the team previously considered the information requirements of the processes in a top-down way; using the understanding gained, the team is able to challenge the manager on whether particular types of information would prove useful, even if their need is not currently recognised.

The project team then seeks to understand the managers' views on the information currently available. This will encompass the parameters which are available, the frequency with which they are reported and the perceived integrity of the information.

Again the managers' opinions need to be challenged. The views on the availability of information may be wrong because of a limited understanding of the systems. Complaints about the integrity of the information may be exaggerated. Therefore the project team need to probe the answers given.

It now becomes possible to draw up an analysis of the gap between the information needed and that which is available, as shown in Figure 3.9.

Databases

There is likely to be a variety of databases maintained in the organisation, resulting in both duplication and fragmentation. It is necessary for the project team to identify the various databases, many of which may be not be computerised, which are maintained in each activity centre.

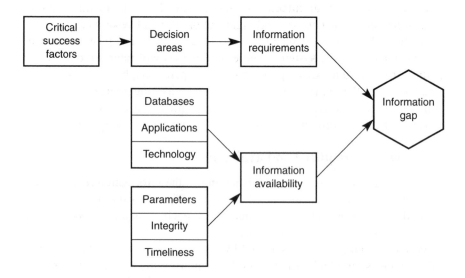

Figure 3.9 Information gap

Once a database has been identified, then its contents are summarised. The contents are the data entities, and these entities can be linked to the applications which draw upon the data.

Applications

When discussing the information requirements, we remarked that it is straightforward for the manager to discuss information needs which are already met, but more difficult to identify a requirement which exists but goes unrecognised. In a similar way, it is relatively easy to identify applications which are formally recognised and implemented on computing systems, but it is more difficult to deduce the presence of an information process which is informally undertaken, but nonetheless forms an important part of the business.

The first step is to catalogue those applications which are formally recognised, extending this where necessary to include manual systems. The next stage is to deduce the less formal information processes, which may merit a more formal application in the future (e.g. the maintenance of a list of approved suppliers, which reflects recent performance). These may be undertaken informally but could merit a special database application in the future.

Once the applications have been identified, the next step is to link their use to particular activities or tasks.

Technologies

Recording the technologies in use is usually a fairly mechanistic task which involves listing the hardware (both processing and storage) and operating systems available to support each activity or task. This exercise should not only cover computers, but also:

- non-electronic technologies, for example a sophisticated manual project monitoring and control system;
- the communications equipment in use, whether for data links or for voice or graphical communication or storage.

While all this is straightforward, it usually emphasises the duplication of systems, their lack of integration and the wide spectrum of technology employed.

Collation of results

At the end of this procedure a large amount of information will have been collected on the information systems and technologies which are in use to serve particular activities or tasks. It is now necessary to begin identifying opportunities for improvement. There will normally be no shortage of such opportunities, involving:

- a shortfall in information requirements, either as a result of information being absent or of inadequate timeliness, frequency or accuracy;
- inconsistent or duplicated data being maintained within the organisation;
- the boundaries of applications reflecting arbitrary organisational boundaries as opposed to those set by the business processes;
- limitations in technology, e.g. the absence of computerisation or modern communication technology.

There is a need to identify patterns in these opportunities for improvement, so as to arrive at a condensed version of the main shortcomings of the current systems for both the current and proposed operations. Once this is done, priorities can be attached to the various shortcomings by relating them to the activities or tasks affected.

The results from this work will be used in Step 3, *Radial Change* to generate a strategy for information systems and technology within the organisation.

IT SUPPORT TOOLS

Need for tools

It will be apparent that a large amount of information is being produced during this programme. The project team can easily become overwhelmed by detail, especially when the cost modelling is being undertaken. We now discuss the various options for IT support that are available.

Spreadsheets

These are of course easily created and very useful for *ad hoc* calculations. There can be a danger, however, that the information in the project becomes fragmented over a series of spreadsheets and proper control of the information becomes difficult. This is especially the case if the information is liable to change, and is recorded on more than one spreadsheet.

Commercial packages

There are many inexpensive packages available for activity-based costing, process modelling information system analysis, project management etc.

These are a great boon to productivity in their particular area of application. The drawback is that the transfer of information between the different packages may not be simple.

The issue of data transfer needs to be addressed when a tool set is being chosen. Sometimes compatibility is not possible, in which case a database application may be appropriate.

Database applications

Since the basic objective of the PC support tools is to store data in a structured manner and to identify links and patterns, there is some logic in constructing an application to run on a PC database system. This has the advantage that the data are integrated and can be drawn upon as required.

The disadvantage is that it takes some effort to write such an application the skills may not be readily available. Furthermore the work needs to be done prior to the start of the project, otherwise the lack of PC support will form an impediment.

LIFE-CYCLE COSTING CASE STUDY

Background

The company manufactures and sells garments. This apparently simple mission in life is, in fact, extremely complex. Some of the garments are 'plains', which do not vary from season to season; others are 'designs' which are unique to a particular season. Many of the customers are small and deal on standard terms but can be costly to service; some are major large companies who have immense negotiating power and demand special arrangements, some of which incur cost, while others reduce it, e.g. not returning goods. Some of the garments are made in-house from purchased fabric, while other garments are purchased as finished goods. Finally there is great variety in the business, due to the large number of combinations of garment sizes, fabric designs and fabric colours; the result is that the business has to manage tens of thousands of stock keeping units and manufacture is carried out in very large numbers of small batches.

The demand this places on the company's management is heavy and responding to this demand forms of the basis of our next two case studies. This case study is concerned with the improvement of the product life cycle of the designed garment; the second case study (at the end of the next chapter) is concerned with the calculation of product and customer profitability.

The foundation for both was a major activity-based costing exercise, which we describe below. First, however, we define the objectives of the present case study.

Objectives

The objectives are to identify, for designed garments:

- the key points in the life cycle, at which cost is either committed or expended;
- changes to the life cycle, with a view to shortening it.

These objectives are critical to the profitability of the whole company. We will see that a major opportunity cost relates to 'clearers', which are garments which have to be sold at a discount at the end of a season. If clearers are to be reduced, the costs and lead-times within the life cycle need to be changed so that better decisions on design are taken closer to the season during which the garments are purchased by the consumer.

Approach

Naturally, the first step is to define the product life cycle. Fortunately, this is straightforward. To ensure that the designed garments are available on time, a critical path analysis has been carried out by the company, which states

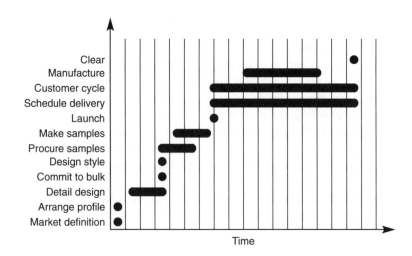

Figure 3.10 Product life cycle

what has to be done by when, in order for the shirts to be available on time. An abbreviated version of this is shown in Figure 3.10.

The second step is far more complex. It is to carry out the activity analysis programme described in Step 2. There is no need to repeat the description of the procedure here, only to summarise the results. A total of some 180 activities was identified, though a strong Pareto curve was found, with a few activities amounting to the majority of the cost; nonetheless the full complement was included in the analysis to reassure the managers that the activity analysis was fully their own.

The third step is to allocate each activity to the stage in the life cycle with which it is concerned, where possible. For most of the cost, some two thirds in this case, it is possible to associate an activity with the life cycle. For some costs, this cannot be done, e.g. administration costs. Rather than attempt an apportionment these were simply left to one side. Furthermore,

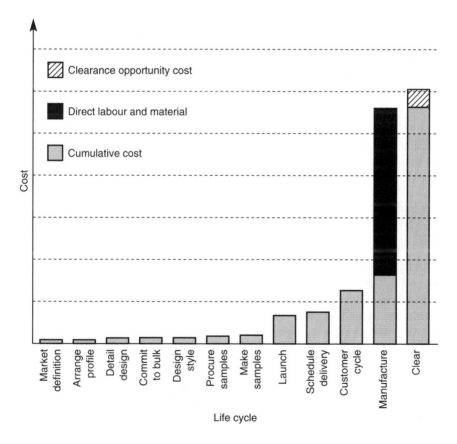

Figure 3.11 Profile of cost commitment

some of the activities which support the life cycle of a 'design' garment will also support a 'plain' garment; this can be accounted for, by separating out the latter costs.

Once these steps have been carried out, we can calculate the accumulation of cost during the product life cycle; this is shown in Figure 3.11. It is a common pattern, which is observed in many industries, e.g. mechanical and electrical engineering.

Life-cycle costs

The first conclusion from Figure 3.11 is that major commitments of future expenditure, namely on the purchase of fabric, are made very early in the life cycle, when very little money has been spent, in terms of the total cost of the garment, on researching the market and designing the fabric.

Given the high opportunity cost of 'clearers', shown on the right of the figure, it may be justified to considerably increase the expenditure on early market research and design to reduce the clearers. Furthermore the manufacturing cost, in terms of the labour input will also have been determined very early on, with relatively little expenditure.

There are two major conclusions for the company:

- the cost of good design is cheap, when expressed as a proportion of the total life-cycle cost and the company may wish to spend in this area for later benefit;
- the cost of bad design is dear, and the quality controls on the design function are critical to profitability.

Incidentally, these conclusions are not unique to the garment industry.

Life-cycle timing

The timing of the life cycle is also crucial. Figure 3.12 shows the life cycle, but marked to illustrate when funds are committed, when orders are received and when payment is actually made. For the company, a worse situation could hardly be imagined: major commitment and expenditure is made on fabric months before a single order has been received; there is then a further period of several months before delivery is accepted by the customers and payment for a garment is received.

Of all these delays, it is the one between commitment to fabric and the receipt of orders which is the most serious. There is a vast opportunity to forecast badly the fabric designs and the quantity of fabric needed; this may not be due to poor forecasting practice but simply because the market radically changes beyond all reasonable expectation.

Figure 3.12 Financial commitment

Therefore the objective for this company is to move from a 'buy before you sell' situation, to 'sell before you buy'. This is not out of the question, due to the long interval between orders being taken and delivery being expected.

Segmenting the product life cycle

A single life cycle, defined by the critical path analysis, has been defined for the whole product range. This simplifies the operation of the business but needs to change. There will always be some parts of the product range, the genuinely unique part, which will have to be individually designed and fabric ordered in advance. Much of the design range is, however, far from unique. It either uses fabrics which are relatively conventional, or it uses yarns of a standard colour and composition. The company therefore has the option to divide its life cycle into three parts:

- A life-cycle along the lines of current practice;
- A life-cycle which uses standard fabric designs. An order is then placed upon the supplier for the appropriate quantity once the initial orders for the garment using this design have been taken;

- A life-cycle which uses standard yarns, but which are woven into unique fabric designs. An order is placed for weaving capacity, but the use of this pre-booked capacity is left open until initial orders for garments have been taken.

The product life cycle also has an impact on the manufacturing strategy. One reason for the early ordering of fabric is to receive it long before delivery of the garments is expected. In this way the manufacturing demand for the season can be spread evenly across half the year, even though the delivery to the retailers is concentrated in a small proportion of the year. The exercise in segmenting the life cycle must therefore go hand in hand with the specification of the manufacturing strategy. This itself is a complex area with several variables, including:

- the option to subcontract out manufacture of the garments or to buy in work from other manufacturers who wish to subcontract;
- the phasing of the 'plains' and the 'designs' through the factory;
- whether to use the factory for short runs, offering high responsiveness, or for high volume/low variety work to minimise costs.

This manufacturing strategy work cannot be carried out in isolation. It must be done with awareness of the manufacturing capabilities of both suppliers and competitors.

Conclusion

The life cycle analysis has suggested that the fundamental operating cycles of the company be radically altered. Not only should the design function be better resourced, controlled and equipped but also the approach to the procurement of fabric be radically changed.

The effect of these changes will also affect the relationship the company has with its suppliers. At the moment it deals at arm's length and specifies its requirements uniquely and independently, but if it is to start using fabrics designed elsewhere, yarns specified by others and ask weavers to hold open capacity for fabric designs yet to be specified, then it will need to build closer relationships with its suppliers.

4

RADICAL CHANGE

To every thing there is a season and a time to every purpose under the heaven. A time to be born, and a time to die; a time to plant and a time to pluck up that which is planted ...

ECCLESIASTES 3:1, 2

INTRODUCTION

Objectives

The objective of Step 3, *Radical Change* is to exploit the understanding provided by the combination of Step 1, *External Review* and Step 2, *Activity Analysis*. The emphasis is on identifying the priorities for change, generating ideas for process improvement and defining gains in the area of cost, lead time and quality. To these are added improvements deduced from analysing the attributes and drivers of the organisation and the potential for rationalisation of segments of the business; we also consider the effectiveness of the information systems and the organisational structure.

At the end of this step, the terms of reference are defined for a small number of task forces to carry forward the work once the project team has completed its work.

Figure 4.1 Step 3: Radical Change

Deliverables

During this stage of the work, illustrated in Figure 4.1, the project team will provide:

- priorities for comprehensive change to the processes of the organisation;
- ideas for improvements to these processes and models of the processes on which the proposed changes can be tested;
- an analysis of the attributes and drivers to generate additional ideas for improvement;
- proposals for:

  – new trade-offs between cost and lead time;
  – shortened lead times within processes;
  – improvements in quality within processes;

- options for the ratonalisation of certain business segments, e.g. products, customers or distribution channels;
- plans for the improvement of the information systems and technologies;
- changes to improve the organisational structure;
- fully briefed task forces to carry forward their proposals, in preparation for implementation.

Issues

The key to this step is the comprehensiveness or breadth of the change which is being considered. Most improvements to corporations are undertaken locally or within departments, because their area of application is limited to the span of control of the manager initiating the change; we consider this type of change in the next step of the programme. In this step, however, we consider the wider possibilities. Compared to local change, radical change tends to be:

- more comprehensive, in that it requires a greater degree of change in the way the organisation operates;
- more rewarding, in that it delivers a greater improvement in performance or reduction in cost.

This step therefore counters the temptation to consider the existing structure as a fixture and to confine increases in performance to improving the current arrangement. It needs to be considered whether a radical approach would yield benefits and to challenge whether an overhead function has to be done in a particular way, or even done at all. The recommendations will include changing the business processes and rationalising the business so that the need for certain activities, or scales of activities, is no longer present.

ASSESSING PRIORITIES

Need for priorities

The need to prioritise is a consequence of success. If there were only a small number of necessities or opportunities for improvement, all of them could be put into effect. In practice, there will be limitations because the number of potential improvements will be too great for the project team to examine and the organisation to absorb.

Given that it is impractical to deal with every possibility, we need guidelines on how to select priorities for improvement, from the various changes to information systems processes and organisation which could be developed in this step. We now outline how these priorities are to be decided.

Setting priorities

The influence on setting priorities was considered during Step 1, *External Review* and Step 2, *Activity Analysis*. There are two conditions which are relevant:

- the shortfall between the required and the actual performance;
- the degree to which the shortfall affects the performance of the business.

During Step 1 the critical processes were defined on the basis of their importance to the business. For each of these critical processes, the performance which customers expect and the value they place on this performance being met were also examined. The project team, therefore, now knows the processes which merit special attention, because they are critical and performance needs to improve or the methods used to control them.

The second influence on setting priorities was examined in Step 2, *Activity Analysis*. Information was collected on both the general cost drivers and the attributes of activities, with the intention of identifying common themes. Both can be used to identify opportunities for improvement across the organisation:

- cost drivers show general influences on the level of cost throughout the company;
- attributes, which are defined by the project team, show common features, e.g. the relevance of a quality issue.

By summing the total cost of all the activities for which a particular cost driver or attribute is relevant, the significance of the parameter can be assessed.

There will, of course, be a great deal of overlap between opportunities identified from the two sources. Many of the shortfalls in performance seen by customers will arise from problems identified from the attribute/driver analysis. At this point a decision has to be taken whether to view the problem from a process or a driver and attribute perspective. The choice depends on whether a particular issue affects a particular process; if a single process is affected then a process approach is the most focused.

Summary of priorities

The priorities for action need to be agreed before proceeding. There should not to be too many priorities; the intention is to finally arrive at no more than five simultaneous initiatives which is the limit an organisation can absorb.

Once the priorities are established then the search for improvements can begin. It is possible that in some cases no improvement can be found; in the others however the analysis is carried though to the point where a task force can be set up to implement the improvement once the project team has finished.

PROCESS IMPROVEMENT

Idea generation

We have already alluded to the fact that change which affects the whole organisation is likely to be more radical and result in greater reward. This begs the question of from where these radical ideas are expected to arise. Here we see an opportunity to transfer expertise and techniques from the area of product design to process design.

The first step is to identify the sources of new ideas: these comprise:

- *Individuals within the company.* This is a natural source since many staff will no doubt be harbouring years of dissatisfaction with the way the company's operations make their lives difficult. These ideas represent an internal view of improvement.
- *Customers*, who can be a very useful source of ideas, since they bear the brunt of any problems. The project team will have already canvassed the customers on their requirements and this can be extended to their views on how requirements can be met by a change in operations.
- *Suppliers*, who can occasionally offer useful ideas on how to integrate their operations with those of the organisation. Much of the emphasis on partnership sourcing is concerned with this topic.
- *The press.* Regular reading of the business press reveals reports on how other companies have achieved success or of new systems and technologies that are becoming available.

The second step is to agree the forum in which the new ideas can be canvassed. One obvious route is to set up a short meeting with the originator of the idea. This is excellent for examining the idea because its substance can be carefully picked over during a dialogue; this is far more effective than relying on reports of new ideas where only one-way communication is possible.

'Brainstorming' sessions also have a role; their advantage is that many ideas can be generated by individuals bouncing ideas off each other and combining them. The disadvantage is the natural disorder of the event; however, on no account should this be countered since it will destroy the spontaneity of the meeting on which its success depends! Once the meeting is ended the ideas need to be explored further.

At this stage, the level of documentation and bureaucracy needs to be kept controlled to the minimum necessary to assure the quality of the work. Most of the best ideas will arise form informal meeting of minds and this can be suppressed by endless chairing of sessions and minuting of actions.

Assessment

A careful balance has to be struck between generating radical new ideas and ensuring they are practical. If the balance is not met, there will be either a set of startling ideas which cannot be implemented or a rather dull set of proposals which closely resemble current practice. To avoid the latter fault two steps are necessary:

- Idea generation needs to be separated from idea assessment. Early assessment stifles creativity as potential contributors see ideas being knocked down.
- Idea assessment should be postponed until the full results from the external and internal analyses are known. This is assured with the proposed programme, because these tasks are undertaken in the first two steps. It needs to be stressed, however, that pressure to deliver early solutions will result in these solutions being relatively conservative.

Nonetheless, eventually an assessment of the ideas is essential. To be useful, this assessment needs to develop as opposed to criticise the ideas. One technique that has a long pedigree in the design field is the use of peer group review. The roles which are relevant to designing new processes are:

- The project team which has now collated its proposals for change.
- The steering group whose purpose is to comment on the new processes.
- A chairman. The chairman of the meetings should not have any vested interest in the discussion. Therefore he should not be the project manager. An ideal candidate is the Chief Executive of the company. An absolutely necessary skill is to be able to steer the discussion constructively so as to enhance the original proposals.

The meetings should last no more than a few hours, and a follow up meeting arranged to occur within a few days, when the recommended changes will be examined. In this way the iterative process of developing the ideas can operate as rapidly as possible.

Carts and horses

When it comes to implementing process improvements a choice will have to be made between:

- pursuing the ideal solution and designing the tools to support that solution;
- researching the market for the tools which are available and moulding the processes to use them.

The first course of action may seem the natural course, namely putting the horse before the cart; however, in the real world the horse often takes second place. The reason is the high cost of customised vehicles, namely the customised information and distribution systems needed to support an individual process design.

Even major organisations, e.g. large utilities, can come to regret customised system development. The costs of ensuring the system is kept abreast of modern developments can be exorbitant when the IT is not amortised across many installations. The 'packaged solution' is now accepted as at least the first step for systems as diverse as general ledgers and manufacturing resource planning; it may also be the last step, i.e. the company accepts its procedures will match the needs of the package completely, or alternatively some degree of custom development is accepted as inevitable. The extent of this development has to be controlled; if it is too great the potential for upgradeability will be destroyed.

Therefore any search for improvements to a process has to take account of the standard systems which are on the market. These standard systems may be confined to the processing of information or involve physical processing, e.g. physical distribution systems.

This issue is not confined to the application of packaged systems. More generally, there is the question of whether the business ought to drive technology or the other way around. Posed in this form, there seems only one answer: the business issues should determine which technologies are adopted. In practice, however, many improvements in business operations are made by observing the technologies which are emerging and asking 'How can I apply this?' either to an existing business or to a new business. So for example, the fax machine and the Walkman were businesses created by searching for new purposes for the available technologies.

Matters become even more complicated when the company has the resources to develop the technology. The technology development then becomes one part of the corporate strategy and decisions need to be made on whether to incur the costs associated with maintaining a technological lead or to apply the technology developed by others. Either route is viable, but if the decision is made to develop a technological lead the management of this process is key.

In summary, when seeking process improvement one eye has to be kept on the business itself and the other on the systems or technologies which are available off the shelf or for an economical cost of development.

Idea generation – summary

Any programme to seek radical change will fail if new ideas are not forthcoming. To succeed, there needs to be a:

- forum for the generation of ideas;
- means of assessment of those ideas, which does not interfere with the idea generation;
- recognition of the availability of off-the-shelf solutions on offer in the market.

These influences are summarised in Figure 4.2. We now consider specific ways in which the ideas for improvement can be developed.

Specific types of improvement

Generally a process may fall short of required performance in three ways:

- *Cost and service levels.* The costs involved in operating the process do not justify the value of the services delivered in terms of the customer, i.e. there is a need to strike the best trade-off between cost and customer service.
- *Time.* The time taken within the process is too long to satisfy the requirements of the customer.
- *Quality.* The quality of the product or service delivered is impaired.

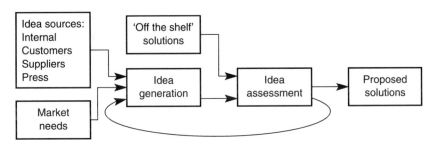

Figure 4.2 Idea generation process

Quite often, these problems are interrelated. For example, a quality problem can give rise to unnecessary iterations within a process, which result in lengthy lead time and unnecessary cost.

Focusing attention

It is instructive to take the $IDEF_0$ process model, which has been decomposed to its constituent activities, and annotate the model with the activity costs, lead times and a measure of quality (perhaps quality cost or failure rates). An example is given in Figure 4.3 for the supply chain management process.

This immediately helps focus attention on where within the process effort should be concentrated. So for example with the supply chain management process, it may be that accepting orders is a relatively inexpensive activity compared to the clerical or manual tasks involved in their execution, but it can take an undue length of time. If the emphasis is on cost reduction, the order-taking activity may merit only scant attention (except if it caused quality cost elsewhere); however, if the object is lead-time reduction, then a detailed analysis is justified. For manufacturing companies, the sales office is often an area where substantial reductions in processing time can be achieved at minimal cost compared to investments required elsewhere; for example, equipping salesmen with personal computers and modems for daily direct entry of orders is far cheaper than installing flexible manufacturing technology to reduce set-up times on the shopfloor.

Figure 4.3 Process diagram

The advantage of examining cost, timeliness and quality along the process is that attention is focused in the locality where the most can be gained, on the Pareto principle, that 80 per cent of the benefit will be gained in 20 per cent of activities.

Detailed process modelling

Once the areas which merit the closest attention have been established it then becomes worthwhile to carry the process modelling down to a closer level of detail in these areas. The purpose of the detailed process modelling is to:

- define what is undertaken in a concise and unambiguous way;
- act as a medium for communicating when discussing potential improvements;
- provide a means of modelling the effects of possible changes.

The process modelling can be done simply by carrying out the $IDEF_0$ decompositions to a lower level of detail. There are however alternatives. We have already commented that although $IDEF_0$ is a useful tool for describing mixed systems, it does not capture all the information on a process, e.g. the decision points within a process, so it may be useful to adopt a different method for the detailed process modelling. These alternatives were outlined in the previous chapter, for example, flow-charting or simulation.

String diagrams

Another technique for simplifying process flow has been taken directly from the work study method used to improve physical distribution. This is the 'string diagram', which is illustrated in Figure 4.4, where the progress of an item during manufacture and distribution is charted on a peg board using a piece of string. Unidirectional flow over a short distance is evidence of a good organisation of the process; a plate of spaghetti is evidence of quite the reverse!

In a similar way it is possible to plot the process flow as it moves from department to department, and back. In general, numerous crossings of boundaries should be avoided, because:

- There is often a cost, delay and risk of error associated with the transfer as the process moves from one system to another.
- There is a loss of accountability as more managers become involved in the process. Where there is failure the cause can be obscured in a fog of complexity.

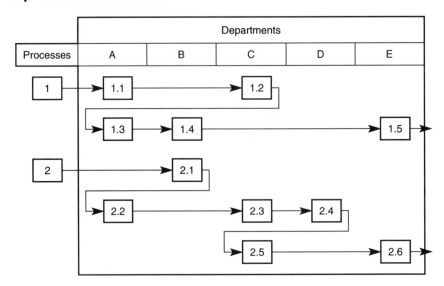

Figure 4.4 String diagram for clerical functions

The process flow, which may involve physical movement, information flow and authorisation is plotted on a chart. Different departments are distinguished by either by the use of different locations or in some other way such as the use of colour or cross-hatching. Unnecessary crossings of departmental boundaries become apparent and opportunities for streamlining the processes can be investigated.

Process simplification

Whatever method is employed an immediate advantage of the graphical representation is that possible simplifications become apparent. These may arise from:

- Elimination of duplicated activities. If the process is complicated duplication is quite possible, especially where it involves the checking of information which has been checked before.
- Avoiding generating unnecessary information. Especially where paper forms are involved, there is a huge inertia in changing data collection procedures. Information may have been collected in the past to support a procedure which is no longer carried out.
- Avoiding unnecessary decision points. In most flow diagrams there are conditional points, where the route taken within the process depends on a piece of information. The conditional paths can be unnecessarily complex and this offers the chance for simplification.

- Combining or separating process flows. In some cases similar processes exist side by side, and it would be possible to combine these, perhaps with the addition of some conditional tests, to achieve economies of scale. In other cases separation of processes is called for; this is particularly the case where the same process is being used to support both high volume/low variety and low volume/high variety flows. The process complexity needed to support the latter type of work can result in unnecessary cost when the process is used for the former type.
- Avoidance of unnecessary movement. Sometimes this is physical movement, in other cases it involves crossing departmental boundaries.

Once the options for improvement have been identified, using the approaches described above, the next step is to test their practicality. We now describe how this may be done.

Quality Function Deployment

We now consider a technique to link the internal operations of the process with the needs of the customer, since in simplifying processes there is a need to judge which activities are relevant to meeting the customers' needs and which are not. In this way a 'value' is attached to an activity.

This is a crucial point often missed. It is common to distinguish between high value and low value activities. Sometimes the distinction is obvious, but in other cases an activity only acquires value though being part of a process which serves a customer. There is therefore a need to associate a part of a process, i.e. an activity, or a characteristic of a process with the customers' requirements, so as to judge the relative importance of those parts and characteristics.

This is a familiar problem. In product design there is the challenge to relate the physical features of the product, such as its weight, power consumption and features, with the needs of the customers. If this is not done the efforts of the design engineers will be unappreciated by the eventual customer. There is a clear parallel with the specification and design of processes where there is a similar requirement to connect the internal and the external view.

A tool which has demonstrated some success in the product design area has the name of Quality Function Deployment. It originated in Japan and has also been developed under the banner of the 'House of Quality'; a detailed account is provided in *The House of Quality* (Hauser and Clausing, 1988). The heart of Quality Function Deployment is a matrix as shown in Figure 4.5: the method is a way of compressing diverse information into a small space in a way that is easily understandable and attractive to those who receive it.

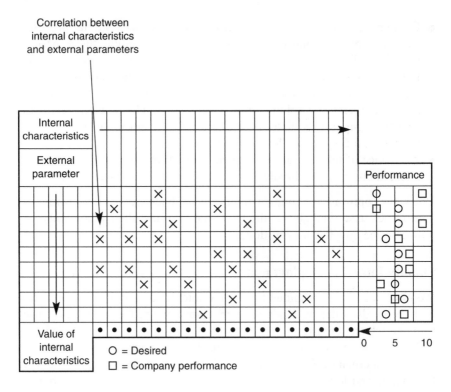

Figure 4.5

The sides of the matrix are a statement of the customer requirements and the values which the customer expects and actually receives; This information was gathered in Step 1, *External Review*. The top of the matrix lists the internal characteristics of the product (or process); at the bottom is a measurement of the characteristic, comparing the product (or processes) under development with its rivals. Finally an optional roof can be added (to build a House of Quality), which consists of a matrix showing the interdependency, both positive and negative, between the different internal characteristics.

We therefore have a means of being able to relate the internal characteristics of the process to the external requirements of the customer. A proposal to introduce parallel processing to reduce lead time, to restrict the variety of work being undertaken, to move to electronic media, or any other change can be examined and discussed using the Quality Function Deployment matrix. The strength of the method does not derive from any special method of analysis, but rather in its ability to display information in a form that is accessible to all and thereby encourage debate.

Process testing

Finally, before proposing changes to processes a view has to be taken on how the changes will be tested, since the practicalities of testing may affect the proposed solution. The alternatives are to have the changes:

- Implemented in one go, the 'big-bang' solution.
- Implemented gradually, so that a change in one area is tested before the next change is made.
- Tested in a parallel system, which mimics the operation of the live system until there is sufficient confidence in the new system for it to assume the operational workload. At this point the original system becomes the parallel back-up as the new system goes 'live'. When no doubts remain of the new system's performance the old system is finally dropped.
- Tested in a pilot system, before adoption.
- Simulated using a computer simulation language. This has the advantage of being able to test the new proposals without affecting the organisation as a whole.

The first option should only be adopted for non-critical systems, i.e. where a failure is not serious and the damage is repairable. Gradual change also has its dangers, as some parts of the company work to the old systems and others to the new; however, if the various components of the proposed changes are relatively independent, it is possible.

The last three options are all feasible. Parallel working is the surest way to ensure the new processes work correctly, but it is expensive; hence the adoption of a pilot study in many cases. While the simulation approach can be cheaper still, there is a need for the simulation to be sufficiently realistic.

ATTRIBUTES AND DRIVERS

Application

So far, we have emphasised the process view when seeking methods to exercise tighter control over the overhead functions of the company. We now consider the use of attributes and drivers. These were introduced during Step 2, *Activity Analysis*, when attributes, cost drivers and activity drivers were discussed. They are used to spot common issues or problems that may not be confined to a single process and which, while they may not merit attention if their impact on individual processes is considered, do merit action when their overall impact is understood.

Attributes

We have also explained how attributes can be used to investigate lead time or quality, mark candidates for a make-versus-buy analysis or group the activities into certain classes. We will dicuss lead time and quality improvement later in Step 3 and consider the make-versus-buy decision in Step 4. We consider here the use of attributes in linking together similar activities.

If activities are in some way similar, there may be an advantage in acknowledging this within the organisation; problems can arise when activities with common attributes are dispersed throughout the organisation. The factors to be considered when activities show common attributes include:

- *Installing common monitoring mechanisms.* For example, if there are activities which have an environmental impact there may be a need to install common systems; alternatively, if there are several activities responsible for purchasing material from suppliers, this too would require some form of control. One solution is for, the activities with common attributes to be brought together.
- *Sharing information.* There can be advantage in providing links between staff carrying out similar types of activity to share expertise.
- *Common support.* Activities with the same attribute may require similar support, in terms of training or information systems.

When used in this way, attributes identify common features between activities, with a view to associating them in some way. This can be useful in the larger organisation, where the diversity of operations prevents an understanding of the individual features of the activities.

Cost drivers

The cost drivers collected in the previous step are of two sorts:

- those specified by the project team, in the knowledge that they were factors which were relevant to the organisation;
- one or two open cost drivers, where the interviewee is invited to state the major irritations and obstacles to good performance.

These are now used to identify the relative priorities for cost reduction. Common examples include the availability or the functionality of the information systems of the company and the lack of accurate forecasting within the organisation. The cost driver analysis also reveals the costs associated with complexity; common drivers include the diversity of the product or service ranges or the number of transactions that need processing, regardless of their importance to the company.

The cost drivers named by the managers are also interesting, because where these factors recur they indicate areas which may merit investment to correct a shortcoming.

Summary

The analysis of the attributes and drivers provides additional insights into the ways in which performance can be improved. These are combined with the results of the process improvement analysis and are used to propose changes in the overhead functions, with a view to improving costs and service levels, lead times or quality.

COST AND SERVICE LEVELS

Introduction

Cost reduction is often the primary objective in a programme to control overheads. Nearly all of the techniques which will be described subsequently have a place in reducing costs, given a certain level of service within an activity. The current topic is more general, namely the trade-off between cost and service level within a process.

This trade-off is always of concern, either to understand the degree to which cost reductions will affect the quality of service delivered to customers or, more positively, to question to whether an increase of expenditure in an area will deliver value in excess of the cost incurred.

Measurement of value

The project team have been considering the value of activities of the company's performance in many ways, including the:

- measurement of the customer requirements and the quantification of his needs using conjoint analysis;
- classification of activities using attributes such as value-added and non-value-added, or by the use of other similar categories;
- use of Quality Function Deployment to relate the internal operations of a process to the customers' needs.

Taken together, these perspectives provide the team with a measurement of value to examine different combinations of cost and service level, and judge their attractiveness to the customer.

Constant service level at lower cost

We have already commented that different activities offer different cost versus service level trade-offs, e.g. the sales office example given previously, where lead-time improvements may be particularly economical to obtain, compared to activities elsewhere in the process.

The first step is therefore to examine whether overall process cost reductions can be obtained by increasing activity costs in certain areas while decreasing them in others, but still delivering the same process performance overall. This is investigated using the $IDEF_0$ process diagrams; various opportunities for switching resource from one activity to another while maintaining overall performance are considered. In this way it may be possible to make economies without compromising service.

Changing service levels

If the value of a particular level of service to the customer has been quantified, it is theoretically possible to adopt a mathematical approach to optimisation. The stage in the process which offers the most economical method of improving service is identified and the cost associated with increased performance, e.g. in delivery lead time, is understood. This is compared with the amount a typical customer would be prepared to pay for the incremental increase in service, and an optimum level struck. While the mathematical rigour of this approach is attractive, the number of occasions when the precision of the available information allows this approach to be undertaken is very few.

More commonly, a series of proposals for changing service levels and their associated costs is considered and the impact on the customer assessed. The assessment is based on the insights into the customer requirements gained by the methods listed earlier. Generally, there is an attempt to shift resource into those areas identified as important to the customer and away from the non-value-added activities.

The team needs a means of evaluating these proposals, other than poring over them at a desk. We now describe one method which has the advantage of stimulating real dialogue, namely that of challenge groups, which bring together those responsible for a process and the recipients of its output. The recipients may either be customers or their representatives, i.e. 'devil's advocates', perhaps from the sales function, who can argue the customer view from knowledge of the customer requirements.

Service level challenge

We have said that ideally, when considering the level of process expenditure it would be possible to calculate the costs and revenues if the service levels were changed and compare these with the costs and revenues with the current service levels, but often this objective method is not feasible

If this is the case it is still feasible to retain a rigorous approach while using the skills and judgement of the management. The approach is designed to force choices on the relative merits of different service levels, given their costs. These choices are best made in face-to-face meetings between the managers of the activities and the recipients of their services. In many companies such contact is relatively rare, and by bringing the two groups together many ideas for improvement emerge automatically.

The cost of the different activities has already been calculated, as has their position in the process. The procedure begins by confirming from the customers or their representatives, the value they place on the outputs of each activity. Once this is done it will then become possible to compare the value placed on services and the costs involved in providing them. It will be possible to identify:

- *High value, high cost activities.* Such activities must be provided but consume resource. The priority here is to make their provision more efficient.
- *High value, low cost activities.* In such cases the question needs to be addressed whether the service should be expanded or changed to improve its value further. Possible changes could include altering the timing of the service or its scope.
- *Low value, low cost activities.* These activities need not absorb much time in the study, except to question why they are to be carried out at all.
- *Low value, high cost activities.* This will be the main focus of future cost reduction effort. Where activities fall into this category, the implication is that the organisation is undertaking work, which may be efficiently undertaken, but which is of little use to the recipients.

Most attention will be paid to the last category, namely the activities listed as being of low value but having high cost. In some cases, the minority, it may be that elimination of the activity is the natural response. More usually it is the case that the activity was set up to fulfil a real need, but has failed to do so, and changing the activity can either reduce its cost or improve its value. Specifically, there are choices to change the nature of the activity offered or the level of service provided.

We now describe the operation of the challenge groups.

Operation of challenge groups

In bringing together the managers of an activity with the recipients of its outputs, naturally there is the potential for conflict in these sessions but this is not necessarily a bad thing as long as it does not obstruct the flow of ideas. The premises behind such meetings are that:

- many of the best ideas for improving the effectiveness of overheads will emanate not from the project team bringing an independent view, though some will, but from discussion between those who manage the activity or receive its outputs;
- such ideas will be undiscovered because there is often a lack of discussion between such groups.

Therefore, on bringing the two groups together useful ideas will emerge on the potential for improvement. The prospect of this declines if the exchange becomes too adversarial. Naturally if real external customers participate, then the adversarial element must be tightly controlled.

The chairman of the meetings must either be someone senior to the internal participants or from outside the organisation. The chairman must be able to spot a potential saving as the discussion unfolds; equally, the person must not be so formidable that his presence stifles discussion.

In summary, challenge groups are a practical way of finding the relative merit of activities. The groups highlight the needs of customers, draw on the wealth of experience of the operating managers, and generate new ideas by bringing these people together. The disadvantage is that a subjective element has been introduced, and while the preconceptions and vested interests of any one individual will be filtered out by the group, prejudices held by the whole group may still prevail. Therefore the project team should still assess the outputs independently and judge whether the presence of a support activity can really be justified by the improvement it gives to the core activities.

PROCESS LEAD-TIME REDUCTION

Importance of lead-time

All the methods outlined previously can be used for reducing lead time as well as reducing costs. Sometimes lead-time improvement is the primary issue and we now describe methods which focus on this parameter alone.

More and more emphasis is being placed on reducing lead times, the reason being that short lead times are the key to responsiveness. If lead times are generally short, then it becomes possible to:

- Benefit from faster introduction of products and services, where often the largest cost is the opportunity cost of lost revenue during the development process.
- Win orders by offering prompt delivery. This applies to both manufacturing and service sectors. In the latter case an alternative to reduced lead time would be to hold inventory but this is very costly. To an accountant inventory is an asset, but it can also be a liability: it represents potential obsolescence and is costly to store.
- Provide product variety through the use of short change-over times to move from the delivery of one product or service to another.

This responsiveness is often there for the asking. Low responsiveness may have arisen because low priority was attached to it or the performance measures have emphasised other aspects of performance, such as utilisation of resource or cost.

Cycle time reduction

The concept of cycles recurs in many forms within the organisation. There is a purchasing cycle concerned with obtaining external supplies, a sales cycle concerned with selling goods and services, an operational cycle concerned with satisfying a customer's order and a development cycle concerned with designing new products and services.

Once a process has been modelled attention can be paid to the reduction of the time it takes each cycle to execute. An indication of the scope for improvement is the ratio between the time spent working on an item (adjusted for the number of staff engaged on the work) and the elapsed time between the start and completion of the work:

$$\frac{\text{Time input/Number of staff involved}}{\text{Elapsed time}}$$

This ratio can often be very small indeed; for example, it may be that only a few minutes of work by a few people is spent in actual processing but it takes several weeks for the cycle to be finished. The remaining time is taken up by queuing and storage. This ratio can rise to a value of one, whereby all staff involved work on nothing but a single task until it is completed.

Usually this ideal situation will not be attainable. Nonetheless, some improvement can be made:

- *Identify the bottlenecks in operations.* In some cases there is not a stable bottleneck because the location of the limiting factor is dependent on the mix of work being undertaken. In other cases there is a single stage in the process which limits the entire rate of operation. Queues form behind the critical stage and represent a limit on reduction in cycle time. Queuing is justifiable, if there is an uneven supply of work and a resource with limited capacity which has to operate at an even utilisation. Often though, queuing arises from bad planning. Queues, and hence cycle time, can be reduced through smoothing the supply of work to be handled within the overhead structure and investing in capacity at the bottleneck stages;

- *Synchronise operations.* Frequently buffers between sequential operations are allowed to develop because the operations do not operate in synchronisation. These buffers can be removed if the successive stages in the process are tied into a common timetable, for example, specifing the tasks to take place on each stage on each part of the day on each day of the week;

- *Measure work-in-progress.* There is no better way to ensure work does not flounder within a system than measuring its progress. Each stage in a process can be considered as containing a backlog of work, the number of items outstanding at the start of the period. During the period being measured, units of work will arrive and also be finished. The work outstanding at the end of the period is simply:

Initial units + Received units – Finished units

This measure can be supplemented by others such as the longest time any outstanding item has had to wait in the backlog. Installing such a process measuring system allows management to monitor the flow of work and immediately respond to obstructions. The author installed one such system in the order taking, kitting and dispatch process of an instrumentation company; it allowed backlogs to be driven down quickly and ensured managers became involved in the causes of backlogs, e.g. computer breakdowns, sickness etc.

These three steps form a natural sequence: first attend to the structural issues of limited capacity and uneven supply of work, secondly ensure the process works in unison and finally, monitor the performance of the system to identify problems promptly.

We now turn our attention to one area which is a major cause of excessive lead time, the problem of including unnecessary authorisation proce- dures within the overhead functions.

Unnecessary authorisation

The inclusion of unnecessary checking and authorisation of others' actions has impact in terms of cost, time and quality. The impact on cost is obvious: checking consumes resource and adds nothing. Ironically, excessive use of referrals to higher authority can also have a detrimental effect on quality: those doing the work know they are not trusted and can get away with poor quality without eventual ill effect. However it is in the area of timeliness that the effects are most felt.

When work is referred upwards or to a checking procedure, this involves stopping the task in hand and waiting for the higher authority to brief themselves on the matter and give their approval. When the times involved in transmitting the information are taken into account, the time taken to obtain approval can be longer than that necessary to carry out the work.

Authorisation procedures need to be pruned to the bare minimum. To do this needs recognition of why intervention is necessary; it may be:

- either because a higher degree of skill has to be introduced than is available at the operator level; or
- the scale of the consequences of error make security paramount.

In considering the first point, the question of whether additional training would remove the need for referral has to be asked. There is sometimes a tendency for managers to underestimate the abilities of employees who, given the right training, may be capable of greater responsibility. In reducing the incidence of needless approval the amount of work actually being corrected needs to be analysed. If work is almost never corrected there is clearly little need for checking. If the type of fault is concentrated in a particular area, then a focused training course may be appropriate. If the faults are many and varied there is a fundamental problem in the operation of the process. If the problems are few but varied, the problem is less tractable. A comparative analysis needs to be undertaken between allowing the errors to occur (while ensuring the full cost of bad quality is recognised), staffing the process with higher skilled operators or continuing the approval procedures.

As regards the second point it may be more effective to ensure there is clear accountability for actions and penalties for carelessness. It is probably no coincidence that the sector which offers excellent job security seems to require an inordinate amount of checking and verification! There will always be some cases, however, where the consequences of any mistake or malpractice are so large that verification is required. A risk assessment needs to be carried out and this is another area where the techniques which were developed in product design carry over very well into process design.

The method, called Failure Mode Effect Analysis, systematically considers each possible fault, its probability and the consequences of the failure. With this information a rational choice can be made on the need for approvals and the threshold above which an approval is triggered.

Very often, thresholds are used in approvals procedures, i.e. if an item exceeds a threshold, usually monetary, then referral upwards is required. Slight movement of these thresholds would not affect substantially the risk faced by the organisation, but can dramatically affect the volume of referrals. To check for these opportunities it is necessary to plot the distribution of the number of items against their monetary value. This can then be used to position referral thresholds so as to retain their effectiveness while reducing their cost. A side-effect of this analysis is often to highlight the large number of trivial items, where the cost of processing the transaction, e.g. the cost of raising a purchase order, can be far more than the cost of the item being purchased. In these cases, the answer is to introduce a second threshold, i.e. a minimum value below which a transaction is barred.

Just in Time for clerical operations

The group of techniques which go under the banner of Just in Time (JIT), have been remarkably successful in transforming manufacturing operations and raising Western levels of productivity to Japanese levels. Most of these techniques are equally applicable to 'paper factories' and we now outline the basic principles of JIT.

The JIT principles are intended to counter a tendency amongst Western countries to install ever more complex scheduling, inventory holding and quality assurance systems. These do not add value to the customer and indeed their very size seems to make companies unresponsive. As a reaction, JIT advocates:

- *A perpetual drive to eliminate waste.* It has much in common with Total Quality Management in the way it advocates continuous improvement.
- *Reduction in inventory.* Inventory itself is regarded as a thoroughly bad thing. It is used to insulate the organisation from its faults, such as unreliability, poor forecasting etc. The metaphor which is often quoted pictures the company as a boat floating on a river of inventory; if the inventory level is lowered, rocks appear; these represent the dysfunction within the organisation, which are now visible and can be tackled. By progressively lowering inventory the organisation is forced to reform.
- *Synchronisation of tasks.* Removal of inventory also forces successive activities to become better co-ordinated because inventory no longer acts as a buffer. This ensures all those involved in the process are better informed of the purpose of their work and the external goals.

- *'Pull' scheduling.* JIT advocates that work should be pulled through a process by demand signals being passed up the process, as opposed to being 'pushed' through the system by product being launched at the beginning. The implication is that work is only produced when it is needed by the next stage down the process.
- *Even flow of work.* There are many advantages that arise from an even flow of work, some of which were alluded to when discussing lead-time reduction: queues do not form, the use of small batches allows increased responsiveness, there is a reduction in inventory and if there is a quality problem this is identified immediately. The need for work to be produced in small, frequent batches encourages initiatives to reduce change-over times, which again increase the flexibility of the company.
- *Simple visual controls.* Rather than attempt to schedule or model the whole operation from the centre the preference is for simple signals to be passed between operators on when work should move along the process. One of these is the 'kanban' or storage place for work in progress. When the kanban is clear then those involved in the task upstream of the kanban know to start generating work so as to fill it. A secondary advantage is that work in progress can only be stored in designated places. In clerical operations the equivalent to the kanban would be the old fashioned filing tray, though without a 'pending' facility!

All of these principles are as applicable to the design of overhead processes as they are to manufacturing processes. The elimination of waste is transferable to all areas of activity. The relevance of the reduction of inventory to clerical operations may seem obscure, but there is a work in progress associated with clerical operations; first this inventory has a value (e.g. the value of orders stalled in the sales office) and second the information that is in transit between successive tasks represents a lack of precision in the monitoring of the process. The synchronisation of tasks is a method of avoiding this 'information in transit' by the elimination of inter-task buffers. Pull scheduling is another means for reducing the information in transit by releasing future work only when it can be processed. An even flow of work helps avoid unaccountability associated with work in progress. Finally, the close positioning of related clerical operations encourages the 'little but often' approach and the insistence that work in progress be confined to 'kanbans' or set places ensures that supervisors know exactly the state of any backlogs.

In fact, clerical operations are much more susceptible to JIT approaches than the manufacturing operations in which JIT was developed, not least because the 'set-up time' for changing from one operation to another is usually less significant in clerical operations. The application of JIT principles can be imagined by visualising a good and a bad office. The former is marked by a general lack of paper, in either the right or the wrong places, an orderly flow of work and an understanding of current problems. The latter is marked by general confusion, sudden surprises and unexplained delays. In reforming this situation the JIT techniques explained above are all relevant.

PROCESS QUALITY

Need for the information

When an organisation measures its 'cost of quality', i.e. the cost of bad quality, the typical result is that the cost amounts to about one third of the total costs of the company. At first sight this may seem unlikely, but it is supported by a study of the overhead function 'The Hidden Factory' Miller and Vollman (1985). They analysed the number of transactions, and shown their composition to be on average:

- one sixth 'balancing transactions', matching supply to demand;
- one sixth logistical transactions, which result in the movement of material from one location to another;
- one third change transactions, which deal with alterations to the products and services from their previous state;
- one third quality transactions, which ensure that actions take place as intended. This includes the audit function.

The startling conclusion of this research is the low proportion of the transactions concerned with adding value to the business of today.

Not all the cost of quality will be accounted for by the activities categorised as 'waste' in the earlier attribute analysis. In some cases, the costs will be hidden with the activity costs of core and support activities. Furthermore there may be activities which were labelled as 'policy' whose costs are part of the cost of quality. An example is the cost of carrying out full inspection of finished goods. It is therefore necessary to collate the different costs, where necessary separating out the proportion of activity cost which has a quality aspect. This collation needs a clear definition on what constitutes a quality-related cost; we will provide this definition in the next section.

Measuring the cost of quality is a necessary step to its reduction. However, in itself it is not a sufficient step, since the measurement must be:

- in a form that allows the cause rather than merely the effect of a quality problem to be identified;
- linked to mechanisms for the reduction of quality problems.

The cost of quality information is therefore to be used as part of a quality improvement programme. Typically the information is used to:

- attach priorities to the various ideas for improvement;
- monitor the success of the quality improvement teams.

Quality improvement is of course a major topic in its own right and well covered by current material. Given that over a third of the transactions of the overhead function are related to quality in one form or another, quality clearly has an important role in the control of overheads.

Calculation of quality costs

Quality costs are typically divided into four categories. These are:

- *prevention costs*, which refer to the costs of preventing poor quality from occurring, e.g. assessing suppliers, monitoring of equipment and the training of staff;
- *appraisal costs*, which refer to the costs of test and inspection, e.g. sampling work to check that quality is being maintained;
- *internal failure costs*, e.g. the cost of rework or scrapped work;
- *external failure costs*, e.g. the costs of warranty claims and dealing with customer complaints.

This classification has the drawback that it does not relate to the underlying causes of bad quality within a company. It does however have the merit of defining the broad scope of the cost of quality.

Therefore to measure the cost of quality, four attributes are used, corresponding to the categories of quality cost given above. For each activity the attribute is set to zero if the activity does not relate to the relevant type of quality cost and is set to one if the activity does relate. It is possible, though much more complicated, to have fractional values; so if only half an activity is related to appraisal, the relevant attribute is set to 0.5.

Once each activity has been marked in this way then the cost of quality can be calculated. Since the activities taking place in each department are known, then the cost of quality in each category can also be related to department. However, this analysis will not include the cost of lost sales because of failure to satisfy customer requirements, because it does not form part of the cost base and therefore a separate estimate needs to be made of this quantity.

As well as understanding where quality problems occur, it is necessary to understand why they occurred in the first place. To do this requires analysing the causes of bad work in a particular department and apportioning the cost of quality to the originating activity or department. The results can be start-ling. Most of the cost of quality occurring in activities towards the end of the supply chain is usually the result of mistakes made earlier in the process. Clearly it is pointless insisting to the 'downstream' departments that they reduce their quality related costs, if these are outside their own control.

In general, the most expensive mistake that can be made is one which is made early and allowed to exist for a long time. So the cost of an error in specification that is undetected before the delivery of a product or a service to the customer is exorbitant, whereas the cost of a mistake by an operator which is detected soon afterwards is relatively small. The implication is that quality control needs to be the most rigorous during the initial stages of a process. Ironically, this is seldom the case. Often the early stages are the most intangible and it is wrongly assumed that quality control cannot be exercised.

Fish-bones and dominoes

In tackling quality problems it is useful to clarify how the factors and actions interrelate, both in causing a problem and as a result of a problem occurring. Two graphical techniques enable clarifications of these interdependencies, to encourage debate on their solution.

The first is a fish-bone diagram, whose name is apparent from Figure 4.6; it is sometimes called an Ishikawa diagram. It seeks to trace the cause and effect that lie behind a particular quality problem. While, it may not appear an especially profound analysis, the benefits of using these simple graphical techniques to communicate a concept to management and staff should not be underestimated.

Sometimes the reverse analysis is useful. Rather than seeing how a combination of factors converge to cause a problem, the need is to understand how the effects of a problem in one area have a domino effect on others. This can be examined by a form of flow chart, where the effect of the initial action (e.g. correcting some documentation) is plotted out as the changes ripple through the organisation. This is illustrated in Figure 4.7. Sometimes

Figure 4.6 Fish-bone diagram

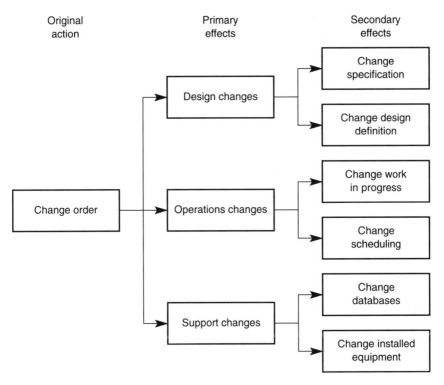

Original action   Primary effects   Secondary effects

Figure 4.7 Domino effect

each of the side-effects can be costed and a view taken of the total cost of the initial action. Usually, the cost is greater than first imagined, since the full ramifications were not previously understood.

SEGMENT RATIONALISATION

Dangers

Before discussing rationalising segments of the business, e.g. products and customers, it is worthwhile considering the dangers of too much enthusiasm in this area. It is far simpler to close down parts of a business than to create new parts, and care is needed when reducing volume (which is implicit in any rationalisation exercise) that there is sufficient contribution, i.e. the difference between revenue and fixed costs, to cover the hard core of fixed costs. The key term here is 'hard core'; many fixed costs are not fixed and can be eliminated if certain products or customers are abandoned; however, there will be some costs which will not go and this needs to be recognised.

With this is mind, we first outline some of the alternatives to rationalising the business and then describe the concept of 'attributable cost' which is a better tool for considering rationalising than the simple fixed and variable concepts alluded to above.

Alternatives to rationalisation

Before considering the deletion of products or customers, thought ought to be given to the alternatives. Some of the options include:

- *Price increases*. If a segment is unprofitable, it may be the case that the company is simply not charging the market rate, either for its products, or for particular customer terms.
- *Price decreases*. Unprofitability may arise from too low a volume and if there is a strong price elasticity in the market, coupled with a high contribution, then the segment could move back into profitability with the volume increase associated with a price decrease.
- *Promotions*. This is another method of increasing volume, while retaining the selling price.
- *Process improvement*. Process improvement has already been discussed, and the discussion on segment rationalisation should always be postponed until the options for improving profitability have been explored.
- *Product redesign*. This is a potent weapon, and is as applicable to the redesign of 'products' in the service industry as it is to manufacturing. In the latter, most of the costs, the usual estimate is 80 per cent, are effectively pre-committed once the design is complete.

These avenues, and others identified by the project team, need to be explored before undertaking segment rationalisation.

Attributable costs

When considering product abandonment as a means to reducing the costs of complexity, the concept of 'attributable' cost becomes very useful; this was developed over thirty years ago in the paper 'The concept of attributable cost' (Shillinghaw, 1963). The attributable cost of a product is that cost which would cease to be incurred if the product ceased to be produced. This is the figure which is needed to understand the net increase or decrease in profit upon the abandonment of a product.

The key point about attributable costs is that they are not additive. So, for example, if a single item from a product range were deleted, then the net cost reduction would most likely be limited to the direct cost of the item. If, however, several items were deleted, then the cost reduction would not only be confined to the direct cost but may well include an element of indirect cost. Therefore the attributable cost of an aggregation of products is at least the sum of the amount for each individual product.

Not surprisingly, calculating such costs on anything other than an *ad hoc* basis is difficult. It is possible, however, to survey each activity within the company and determine the degree to which its costs would fall given the deletion of ever greater aggregations of each product or customer range. Once this is done the management have a tool for 'what-if' analysis on the effects of product abandonment and of losing the business of a particular customer.

Even if this sophistication is not adopted, the key point to bear in mind is that by no means all the 'product cost' will cease if a product is deleted. Even if cost can be directly traced to a product through activity-based costing, for deletions of small elements of a product range staffing levels may not be able to fall. Therefore product deletion has to be handled with great care.

Procedure

The proposals for rationalisation generated as a result of this project will be adopted by a task force for further examination and possible implementation. This will undoubtedly involve discussion at board level.

It is also worth considering the procedures which need to be followed to deal with rationalisation on an ongoing basis, since it is usually the failure of these ongoing mechanisms to function which leads to the need for single exercises to cut back on complexity. Any procedure will need the following elements:

- A specified forum for taking the decisions. In some cases this is centralised into a single individual, perhaps a brand manager, and the views of others are transmitted through cost and price signals. More usually there is a discussion amoung a group of people. The membership of this group and the frequency with which it meets need to be clarified.
- The criteria on which business segments are judged to have failed. In this programme the implication is that segment profitability is used for this purpose, but there are alternatives. Examples include market share, management time or turnover.
- A procedure for considering alternatives to deletion of a segment, on the lines of those proposed in the earlier section.

Most companies will not have such a procedure: it seems that just as baptisms are universally more popular than funerals, introducing new products or customers is more attended to than their deletion.

INFORMATION SYSTEMS AND TECHNOLOGIES

Objective

The team has now obtained two perspectives of the information systems and technologies which are relevant to the organisation:

- The first, gained in Step 1, *External Review* was a top-down view of the information needed to effectively manage the processes, the applications which would support this and the current and future technologies. This was done in the context of a business strategy and an understanding of the critical success factors for the organisation.
- The second, gained in Step 2, *Activity Analysis* was a bottom-up catalogue of the actual information required and provided, the data kept within the company, the applications in use and the technologies employed. From this was distilled a list of areas where improvement is needed.

The task now is to create a strategy for the development of the information systems and technologies, which:

- is consistent with the business strategies of the organisation;
- exploits the opportunities provided by the market in terms of the applications and technologies which are available and being developed;
- tackles the shortcomings in the existing systems and technologies.

This itself is an ambitious task, but the team will be also be constrained by the availability of managerial and financial resource. They must therefore condense their ideas into a series of projects, with stated costs and benefits, which can be considered alongside the other proposals for change.

Consistency with business strategy

In Step 1 we suggested the use of the five forces model to bring views on how information technology and strategy can assist in providing competitive advantage. If this has been done, there should be some initial views on how the technology and the systems are intended to evolve.

In a few cases then the information systems and technology are the centre-piece of how the company intends to compete. Usually this is not the case but there will be a set of critical success factors, already defined, for which good performance is essential. For most of these factors, whether they be linked to cost, time or quality, the use of information technology will enable this performance to be bettered.

Alignment of the business and information strategies therefore involves ensuring that proposed direction for investment in information systems and technologies will assist in meeting the critical success factors and the customer requirements. This will usually imply investing in applications and technologies that enhance the core customer-related processes.

Current and future systems and technologies

This can be a bewildering area for those who are not technically educated, however the key is to probe the benefits and not the features of the systems and technologies. In Step 1, a survey of relevant systems was proposed and there should already be a view of the current and future applications which could assist the core processes. However, it is the area of technology where there is the more rapid change.

The most significant recent change is the evolution of computing from a largely centralised function, requiring specialised staff, to a distributed function. The benefits of this change are immediately apparent, as users are able to develop their own applications to meet their needs, but the potential for loss of integration is greatly magnified. The move is now to create client/server networks, whereby data, the server, is accessed through a network by the client platforms. In this way the benefits of both flexibility and data consistency are obtained.

The other major change is the continual advancement of open systems. In the past, once a user committed to a particular vendor of hardware and closely associated operating system, then the user was locked into that vendor and at a commercial disadvantage in any negotiations on operating costs. This is now changing, most significantly with certain operating systems (for example, Unix and MS-DOS) becoming accepted as standards, with an open market for manufacturers to provide platforms compatible with the standard, and for software developers to develop applications to run on the platforms. Other standards are being developed in areas such as communications.

Communications themselves are a source of great innovation, which is changing the commercial relationships in many industries. The most significant development is electronic data interchange, which is being used to bind suppliers and customers closer together, at the expense of those who do not adopt the standard.

Finally there are many emerging technologies of which expert systems are perhaps the most fundamental. The ability to bring to bear expert knowledge in a consistent and accessible way will change the way responsibility can be distributed around an organisation.

The team can then bring together potential solutions for the organisation, which allows it to benefit from the available or emerging technologies and systems. It will be searching for an overall plan which makes the best of the existing investment and ensures future investment is compatible where necessary and does not itself place constraints on future developments. The potential solutions need to be firm enough to identify particular systems and applications, as well as technical standards for hardware, operating systems and communication interfaces.

Tackling shortcomings

There remains the task of matching the potential solutions and the current and future systems and technologies, to the problems, namely the shortcomings identified in Step 2.

Each of the shortcomings has already been linked to a particular activity and, by implication processes; this is the route to assess the impact of the shortcomings on the core processes and the ability to satisfy customers and to meet the critical success factors.

A series of proposals is generated and their ability to meet the requirements of customers and to enhance performance, as measured by the critical success factors, is examined; the emphasis is on establishing the benefits, rather than dwelling on technical features. Alongside these benefits, the costs of the various options need to be developed. Each option is, in effect, an outline project plan.

Selection of projects

Usually, there will be a surfeit of opportunities, which would overwhelm the financial and managerial resources of the organisation if they were all implemented simultaneously. Furthermore, in addition to the information-related projects there are the other proposals for change that are developed in the programme. In choosing the projects with which to proceed, the team first separates the opportunities into two categories:

- Significant projects, involving changes to systems which will affect the whole organisation. These are considered in this step, along with the changes affecting other areas.
- Small projects, often involving localised change and minimum investment. These are carried forward to Step 4, *Focused Change*.

The intention is to collate the various options for change, so as to rank them for access to resource.

ORGANISATIONAL STRUCTURE

Sequence

We have left the consideration of the organisational structure to the end of Step 3, *Radical Change*. The structure can only be put in place once the processes have been clarified and the effects of the various radical changes assessed. This is in contrast to traditional approaches, which begin with fixing the corporate structure and then work within it. We consider here three aspects of organisational design: centralisation, the structural efficiency of the organisation and the delineation of organisational boundaries.

We discuss the cultural impact of organisation structure in Step 5, *Sustainable Improvement*; in this section we concentrate on the principles behind the design of the reporting structure itself.

Centralisation

It is not only processes which can be split across many different departments; it is quite possible for individual activities to be split as well. This usually occurs when individual departments are not satisfied with the central provision of a service and choose to provide it locally. On occasions the better responsiveness can make this worthwhile, but there are drawbacks:

- There is a lessening of control associated with the dispersal. This is especially the case when the purchasing activity is spread over several departments. In these cases it is difficult to ensure that business is being placed with the most competitive suppliers.
- Information becomes fragmented making coordination difficult. For example, if sales orders are accepted at multiple points there can be a lack of visibility of the business being done with a single customer, with possible deterioration in customer service.
- There is a loss of economy of scale, both as regards the organisation of operations internally and in dealing with suppliers.
- There is a dilution of expertise. Some activities require a 'critical mass' of personnel and skill if they are to attain acceptable standards.

While the arguments for centralising of expertise appear to be strong, the costs associated with poor flexibility can be enormous as well. The challenge therefore is to gain the benefits of centralised expertise while preserving flexibility. Information Technology and creating a 'customer service' culture amongst the providers of central services are both important tools in achieving this.

Structural efficiency

The two traditional measures for organisational efficiency are:

- spans of control, i.e. the number of staff a manager has reporting to him;
- layers of management, i.e. the number of layers in the organisation, from Chief Executive to the most junior employee in a particular area.

It is undoubtedly the case that in the past decade the pressure has been to encourage flatter organisational pyramids, by means of 'delayering', which is a process as painful as it sounds, and which broadens the spans of control. The driving force for this has been the economy which follows from removing levels of middle management. There have been two facilitating factors:

- information technology, which has allowed managers greater visibility for the status of the operations, without recourse to the need for intermediaries;
- greater willingness to allow junior employees to use their discretion and the reduction of the need for referrals upwards for authorisation.

A further benefit from removing layers of middle management is an increase in the responsiveness of the organisation, as the junior staff are able to act without referral and the senior staff become more in touch with the reality of the business.

It is not possible to give ideal spans of control or guidance on the number of layers. Spans of control will need to be smaller where there is a greater variety and unpredictability within a system; they may be large when there is considerable routine work to be carried out by clerical staff. However, in seeking improvement it is possible to:

- Use benchmarking techniques to identify apparent anomalies in the spans of control and number of organisational layers between the company and suitable comparators, whether internal or external.
- Examine the effects of incremental changes on a case by case basis. In this instance questions are posed on the effect of specific changes to the spans of control, in order to identify the precise need for managerial input and the consequences of its absence.

In this way the project team can challenge the level of managerial overheads. In Step 5 we discuss the application of the principles of empowerment, which can also have an impact on the degree of managerial overhead which needs to be borne, and expand on the concepts of crisp and fuzzy structures.

Reporting hierarchy

The division of the company into a reporting hierarchy of responsibility centres is an important step. It is usually observed that difficulties arise from the interfaces between different functions and therefore the location of these interfaces is crucial. Various approaches have been tried in the past; these are outlined with their advantages and their drawbacks:

- *Functional organisations*. This is the traditional form of structure where particular skill groups or functions are identified and departments are formed around them. It encourages functional excellence, as the staff in a single discipline are grouped together and encouraged to develop and compete. As was commented on earlier, it does however lower customer response as most processes have to cross over several boundaries.

  The most extreme example of a functional structure observed by the author occurred in a small socialist republic; it is illustrated in Figure 4.8. It shows a state-planned system which was able to ensure the basic production facilities kept functioning, since each type of facility had its own ministry (e.g. ministry of agriculture, ministry of agricultural buildings, ministry of bread production etc.), but was slow to react to change, partly because of the degree of cross-functional co-ordination required.

FORTY SEVEN MINISTRIES TO GOVERN FOUR MILLION PEOPLE

Academy of Agricultural Science	Foreign Economic Relations
Academy of Science	Gasification
Agricultural Buildings	Internal Affairs
Agriculture	Irrigation & Water Supply
Archives	Justice
Border Policy	Labour & Training
Botanic Heritage	Land Reforms
Bread Production	Material Reserves
Broadcasting	Meterology
Building	National Security
Building & Architecture	Nature Protection
Building Materials	Newspapers
Censorship	Oil Products
Communications	Public Health
Consumer Goods	Religious Affairs
Culture	Road & Transport
Customs	Social Security
Defence	Sport
Economic Planning	Statistics
Education	Supply
Ethnic Press	Supreme Judiciary
Fishing	Trade
Food Processing	Trade Industrial Police
	Wood & Countryside

Figure 4.8 Governance of a small socialist republic

- *Project structures*, whereby a unit is formed for a particular purpose, usually a project, and disbanded thereafter. This provides the advantage of the structure being designed to deliver a particular result, though has the disadvantage of the dispersal of the group and its expertise at the end of the project.
- *Matrix structures*, which are intended to combine the advantage of functional structures in the development of functional excellence and retaining the advantages of project-orientated teams. Individuals retain a functional reporting relationship, which is responsible for developing functional excellence, but are also engaged for project-related tasks. The only disadvantage is the ambiguity involved in dual reporting lines. Nonetheless this form of organisation suits many types of professional organisation well.
- *Process structures*. These seek to divide managerial responsibility along process lines, and in doing so, reduce the number of interfaces that occur within a process. In adopting a process-orientated organisation, an important point is to allocate responsibility so that there is unambiguous responsibility for key parameters, e.g. inventory levels. We raised these issues in our discussion of sample processes in Step 1, *External Review*.

There is, of course, no universally correct form of structure: functional structures are appropriate where functional excellence is paramount, project structures are appropriate where each single project is a new enterprise and matrix structures allow the dual development of skill and project focus. Process structures maximise process efficiency and, by implication, customer satisfaction, but at the expense of functional expertise.

PREPARING FOR IMPLEMENTATION

Context

During Step 3, *Radical Change*, there will have emerged a number of proposals for change. The proposals will usually overlap in some way. Most radical changes will also affect more than one department. There is therefore a need to:

- bring together the overlapping ideas into a small number of programmes;
- carry out a cost/benefit analysis on the programme of changes and create some outline project plans;
- form a task force for each programme with clear terms of reference, and brief it.

The use of task forces is necessary because the proposed changes bridge the departmental structure. Proposed changes that are contained within a particular department are best managed through the line management structure, and should be dealt with in Step 4, *Focused Change*.

Outlining the programmes

Defining the programmes of work to be undertaken needs to be carefully considered. The challenge is to avoid treating the symptoms of a problem, without dealing with underlying causes, or to avoid dealing with an underlying cause in a way that is oblique to the needs of the business.

One way to avoid this is to consider how any proposed programme is relevant to the critical success factors of the business and how it will close the gap between the customers' requirements and the current level of performance. If the programme is not directed to closing this gap, then it is misdirected. The key is to identify an interrelated set of problems which contribute to a shortfall in performance in a particular area and to develop a feasible solution.

Cost/benefit analysis

Once a cohesive group of actions has been identified it is necessary to subject each change to some type of cost/benefit analysis as has been done for information-related projects.

Usually this does not need to be particularly complicated. Often a convoluted assessment process can obscure the fact that the information upon which the assessment is based is relatively speculative. With this in mind, most of the effort needs to be concentrated on forming realistic estimates of the costs and benefits themselves, and the risks attached to both these categories; only once the basics are understood should the finer points, such as the time-phasing of the cash flows, be considered.

The cost/benefit analysis is used to whittle down the proposed ideas to those which are genuinely attractive. In doing so, there are two points which need to be recognised:

- Some changes will be mandatory, if the company is to remain in business. For example, if most of the company's customers are stipulating a level of performance, and can go elsewhere for it, then it must be delivered. Either the cost must be borne, or operations must cease.
- There is likely to be a shortage of funds, with the effect that the number of projects involving large expenditure for comparable savings will be limited. There are formal techniques available for fund rationing, generally

relying on maximising the net present value of the selected projects, however, many of the underlying assumptions of the theory, e.g. the use of unallocated funds, often do not hold in practical situations.

The outcome of the cost/benefit analysis is the confirmation that the set of actions in each programme is financially attractive to the organisation and within its means.

Project planning

Once the content of the programmes has been set, the next step is to create an outline project plan, to check on the feasibility of the proposed programmes and the interdependencies that may exist between the different actions. It is necessary to ensure that the full scope of the tasks has been understood and to form realistic estimates of elapsed time for these tasks. Once this has been done an outline project plan can be drawn up. However at this stage the intention is not to create a detailed project control document; this is included in Step 5, *Sustainable Improvement*. The intention is to enable the plan to be explained to the task force members and for them to accept it as plausible and commit to its success.

We now describe how these tasks forces are created.

Staffing of task forces

The first step is to choose a leader for each of the task forces. It can be a difficult choice: the leader must have a thorough, and recognised, understanding of the topic. However, it is also essential that the leader is not an established protagonist in the area. These two requirements can be contradictory; often the most knowledgeable people are those with an established position. Nonetheless the task force will be unable to draw co-operation from the organisation if its leader is partisan; therefore someone must be selected who will be trusted not to pursue a personal or departmental agenda.

Furthermore, the leader needs to act in the role of chairman, as opposed to an originator or shaper of ideas. The key to success is to develop a working team and this cannot be achieved if the nominated leader begins to domineer. This may beg the question of whether a leader is required at all; in the author's view, this is definitely the case, because once the project moves into the implementation phase, then the company has to hold an individual accountable for achievement.

As regards the members of the task forces, the guiding principle is to achieve breadth of membership. Not only does this ensure a good range of skills are available to the task force but it helps achieve acceptance among the company through wide involvement.

Information systems task force

In nearly all cases there will be a need to set up a task force specifically to steer through improvements in the information systems. One part of their terms of reference is to ensure that the activity-based analysis carried out in Step 2, *Activity Analysis* is kept up to date. Another part of their work will involve the co-ordination and planning of the information systems initiatives which were identified.

The latter may seem the natural province of the management information systems or computer department. Unfortunately this function can often be introspective and interpret its role in terms of data processing as opposed to the provision of management information. For the latter role to be played requires an understanding of the business priorities. Therefore there is a role for the task force in setting the agenda for the development of the information systems department, working with them in implementing the priority developments and monitoring the results.

Briefing of task forces

The stage is now set for the briefing of the task forces. The members need to be told of the proposed programme and its objectives and taken through the outline project plan. Most likely they will have their own comments to add and this should be encouraged because it increases both the sense of ownership of the plan and accountability for the results.

Once financial approval for the changes has been attained in Step 5 the next stage is to announce the creation of task forces to the company as a whole. This has to be done carefully because their operations will cut across the normal management reporting lines; the announcement should be include a brief statement on the terms of reference of the task forces, their objectives, their composition and a summary of the outline project plans.

CUSTOMER AND PRODUCT PROFITABILITY CASE STUDY

Introduction

The previous case study recounted how a garment manufacturer calculated its life-cycle costs. The same company also wishes to calculate the profitability of its customers and products. For reasons alluded to before, the exercise is particularly complex because the company sells to customers with varying powers to negotiate special terms and manufactures both 'design' garments and 'plain' garments, which require different activities to support them.

Objectives

The purpose in calculating the profitability of the customers and the products is to guide:

- the marketing strategy of the company and to prioritise the market sectors it should develop;
- the product strategy of the company and in particular the pricing policies it should adopt.

These are crucial areas for all companies. In many cases, however, decisions are taken on the basis of no information, which is the usual case where customer profitability is concerned, or inaccurate information, which is the case where the calculation of product costs involve substantial apportionment.

Approach

The activity costs were calculated during the exercise to establish the life-cycle costs of the company. The calculation of the profitability of the products and the customers follows the approach defined in Step 2, *Activity Analysis*. The major practical task in implementing this approach is the selection of tracing factors along the lines described in that chapter.

Once the activity costs are traced to products and customers there is also the need to reallocate the product costs to customers and vice versa. The product costs are allocated to customers by means of the product mix which the customers buy. Customer costs are allocated to customers by means of a limited number of cross-allocation factors, also as described in Step 2. Once this is done then the full product cost and the full customer cost is known and can be deducted from the revenue for the product or customer.

The final part of the analysis was to measure the growth or decline of each product, in order to guide the product strategies of the company.

Customer profitability

The customer profitability is shown in Figure 4.9; the graph shows the profitability of significant individual customers, and a general category of small independent customers. The first conclusion is that the profitability of the individual customers is not volume dependent; small individual customers can be more or less profitable than large individual customers. The profitability depends both on the discounts extracted by the customers in negotiations and the special demands the customer makes on the company.

The second conclusion is that the general category of very small customers, who deal on standard terms, has only middling profitability due to the costs of supplying many small size orders. This conclusion was surprising to the senior management, who were painfully aware of the ability of the large customers to extract discounts but who were unaware of the costs of servicing the very small customer on standard terms.

The company is also now able to modify its customer terms to those customers or sectors which are less profitable.

Product profitability

A comparison of product costs, when calculated according to a standard costing system and an activity-based costing system is shown in Figure 4.10. It can be seen that the product costs differ widely. The standard costing systems have overestimated the costs of the plain garments, by not accounting for the lower costs associated with their support. This has a major implication for pricing strategy because the company is experiencing strong price competition for these products and it is now apparent margins can be maintained even with a price reduction.

For design garments, the activity-based costs are both higher and lower than the standard costs. The relationship becomes apparent in Figure 4.11. It can be seen that product profitability is highly volume dependent. There are many costs which are incurred once a product family is created and if the volume is insufficient then the product family will be unprofitable.

A further view is given in Figure 4.12, where we consider the growth rate of the product families. Some unprofitable families with only a small volume are growing so their continuance in the product portfolio is justifi-

Figure 4.9 Customer profitability

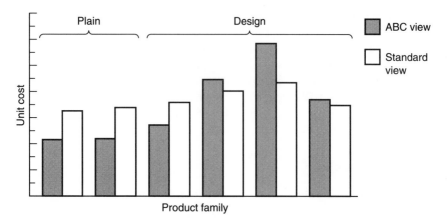

Figure 4.10 Product family costs

able in the expectation that as the volume increases they will become profitable. One family with low volume is, however, shrinking and is likely to become even less profitable in the future. It is therefore a candidate for product deletion.

Production cost

Many of the differences between the standard cost and the activity-based cost relate to differences in the tracing of administrative overhead. However, these differences also reach back to the production functions.

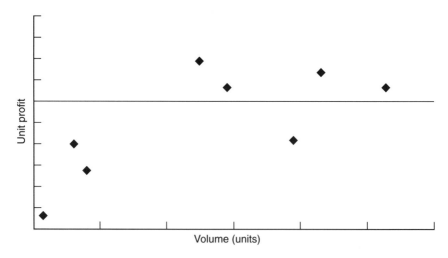

Figure 4.11 Unit profit versus volume

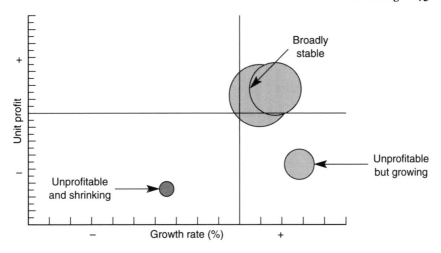

Figure 4.12 Portfolio analysis

Generally the activity-based costing view favours those product families which combine high volume and a large batch size with a low number of production orders and number of individual stock-keeping units. The production overhead cost for these garments is far lower due to the lower complexity of manufacture.

Conclusion

The calculation of the customer and product profitability has given a new direction to the company's marketing strategy and shown the need to examine the product portfolio.

5

FOCUSED CHANGE

. . . a living dog is better than a dead lion.

ECCLESIASTES 9:4

INTRODUCTION

Objectives

The project team will identify improvements in the control of overhead activity by making localised changes to the overhead functions, i.e. within an activity centre. The purpose is to improve the three components of value for money, namely the:

- effectiveness of the activities, or the degree to which the outputs of each activity are aligned with what is required;
- the efficiency with which the activities are undertaken;
- the economy with which resources are procured for activities.

Deliverables

During this step, illustrated in Figure 5.1, the project team will:

- increase effectiveness of support and policy activities;
- identify efficiency improvements; and match resources to workload, as well as establishing the ongoing rate of performance improvement which is possible;
- identify the scope for cost reduction through more economical procurement practices for staff and materials;
- identify opportunities for exerting better control of overheads through the introduction of market forces;
- apply information systems and technology;
- prepare for implementation of the changes.

Figure 5.1 Step 4: Focused Change

Issues

It is helpful to have a framework to place the various techniques within, and to understand their relationship. One such structure is the 'value for money' audit approach. The term 'value for money' refers to a numerator and a denominator. A review is made of whether the right things are being done from the customers' point of view, i.e. whether the activities are valuable, and whether they are being done efficiently and economically. The approach began in the public sector and was developed to examine and enhance the quality of service operations; it has been summarised in a booklet entitled *Value for Money Audit* (Pickwell, 1980). While there is an accepted framework and terminology, the approach does not extend to a detailed methodology; we have however suggested a set of techniques which fit this framework and can be used to improve value for money.

The framework begins with a clarification of the goals of the organisation and then deals with its hallmark, the 'three Es', namely economy, efficiency and effectiveness, whose meanings were defined at the start of this chapter. The usual approach to the audit is to begin with an examination of the inputs and outputs of the activities and then consider their relevance to the goals of the organisation, in parallel with an examination of the procedures and systems used to control the operations. It suits our purpose however, first to consider methods to enhance effectiveness, and then deal with efficiency and economy in that order. We will discuss reporting systems in Step 5, *Sustainable Improvement*.

While it would be possible to force all the available techniques into these categories, there is one important area which merits separate treatment. This is outsourcing and it follows on from the discussion of economy in the procurement of resources. This refers to the growing practice of subcontracting out whole areas of activity, and trimming back the corporation to a small core; it is equally applicable in the public and the private sector.

Links to Step 3, Radical Change

Many of the techniques described in Step 3, *Radical Change* will be equally relevant here. In the previous step, we considered the major processes and ways to make them more effective in the eyes of the customers and to make them more efficient and economical, through the analysis of cost drivers and other methods.

This is exactly our objective here, but we are seeking more localised improvement and will be concentrating on those activities which are not part of the key processes. The sense of *déjà vu* will be strongest when considering the effectiveness of the activities. This implies putting some value on the output of the activities and considering their worth to the customer. This, of course was the central theme in Step 3.

There will also be some ideas for improvement generated in the earlier step which will have been marked for consideration in this step, e.g. enhancements to the information systems which only affect a localised area.

Differing emphases

It is commonly heard that too much management attention is spent on examining the efficiency of operations and not enough time spent on considering their effectiveness, with the result that people become 'busy fools'. The right emphasis depends on the type of activity.

The different types of activity were discussed in Step 2, *Activity Analysis*. A quadripartite classification of core, support, policy and waste was suggested. The use of these classifications can show if there are too many activities which do not supply value to the customer and allow different activities to be treated in different ways.

Core activities are the essential minimum overhead. Core activities are best improved through better efficiency, since their effectiveness is already assured. There would also be concern if the amount of cost incurred in 'core' activities is relatively small since these are the activities which are mandatory to the supply of a product or a service to the customer; if they are a small proportion of the whole, there is obviously the threat from competitors who concentrate only on the bare essentials.

Support activities have been defined as those which facilitate the core activities. While this may appear to cast them in a positive light, support activities can be of differing values to the organisation or its customers. It is in this area that the major questions on the effectiveness of different activities are raised.

Policy activities are not dependent on a level of output but have been incurred through decisions made within the company or outside; e.g. the costs involved in producing audited accounts for a private company is a legal obligation, but the decision on the level of research and development expenditure is a corporate decision. In the long term though, most of these costs are discretionary: if externally imposed obligations are too costly the organisation can choose to locate to an area where such costs are lower, and if it does not it will have to compete at a disadvantage against organisations who are in these areas. Setting policy expenditure is partially concerned with effectiveness but is also influenced by the strategic direction of the company.

Waste represents expenditure which is no good for anyone. This is of course a rich opportunity for improvement. By reducing waste, in fact by making it a cultural theme, the biggest savings of all can be made. This is the source of interest in topics such as 'total quality', which we consider in Step 5, *Sustainable Improvement*.

EXAMINATION OF EFFECTIVENESS

Value of support activities

We have defined effectiveness as how appropriate the outputs of the activity are to the goals of an organisation, which for commercial organisations will encompass the need to satisfy customers. Implicit in such a definition is the concept of 'value': it is necessary that the outputs of the activity are valuable to those who receive them. We have already discussed the measurement of the value of activities within processes which satisfy customer requirements. It is also possible to examine the value of isolated activities, as long as the activity has an identifiable output which is used by identifiable recipients.

When an activity is considered in this way, the value placed on it can be:

- Treated as a binary choice, i.e. an activity is considered to be of value or not. This is appropriate for only the simplest decisions. This information has already been collected during Step 2, *Activity Analysis*.
- Ranked or scored by the recipients of its outputs according to their value relative to the outputs of other activities.
- Measured as the amount someone is prepared to pay for the output. This is difficult; even if the output can be quantified, which is often not the case, a market price cannot develop where there is a limited number of suppliers or customers for the output. Indeed there is often only a single supplier or customer.

Whichever method is used, the objective is to make some estimate of the numerator of the 'value for money' expression. The denominator is, of course, the cost; the activity costs have been calculated during Step 2. It may be possible to extend this by calculating the cost per unit of output.

Initial elimination

Very often the information on how much is being spent on each activity is sufficient to generate some initiatives for cost reduction, without further sophisticated analysis by the project team. This is especially the case where activity costs have not been calculated previously. The project team may believe savings can occur where there is:

- Agreement that an expenditure on a particular activity is simply not appropriate for the business. Taking an example, one organisation was surprised by the amount of money being spent on 'project appraisal'. Upon further investigation it became apparent that a far higher number of projects were being appraised than it was possible to implement. A pre-selection procedure was then put in place, so as to ensure that only the best of the proposed projects went forward to full appraisal. The high expenditure was not apparent previously because the expenditure was dispersed across several departments.
- Realisation that the resources spent on a particular activity do not translate into tangible output. For example, if a new product has not been developed for years and the product development cost is exorbitant, then questions may well be asked on the value of the activity.
- Recognition that a large but dispersed expenditure needs major reduction. For example, the cost of arranging and paying for travel and subsistence is often dispersed and is not always traced by the costing systems. Once the amount spent is recognised then the potential for saving by coordinated procurement becomes apparent.
- A cost/benefit analysis which indicates a support activity should be withdrawn because of insufficient benefit. If costs and benefits can be quantified, the support activity can be subject to a cost/benefit test: would the costs of the core activities rise by a greater or lesser amount than the support cost, if the support activity were to be removed? In many cases, this simple test is too blunt or the information does not exist. However in other cases, the cost/benefit test can create options which are worthy of further consideration, e.g. is it preferable to maintain a substantial personnel department, or have line managers fit personnel duties into their daily timetable.

The first step is to discuss these views with the line manager responsible for a particular activity centre. If there is agreement that savings can be made, then the savings can be noted and incorporated into the financial plan to be used to monitor each department. If there is not agreement, then the proposal needs to be discussed more widely; one method of achieving this is to set up challenge groups which will be set up to discuss ways of improving value for money.

Value-for-money challenge groups

The use of challenge groups was described in Step 3, *Radical Change*; at that time they were used to investigate changing service levels within key processes and the likely impact on customer satisfaction. They are also very useful in this step where the purpose is to bring together the providers and users of internal services, i.e. the managers of activities and the recipients of the outputs of those activities. The objective is to generate options for improving value for money, either through increasing value by focusing the activities on the internal customer's requirements or by reducing costs through the elimination of the lower value outputs.

Previously we spoke about the value and cost of activities; here it is more convenient to refer to the outputs of the activities, that is services, and to the value and the cost of the services. The four combinations of value and cost however remain the same; it is worth reminding ourselves of these and the necessary actions:

- high value, high cost services, which need to be made more efficient;
- high value, low cost services, which may be increased in scope or frequency;
- low value, low cost services, which are not important, and could be deleted;
- low value, high cost services, which is where the major opportunities for saving arise.

If cost reduction is an explicit objective it is also useful to start off with a series of hypothetical cost levels perhaps representing increases or decreases of 10, 20, and 30 per cent of the total cost of the support services. The targets are used to add tangibility to the process, and allow those involved to visualise what the overhead structures would look like for different levels of expenditure and to force choices to be made between particular services.

Many such challenge groups can be held. The project team needs to document the discussion, noting points of agreement and disagreement. There is then a major collation task to bring together changes which the team believe are feasible; this should be done in conjunction with the steering group, because it is essential to carry the organisation along with the proposed ideas. The final decisions on which savings to adopt can only be made at the highest level within the company, either with the Chief Executive personally or with the board of directors acting collectively.

Controlling policy expenditure

All expenditure in the policy category is controllable, but of course some may be more easily changed than others. To take the extreme referred to earlier, the expenditure on meeting regulatory requirements may seem obligatory, but there is the choice of moving to areas where regulation is less severe or costly. For practical purposes however, there will be some costs, such as the above, where the change required to avoid them is so immense that it is not realistic.

Other costs are incurred on a wholly discretionary basis and the question arises of whether this discretion has been exercised wisely. An important influence is the overall strategy of the organisation, which was examined in Step 1, *External Review*, which gives the foundation on which to examine policy expenditure. In examining this expenditure, the basic questions that need to be asked are 'What are the benefits?' and 'How do these benefits relate to our objectives?'. We now discuss the common areas of policy expenditure.

Development is perhaps the most important element of policy expenditure, where profit is forgone today for the prospect of future benefit. The most obvious examples are research and development, and product design. Unfortunately such activities are often undertaken in an undirected way at an arbitrary level (perhaps some proportion of turnover) and viewed as an expensive overhead rather than the foundation of the future corporation; when this is the case, these budgets are often the first to be cut. The way to avoid this is to treat development expenditure as a series of projects or tasks, each with its own expenditure and with its own deliverables and timescales. Once this project-orientated approach is adopted it becomes possible to:

- Carry out an appraisal for each project to find out if it is beneficial financially.
- Monitor the delivery of items against timescales. This at least ensures something is delivered in a regular pattern, rather than the situation where every project will deliver something sometime in the future.
- Review the original assumptions for subsequent changes in the company and its environment.

For organisations that carry out development work on a regular basis all this should be contained within existing procedures. However in many organisations where development work is a peripheral activity, these basic controls are often unapplied, especially the last item – review of the original assumptions.

Marketing expenditure also benefits from close examination. The old adage that half the marketing expenditure is wasted, but no one knows which half, may be accurate but it is not satisfactory. It is necessary to examine if any expenditure has actually increased sales. Any reply to the effect that this is impossible should meet with the response that the expenditure will be suspended to see if there is any difference. To take one example, the author had some experience of evaluating the marketing expenditure of energy utilities, where very large advertising budgets are justified on the grounds of increasing sales. On further investigation, it appeared that the sale of energy, adjusted for weather, followed Gross Domestic Product and seemed unrelated to the advertising budget. This anecdote is provided to encourage the project team to ask simple questions and demand simple answers: even the largest of marketing budgets can be founded on conjecture.

Community support is another common area of expenditure. Small amounts of expenditure given to local causes can generate benefit and goodwill that seems far out of proportion to the amount donated. Beyond these small amounts, however, the gains are questionable and it can be argued that organisations should attend to their primary purpose and use their resources accordingly.

Of course, before the project was started, discussions similar to those outlined above will have taken place to justify the policy expenditure being incurred in the first place. However, there remains a role for the project team to collate information on expenditure, so that priorities can be attached to each item and decisions on whether to continue it can be made at the corporate level. This avoids the funding of numerous pet projects within different parts of the organisation.

EFFICIENCY IMPROVEMENTS

Introduction

So far we have considered the effectiveness of activities, i.e. whether activities are directed to meeting the organisation's objectives. For support and policy activities, this is the first stage and often the one which yields the greatest savings. Having ascertained that an activity does serve a useful purpose, the next stage is to consider whether it can be done more efficiently.

We begin by reconsidering the activity drivers which determine the amount of work which has to take place. This leads to a discussion on the matching of resource to workload, namely setting staffing levels in a realistic way, and to a discussion of experience curves, which can be used to project rates of improvement.

Drivers

We have already considered the use of cost drivers in Step 3, *Radical Change*. They were particularly relevant to this step because they indicated influences on cost which affected the whole company, perhaps justifying investment to remedy the problem. When examining improvements at the activity level, it is more useful to consider the more specific activity drivers.

Activity drivers have been defined as measures which are proportional to the amount of work carried out. Ideally they are related to the input of work to a department, though if this is not possible they may measure the amount of output produced. Activity drivers have two contributions to the improvement of efficiency within an organisation:

- by identifying what creates work, it becomes possible to see how to reduce it;
- it becomes feasible to scale the resources for each activity in a rational way.

The second point is now discussed below.

Workload modelling with standard times

Resource to workload modelling is a relatively mature discipline. It has been the cornerstone of estimating and scheduling of industrial operations for over a century. More recently it has been applied to the measurement of repetitive clerical operations.

In this traditional form, the approach has entailed breaking down a task into its constituent tasks, applying standard times to each of these tasks and calculating a work rate, given various allowances for rest times. The approach has received mixed views from both managers and those to whom it has been applied. From the view of the employees, the method can be used to reduce a task to the minimum series of mechanistic components and then ensure these are carried out at the required rate, thereby creating monotonous employment; on the other hand the existence of detailed task descriptions and standard times acts as a barrier to those who might make arbitrary demands for increased production. Managers welcome the existence of clear information on the work being carried out, since it enhances control; however the existence of formal task descriptions and timings does limit their capacity to implement quickly any improvements they may have identified, subsequent to the standards being set.

The advantages and disadvantages of these systems differ according to whether workload is rising or falling. If workload is rising, staff will often take on the additional work without an increase in resource, unless of course standard times exist which prove that more staff are required! If workload is falling, the effects are often well disguised for fear of redundancy; in these circumstances standard times can be useful for identifying where there is spare capacity.

Despite these different perceptions of standard times, if we are concerned with searching for better ways of controlling overheads, there is no doubt that detailed information on activities is better than no information. With this in mind we now discuss the review of existing standard time systems which may have been installed to control the overhead functions.

In calculating standard times, the first stage is to examine the component tasks of the activity, and consider whether they are necessary. Some simplification may be possible using the process modelling techniques that were described in Step 3, *Radical Change*. Simplification could also be achieved by applying the techniques of work study to improve efficiency at this detailed level; these techniques are well established and those interested in them will find them covered in specialist texts. Even if a previous work study has been carried out, it is worthwhile revisiting this area because further opportunities for saving regularly appear through improvements in technology.

The second stage is to examine critically the standard times themselves. Two issues need to be considered:

- *The absolute amount of time allocated.* If it is possible to draw comparisons with other organisations on the times taken for specific tasks then a view can be taken on whether the allotted times are realistic. This is quite unusual; even small differences between different circumstances, causing say a 10 per cent difference in the amount of time required, can render the comparisons useless. In making this comparison there is an adage 'Don't separate the numbers from the people'. In other words make sure that when external comparisons are being made that this is backed up by personal experience of the comparator organisations.
- *The trend in performance.* It is a matter of fact that productivity continues to increase with time. This can arise from the increased use of capital equipment, better working methods or experience-curve effects (which are discussed in the next subsection). If the standard times have not shown an improvement over the years then this must be justified. One reason may be that the work involves a set of tasks requiring minimal learning, but even here better support equipment can make a contribution to improved productivity.

In summary, the use of standard times for workload modelling is very well established. It is now starting to fall out of favour as more flexibility is expected from staff and the tasks become less well defined. There remains a role however for the use of standard times for repetitive clerical work.

Workload modelling with linear regression

So far the discussion on workload modelling has been confined to the case where the tasks involved in an activity have been very closely defined and measured. There are many overhead activities where the tasks are indefinable, but the activity drivers are identifiable, e.g. customer support activity costs may be proportional to the number of customers being supported. Often there will be more than one activity driver, so in the previous example the activity cost may be proportional to both the number of customers and the number of products. Although the activity drivers are understood the tasks involved in the activity may be too vague to allow the use of standard times, e.g. answering the telephone, making investigations.

In such cases it is still possible to compare relative resource levels where the same activity takes place in many places across the organisation; this is common in large, dispersed organisations where there are many similar branches, e.g. in retail organisations. The technique which can be used to good effect is multiple linear regression, which is a technique for obtaining the relationship between a number of input variables, in this case the activity drivers, and an output variable, such as the activity cost or staffing levels. Rather than provide any further explanation of the theory of regression techniques, the best guidance is to obtain the manual for any common spreadsheet, where instructions on how to carry out regressions will be given.

The output from the regression analysis will be a set of coefficients relating the observed resource level, to the levels of workload drivers. There will also be a correlation coefficient, indicating how good a relationship actually exists. Rather than study the coefficients which are obscure for all but the most determined, the best course is to compare the actual level of resource, with that projected from the regression analysis. Too large a difference between actual and projected resources suggest that the workload drivers have been wrongly identified; if there is an ideal match then this suggests that resources are evenly distributed. Where there is a generally good match but with some exceptions, this suggests that there are some anomalies in resource levels. When anomalies such as these are identified, the next step is to investigate them for special circumstances, rather than automatically adjust the resource level on the basis of a mathematical model.

Although the technique is useful for comparing manning levels across large organisations and is relatively quick to perform, its main disadvantage is that it can only identify relative disparities and does not examine whether the absolute levels of resource are appropriate. This cannot be done without the use of standard times or costs, and this itself requires a definition of the tasks required to carry out an activity.

Experience curves and volume effects

In the discussion below, we assume that the basic principles of experience curves are understood, namely that the time taken to carry out a particular activity decreases with each repetition. An experience curve is characterised by a factor, typically between 60 and 85 per cent; an example of an 80 per cent curve is given in Figure 5.2 whereby unit costs falls by 20 per cent for every doubling of cumulative production. Experience curves are a valuable method of predicting the future costs for an operation, especially when there is some information on the costs of a pilot operation available.

Although experience curves had their origins in production, they apply neither to products nor services but to activities. The ability to distinguish where particular activities lie on an experience curve for particular activities becomes important when a new product or service which is partially based on a previous model is launched. The new operations can expect to experience greater improvements with time than traditional oper-ations. Distinguishing between the costs of the new and traditional activities when making projections of future costs is straightforward if the product or service costs have been prepared on an activity basis.

Given constant technology and investment the rate of improvements slows. However, in practice improvement in both these areas ensures that improvement is continual. Economic statistics and independent research suggest a continual improvement in both white-collar and blue-collar productivity, though the latter grows at a faster rate because of the direct impact of capital investment. We now discuss the rates of improvement of which can be expected.

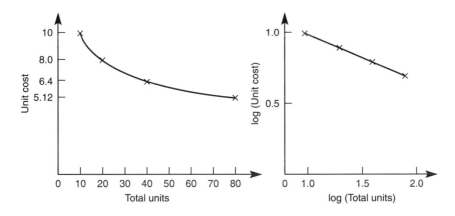

Figure 5.2 Experience curve (80%)

The evidence on while-collar productivity improvement is mixed. Since white-collar workers are mostly involved in the creation and manipulation of knowledge it would be reasonable to expect productivity to rise at the greatest rate where there has been investment in information technology (IT). In fact this causal link is not observed. Despite this, we nonetheless see continual improvement in productivity in both the public and private sectors:

- the Civil Service within the United Kingdom has required a 1.5 per cent per year fall in operating costs for the achievement of a constant volume of work;
- in newly privatised agency functions of the government, annual rates of improvement in productivity have ranged between two per cent and three per cent per year;
- research in both the public and private sectors showed productivity improvements of the order of two per cent per year, albeit with significant variation.

Paradoxically many of the improvements listed above were achieved with minimal investment in IT; the absence of a correlation between white-collar productivity improvement and the investment in IT is itself a major reason for the interest in business process re-engineering.

By comparison, blue-collar productivity has risen at a faster rate, possibly because of the more reliable links between capital investment and the increase in productivity. Typically blue-collar productivity rises at a rate of about 4 per cent per year, as illustrated in Figure 5.3; the period has been chosen to span both an economic boom and the start of recession. Productivity grows faster in a boom as fixed costs are spread over increased production.

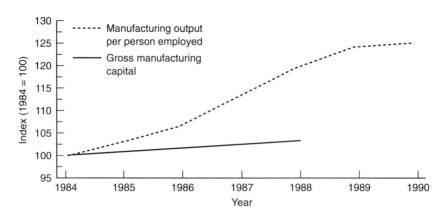

Figure 5.3 Manufacturing (blue-collar) productivity relative to capital stock

The impact of learning curves needs to be understood when formulating the business strategy, which was the foundation for the work in Step 1, *External Review*. Substantial learning is a barrier to entry by new competitors into a market, and a decision can be taken to price a new product to gain large market share and maximise learning opportunities, and therefore to be ready to compete on a cost leadership basis against subsequent entrants.

Scale effects

In making comparisons of the resource levels of activities in similar circumstances, the issues of scale always impinge. Many comparisons are made on a unit basis and the unit parameters are often scale dependent. In examining the behaviour of unit cost it is often useful to separate out the pure volume dependencies, and those dependencies which relate to the rate of production.

The first category, volume dependencies, would consist of costs such as development costs and set-up costs which need to be made regardless of the volume of production. The effect of higher volumes is simply to amortise these costs over a larger number of items. Learning, or experience, is a further volume effect and this has already been discussed.

The second category, rate-dependencies, is more complex. There are some economies of scale which depend on rate of operations, relating to:

- the spreading of a time-based overhead over a facility which is able to operate at a higher throughput;
- the justification of increased capital equipment to make overhead operations more efficient.

There may also be diseconomies of scale, perhaps associated with organisational complexity or through pushing up prices of bought-in services. The most common situation is that there are initial economies of scale, but these tail off and there is no net benefit for subsequent increases in rate of production.

When organising overhead processes, the lesson is always to evaluate the processes with the volume in mind. In many cases the effect of economies of scale may affect the viability of the entire project. For example there is little point in proceeding with a process whose economic scale, in terms of both rate and volume, is so large that the financial and organisational resources of the company would be inadequate. In such a case after initial success at a small scale, a larger competitor would move in and obtain lower unit costs simply by achieving economies of scale not available to the initial entrant.

ECONOMY

Scope of resources

The final element of the three Es is Economy, which refers to the cost-effective acquisition of resource, which we have divided below into staff and bought-in material or services.

We also discuss the principles of effective procurement of external material or services, and extend this to the option to subcontract out an entire group of activities, which we consider in a later section on market testing.

Staff costs

During Step 2, *Activity Analysis*, the project team will have calculated, for each activity:

- staff costs, split between direct and indirect staff;
- number of staff, split by category.

This data provides the basic information needed to calculate unit salary costs. The resulting figures, with the management group and the computer department usually leading the field by a large margin, allow:

- comparisons to be made with outside norms;
- attention to be paid to the costly posts, if there is an intention to reduce manpower.

It needs to be said that controlling staff costs is not just a matter of obtaining the lowest price; nothing is truer than the adage 'If you pay peanuts you get monkeys'. The most important step to controlling staff costs is the elimination of bad personnel practice. The most extreme example of this in the author's experience occurred in a manufacturing company which had the dubious distinction of turning over staff faster than it turned over stock (four and three turns per year respectively).

Good personnel management is a subject in its own right, and cannot be summarised here, though we do touch on some aspects when we discuss cultural issues in Step 5, *Sustainable Improvement*. Instead we summarise the measurable signs of bad personnel management – labour turnover, sickness and absenteeism, and wasted time – and discuss the consequent costs.

Labour turnover

The costs associated with labour turnover are immense; if we suppose that for the first six months employees are operating at half efficiency because of the need to learn the task, and for the last six months they are operating at half efficiency because they are looking for another job, then if they remain for a year only, output will be half of the nominal, and if they remain for two years output will be three-quarters of the nominal. Measurement of labour turnover is best achieved through two indices:

$$\frac{\text{Number of leavers in the period}}{\text{Average number of employees during period}}$$

and:

$$\frac{\text{Number of employees with } x \text{ years' service}}{\text{Average number of employees during } x \text{ years}}$$

The former ratio measures the total turnover of staff, and is a measure of the recruitment and training costs being incurred through turnover. The second can provide a slightly different view, by measuring only those who have remained for a period of time, say one or two years, and is a measure of the stability of longer-serving employees who represent the skill base of the organisation. When these ratios are calculated, this should be done for each activity centre and class of employee. There is likely to be wide variation between different parts of the organisation.

Sickness and absenteeism

The amount of absenteeism is easily measured as:

$$\frac{\text{Number of days lost during period}}{\text{Total number of days available in the period}}$$

Many compare this ratio with industry norms to identify if their own situation is satisfactory or if their organisation is better than average. In fact, any absenteeism is worrying except where there is genuine illness, because it implies the corporation is employing people who would rather not be there. It is not so much the time lost when a person is not at work, but how little they will be doing when there are present that is the main concern. Severe action against malingerers is associated with backward management styles, but it is fair to say that advanced companies require committed employees who do not need to be watched over, and that if commitment is no longer present then neither should be the employee.

Wasted time

It is revealing for someone to take a piece of paper in their hand as a decoy and walk around the organisation, counting mentally how many of the people seen are actually working and how many are reading a newspaper, chatting or enjoying a social telephone call. In the author's experience this activity sampling can show the ratio of wasted time to total can sometimes exceed 50 per cent, though this can soar at critical parts of the day, such as just before lunch or finishing time, with people being unwilling to start a new task. This is really a function of weak management. In extreme examples some managers strike a truce with their staff, and bury themselves in their office at certain times so as not cause undue embarrassment.

The three measurements given above do not consider how much is being paid for the staff, but whether the money is justified given the quality of staff behaviour, which is the better emphasis. Nonetheless sometimes the level of staff benefits does become an issue, and in this case the organisation needs to examine whether the remuneration for the posts is wrong.

There may have been a mistake in setting the required skills for the post. This goes right back to the question of what the job entails, which may not have been considered formally. For example, in a purchasing department is 'the buyer' meant to set the overall purchasing policies (on matters such as number of suppliers), conduct negotiations with suppliers, or process the purchase orders? If the job has been either formally or informally overspecified, then the staff costs will be too high. Conversely, sometimes important tasks are left undone because various staff interpret their job description simply as what they are able to do, and certain tasks fall in between; continuing with the previous example, one person may set purchasing policy while another processes the orders, but no one negotiates with suppliers.

Even if the job has been correctly specified, there may be an inappropriate pay rate for the required skills. This is easily settled by contacting local trade associations, or relying on salary surveys.

If after this analysis, staff costs still appear too high, relocation of some functions offers one solution. Lower pay rates can usually be obtained within in the same currency zone because of the wide variation in regional pay rates. A more radical alternative is to move to another currency zone. If this is being considered, it needs to be appreciated that the key parameter to consider is not the current level of unit wage costs, given present levels of productivity, but the projected levels of productivity relative to others in the same currency zone. This is because it is the average level of productivity within the currency zone which will affect the eventual exchange rate, and consequently the eventual unit labour cost will depend on the company's performance relative to others in the same zone. If there is a move to relocate operations, the question should be asked whether the prospective location is destined to be a high productivity/high wage area or the reverse and to examine the implications for the organisation's own productivity levels.

Bought-in costs

The proportion of costs formed by bought-in material and services will vary between corporations, but at the very least there will be an expenditure on 'consumables'. The purchasing of material for overhead functions is often not tightly controlled, since the amount of cost involved is not significant to any one department. This can be most evident in the purchasing of travel and accommodation, which is usually performed on an *ad hoc* basis where individuals make their own arrangements. The loss of potential discounts can be a major cost.

To control the cost of purchased material, several points need to be considered:

- *The purchasing strategy*, which will dictate the views on the number of suppliers, their location, the acceptability of singlesourcing and the preference for centralisation or decentralisation.
- *The purchasing cycle*, from research, specification, supplier selection, ordering, expediting, storage and making payment. The time spent on any phase of the sequence will of course depend on the amount of expenditure being considered, e.g. the amount of time spent on researching the paperclip supply market is likely to be small; nonetheless all the phases need to be considered, even if some consideration is momentary.
- *Controls and procedures*. Managerial controls determine who is authorised to commit the organisation to expenditure and how this is controlled. Procedural controls are often concerned with the avoidance of fraud; this is not an imaginary threat: procurement is the most fertile ground for fraud within an organisation.

If these issues are all addressed, this will form a sound foundation for the operation of a professional purchasing operation. Effective control of cost also requires information on:

- *Monitoring of performance*. Too often those responsible for purchasing are allowed to take the credit for 'always beating inflation', without being challenged that the price of most materials fall in real terms. The monitoring of the competence of the purchasing function therefore requires the uses of indices.

- *A measurement of total acquisition cost.* It is not possible to control bought-in costs using information on levels of current expenditure. When examined at a single point in time much of the expenditure on material cost is seen to be fully committed: the point of control existed in the past when a particular piece of equipment or way of operating was decided upon. To exercise effective control it is therefore necessary to understand the costs which will be incurred over the entire use of an item when it is purchased.

We now consider each of these five points in more detail.

Purchasing strategy

To speak of a 'purchasing strategy' implies there is an overall plan as to how, and from which source, materials are to be purchased. It might be thought that the best plan is to buy on the open market at the cheapest price, and no further sophistication is required. For a single purchase this is the case, though where there is an ongoing requirement to buy items it pays to consider how it is to be best done.

The first decision is over who should be responsible for purchasing. In a small organisation operating from a single site, it will be possible to nominate a single individual who can be provided with the necessary support; in a larger organisation, there is the option to divide responsibility on:

- *Geographic basis.* The main advantage of local procurement of consumables is flexibility and responsiveness. If local retailers hold stock of an item it can be obtained rapidly. As for costs, the picture is less clear. Buying centrally should allow better prices to be obtained and lower stocks to be held, but there are also administration costs involved. The best solution can often be found in compromises, such as negotiating national call-off contracts with a national supplier and using the supplier's distribution network for storage and delivery, but permitting the use of local sources if this is economic.
- *Purchasing cycle.* The purchasing cycle is detailed in the next section, and it is feasible to divide the purchasing function along these lines. As with all such division, it promotes technical excellence in areas such as negotiation and stores control but it fragments responsibility for particular types of material.
- *Range.* This option has the advantage of providing clear accountability for certain materials, which is a benefit. On the other hand the individual responsible for a range now has to be a generalist.

The purchasing strategy also encompasses making decisions on the number of suppliers, which is a major issue. Very different approaches can be taken with suppliers. One approach is to maintain an arms-length relationship and repeatedly invite competitive quotation; the other approach is to concentrate purchasing through a particular supplier in the expectation of reducing overheads, obtaining discounts and preferential service.

Finally, the stock-holding policies have to be defined. While less critical for overhead activities, where there is usually not a major need to hold stock, the costs are nonetheless large when expressed as a proportion of the value held; typically stock costs an organisation annually about twenty-five per cent of its value.

Purchasing cycle

The purchasing cycle is a familiar concept (for example, *The Purchasing Handbook* (Ferrer, Dobbler and Killen 1993)), though the names given to each phase in the cycle vary. For our purposes, we have defined the purchasing cycle as comprising research, specification, supplier selection, ordering, expediting, storage and making payment; this is illustrated in Figure 5.4. For the common consumables many of these stages can be given a moment's thought, but in other areas, staff can be responsible for the purchase of expensive equipment, most notably capital equipment such as computers. Even when amortised over a number of years the costs can be considerable so basic procedures need to be followed.

- *Researching the market* prior to specification can result in large savings. Even if a custom solution is inevitable, minimising the customisation will reduce costs. Depending on the formality, the research can range from a casual examination of the trade press, to issuing requests to potential suppliers to issue a 'statement of qualification'.
- *Specification of the item* can proceed once an understanding of the features which are available within the market place has been obtained. The functional specification is a statement of what is required of the item. At this stage a degree of formality is often required, particularly if there are going to be several users of the purchased equipment. This is particularly the case with computer systems where an unambiguous specification is mandatory to avoid the purchase of a computer system which despite considerable customisation, does not do what is required.
- *Supplier selection* starts with inviting several companies to submit tenders, perhaps through issuing a formal 'invitation to tender'. From the initial research there should be a good idea of potential suppliers and this will avoid contacting large numbers of inappropriate companies. On receiving their responses they should be tabulated for comparison, in terms of total acquisition costs (which are discussed later), the number of

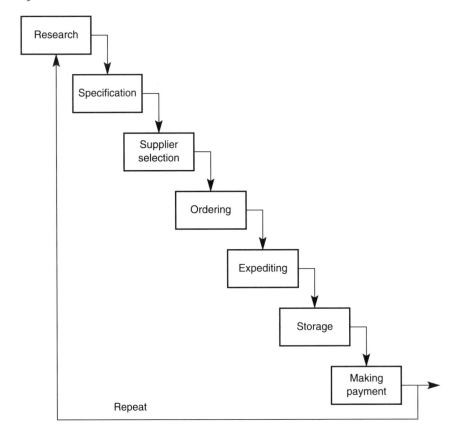

Figure 5.4 Purchasing cycle

non-conformances to specification and the quality and stability of the
supplier. A short-list process can be undertaken if necessary, as can visits
to both the supplier and reference sites if significant expenditure is
involved.

- *Ordering* is not as mundane as it sounds. First it offers the opportunity for
post-tender negotiation to drive prices down further or to exact special
conditions with the favoured supplier. Second there needs to be an understanding of the contractual terms involved.
- *Expediting* can be a mundane task but it should not be left to the last
moment. Expediting should not necessary if an effort has been made to
build relationships with suppliers, but where there are problems, it is the
squeaking hinge that gets the oil. For large items it may pay to be more
attentive than making a periodic phone call, and arrange visits to the
supplier.

- *Storage* is a costly task and we have already emphasised the importance of clear stock-holding policies. Beyond that however, the main concerns are to avoid deterioration and to ensure accessibility.
- *Payment* will conclude the normal cycle. Obviously, late payment could result in discounts being forgone and a disgruntled supplier.

The degree of rigour which a company wishes to adopt on its purchasing policies depends on the proportion of the total cost which material forms. For all significant expenditure this purchasing cycle should be recognised and followed.

Controls and procedures

Purchasing requires special care to avoid the risk of fraud. The most obvious example is a corrupt buyer who awards contracts in return for backhanders. This can be avoided by enforcing strict rules on the dealings between suppliers and buyers and dividing responsibilities within the purchasing department.

More subtle are the schemes where suppliers form cartels, either with or without the connivance of those in the buying department. Even without connivance these can form very easily where there is a stable pattern of suppliers being invited to tender. Where the volumes of business are sufficient, there may be an agreement not to drop below a certain price and suppliers may bid at different levels above this according to their need for the work at the time. Sometimes this is advanced to the point of collusion between suppliers in selecting who should win the next contract. One way to avoid this is to introduce new suppliers into the tendering process. Where this is not possible, because of a limited range of supply, a further check is to examine the accounts of the suppliers. On one occasion when the author did this, it was found that the return on capital employed by one long-standing supplier amounted to a remarkable 49 per cent!

Monitoring of performance

On appointment a new purchasing manager will generally seek to justify his existence by negotiating a few plum discounts amounting to his annual salary. This, of course, is to demonstrate his worth in the short term; of more interest is the long-term performance.

However, it is difficult to measure how effective the purchasing function is. Those responsible will justify their competence by comparing this year's prices to last year's adjusted for inflation; if there is a decrease in real terms this is taken as evidence of competence. However, in the long term the price

of materials usually does decrease relative to inflation, because of technological improvements in the manufacturing processes of suppliers leading to
the experience curves discussed earlier. This decrease is typically two per
cent per year, but for some categories can be much larger for items such as
electronic office equipment.

Total acquisition cost

An understanding of total acquisition cost is essential for the control of
bought-in overhead costs. It has two areas of application, namely:

- The appraisal of capital purchases. Two major components of overhead
  costs are usually the capital and running costs of significant purchases,
  such as buildings and computer systems. Many of these costs, which are
  virtually uncontrollable once a system has been selected, may not have
  been considered when the particular system was selected.
- When making decisions on whether to carry out an activity in-house or to
  sub-contract. It is important to research the full costs of both options. In
  particular, the costs associated with subcontracting can often be underestimated.

Total acquisition cost, which is connected to life-cycle costing, addresses
these points. Life-cycle costing has found an application in the military field
where equipment has to be supported for many decades and the choice
between systems has to account for these costs.

In calculating total acquisition cost one controversial point is the use of
net present value (NPV) techniques. These are an accepted form of accounting for costs and revenues which occur at different times. Underlying the
techniques is an assumption that money available in the future is worth less
than money available at the present, and for a comparison to be made the
future money must be discounted; the interest rate used to discount the
future receipts or payments approximates to the prevailing interest rate. The
result is that any positive or negative events in the distant future have a relatively minor effect. The clear implication that purchasing decisions ought to
be focused on the short term seems to run counter to common sense. It
should be borne in mind, however, that first, once inflation is taken into
account, long term real interest rates are less than the discount rates which
are often proposed; second, substantial price rises can be expected for the
support of equipment from a supplier of troublesome equipment when there
is no other source of supply. While the NPV method is valid, it should not
be used to suggest that only the immediate future matters.

In calculating a total acquisition cost, the principle is to take full account
of costs. This will include:

- *The initial non-recurring cost of the item or service.* For a capital item this non-recurring cost may be the predominant item. Where a service is to be subcontracted, then the non-recurring cost is likely to be small, but will encompass the costs of going out to tender.
- *The ongoing recurring costs.* For a capital item this will include the maintenance costs, which may be considerable. The scope of the recurring costs can be very broad, including the cost of buying, inspecting and correcting the goods or services. These can add substantially to the cost of subcontracting.
- *The liquidation costs of the arrangement.* These can be negative if there is a resale value, or positive if there is a disposal cost for the asset or a termination fee for the service.

When buying capital equipment, once the total acquisition cost is understood, then a realistic choice can be made between the various options. When subcontracting services, the total acquisition cost gives a realistic view of the additional cost which will be taken on when subcontracting; this can then be compared with the cost reductions to be expected from the cessation of in-house operations; the latter will include not only the direct costs but also the indirect support costs, which have been calculated during the activity-based costing undertaken in Step 2. This balance is illustrated in Figure 5.5.

MARKET APPROACH TO SERVICE PROVISION

Introduction

The methods described so far for controlling overheads have been largely deterministic, involving analysis and the setting of service levels and

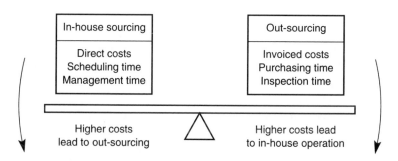

Figure 5.5 Total acquisition cost

resources from the centre of an organisation, after data collection by the project team. There are many cases where this is not possible because:

- either, the organisation is too large or complex to be analysed in sufficient detail;
- or, sufficient authority does not exist at the centre for resource setting to occur.

The former situation is unsatisfactory since it implies the organisation is too large to be effectively controlled, and by implication should be subdivided. However the second situation is quite a common situation in public sector organisations where there has been a deliberate devolution of power, often justified on the grounds of improving the democratic process. The situation can also occur in decentralised private sector companies, where the heads of divisions, in concert, are able to resist attempts by the centre to impose its will.

In such a situation it becomes necessary to devise a means of controlling overheads which does not depend on central direction. This can be achieved by creating a market, whereby managers of one profit centre have the discretion to purchase services internally or externally. In this way a monolithic overhead structure becomes broken up into a series of smaller independent 'businesses'. Overheads become controlled in a similar way to those in a group of small companies, by managers taking decisions over a narrow range of activities under their control, and being penalised by competitive forces if these decisions prove to be incorrect

In some circumstances a market approach may not be feasible. For a true market approach to be a viable option:

- it must be possible to specify the amount of output, or the level of service, which is being delivered, otherwise it is not possible to know what is being purchased;
- there must be a means to exchange information and a space (not necessarily physical) to trade;
- there must be multiple suppliers or consumers of the service, and preferably both.

If all these conditions are met then a market driven approach is viable; if the last condition does not hold it may still be possible to simulate competitive pressures by regulation of the market.

This approach has proved popular in recent times, though there are many disadvantages as well as advantages, and the adoption of a market-orientated approach to the provision of services certainly does not necessarily imply an automatic reduction in cost. These advantages and disadvantages are now discussed below. Although the use of markets is being considered here, this is to allow it to follow the discussion of the purchasing cycle; applied on a large scale, the effects are as radical as the changes discussed in Step 3, *Radical Change.*

The costs and benefits of a market approach

The first point to make is that the choice between a market driven approach and a directive approach is not always an obvious one. This has been apparent at the national level, where for much of the twentieth century there has been debate, to put it mildly, on the best form of organisation of national economies. At one end of the spectrum there have been totally directed economies in which output was directed centrally, while at the other there have been very *laissez-faire* economies where there has been minimal central direction, except for the provision of such functions as the armed forces (though this is a relatively recent phenomenon, until recently these were firmly based in the private sector). This debate seems now to have reached a conclusion, albeit an unclear one, in which the most successful economies are those which allow the operation of a market in some areas (e.g. the provision of common goods and services), but retain central direction in others (e.g. through industrial and energy policy).

At the more mundane level of the provision of overhead services, the situation is just as complex, and it is important to chose between a market approach or a directed approach on pragmatic grounds rather than on dogma. There are now enough recorded cases both of 'market-failure' and the failure of directive systems to make it clear that there is no assured solution.

The disadvantages of a market approach include:

- the duplication of activity between competing organisations;
- the potential loss of economies of scale overall. However, where an activity is already fragmented subcontracting allows greater economies of scale from specialist suppliers;
- additional activities, such as the need to generate price lists, or pay for advertising or other forms of promotion;
- the administration of the market place, whether in electronic or physical form.

There is also a loss of top-level control and oversight. As more services are subcontracted the management's view of the entire range of activity on which they depend becomes restricted.

Set against this there are certainly some advantages of the market approach, especially:

- greater flexibility in responding to new needs;
- higher staff motivation as they can link the provision of a better service to the growth of their own organisation and increased personal reward.

If a market driven approach is considered viable for controlling some of the overhead services, there is a choice of creating an internal market or simply trading on external market. The use of an internal market is less radical, but the company has to carefully consider whether the extra cost associated with the market, or 'playing at shops' as its detractors would call it, is worth the likely savings, especially as it very difficult to create a genuine market internally. It may be the only choice if the organisation is unwilling to allow an activity to leave the organisation; this may arise because the activity may involve a strategically important skill or there may be a substantial risk associated with them, since the act of subcontracting does imply a lessening of direct control.

Setting prices

We have already outlined the basic requirements for a market to operate. Perhaps the most fundamental is that the unit of output, or the level of service associated with it, is measurable. This equally applies to internal markets as to external markets.

Where there is a quantifiable output, then it becomes possible to produce unit prices and collect payment for each item delivered. For example, this can often be done for computing departments, where the department will charge a price for a particular operation or for a unit of processor resource consumed; another very common example of such charging is for training provision, where each course will have an attendance charge associated with it.

In deciding the transfer price, the first question that arises is whether prices will be set following the negotiation of a price between the provider and the recipient, or on the basis of a cost-based formula. Negotiation of transfer prices forms an uncertain middle ground in the control of overhead costs. If staff are under a manager's control, then the manager can control their efficiency; if a material or a service is to be purchased on the external market, then the efficiency of the service is disciplined by the market, and the quantity purchased is under the managers's discretion. When services are purchased through transfer prices the costs are out of reach of both means of control. While provider and recipient may go through the motions of negotiations these have the character of a phoney war.

The negotiations become more real if there is more than one source of supply. Occasionally more than one source of supply will exist internally, though if this is not the case then the option can be created to go on to the outside market, if lower prices can be obtained. Sometimes this is prohibited, however and there is a directive to use in-house resource.

It is not always possible to identify individual items of output. However it is usually still possible to measure the level of service, defined in terms of its timeliness or quality, and perhaps even make the cost charged for the service depend on this. These measurements are encapsulated in a 'service-level agreement', which is a formal agreement by one part of an organisation on the level of service it will provide to another. 'Service-level agreements' are an important part of the drive to break up large monoliths into smaller elements which can be held accountable.

Service-level agreements

Service-level agreements offer an opportunity to clarify the responsibilities in a monolithic overhead structure without resorting to the creation of a full market. The approach recognises that activities are carried out for the benefit of the recipients of their outputs, which may sound a truism but which can appear radical in some circles. These relationships between the providers and recipients of a service are identified, and the level of service formalised into service-level agreements.

Compared to the adoption of internal markets, these agreements have the advantage of avoiding the administration, and the costs, involved in setting prices and trading. On the other hand the agreements cannot usually reward success and penalise failure; if the provider of a service fails to meet an agreement, the consequences are rarely oblivion as is the case for unsuccessful companies. Furthermore, unlike a market, they are not dynamic: they only capture the level of service, as negotiated with the customer, at a particular time. This falls far short of a market situation, which delivers a response to a customer demand, albeit at a negotiated price, which shifts according to the changing need of the customer.

Nonetheless the introduction of service-level agreements do provide two advantages at relatively little cost:

- They can create a shift in attitude in those providing a service, from an inward looking approach where the providers of a service judge themselves on their own standards, to considering the requirements of those who receive the service. To describe an activity as 'inward looking' is not to condemn it entirely; those who operate activities in this way often place great emphasis on technical excellence, although without particular consideration as to how the results of their effort affect the organisation as a whole. In practice it is the application of an expertise that gives it worth, so for example, technically excellent management accounts or research and development are of little use if they have no value to those who have access to them. The existence of a service-level agreement reminds staff what they are there for.

- The process of setting up a service-level agreement also provides an opportunity to understand who is receiving a service and what they expect. While this may have been understood when an activity started, as time goes on the original purpose can be forgotten and staff continue a routine out of precedent.

In creating service-level agreements, managers should only be held accountable for items under their control. This may be an obvious point, but given the degree of interdependency in overhead activities, it is a major restriction on providing service-level guarantees.

Out-sourcing

In introducing market driven principles into overhead control, there is the option to make use of external as well as internal markets to exert control over overhead activities, i.e. to subcontract out some activities. We have already discussed the purchasing of materials and services required to support the business processes. We now consider a wider issue, that of subcontracting parts of the processes themselves. The use of the word 'process', defined as a series of activities which link together to satisfy a customer requirement, is significant. The intention is for the subcontractor needs to take over a structured set of activities, in fact a substantial or complete part of a business process. This approach is proving particularly popular in the public sector, where there is a move to reduce the public sector function to a core policy-making organisation, and devolve the execution of tasks to the private sector.

The benefits of out-sourcing are:

- *Access to a fresh set of skills* which may improve the efficiency of the operation.
- *The potential for economies of scale* by subcontracting to a specialist. These economies of scale may arise from the ability to justify specialised capital equipment.
- *The ability to reduce reserve capacity* to cope with peaks in demand, because there may be the option to carry out the activity in tandem with activities having different, perhaps opposite, demand patterns.
- *The ability to devise specialised reward systems*, suitable for a particular type of activity, to motivate the work-force.

As with the operation of internal markets, there are however costs associated with out-sourcing of overhead activities.

A recommended procedure is outlined below. It is simply an adaptation of the standard purchasing cycle we have already described.

Research

The first step is to research both the market and the organisation itself to decide upon possible candidates for subcontracting. There are two basic requirements that have to be met for out-sourcing to be effective, which are similar to those necessary for internal markets to be effective:

- the service to be provided must be measurable;
- a market must exist for the service.

Using these criteria, it is possible to survey the various activities carried out by the organisation and identify potential candidates for out-sourcing. Each potential candidate needs to be subject to a cost/benefit test, to estimate the likely benefits from out-sourcing and the costs associated with the process, including any substantial risks.

Output specification

The second step is to specify the outputs, or services, which the activities provide, in sufficient detail to allow performance to be measured. Any dependencies the activity may have on the organisation as a whole also need to be clarified; these are, in effect, inputs to the activity from the organisation and in drafting a contract, provision has to be made for recognising these inputs and assuming they are of adequate quality It some cases the interdependencies between the activity to be subcontracted and those which will remain within the corporation are so complex as to make subcontracting impractical. The specification of the outputs of the activity and the inputs to be received from the organisation need to be formalised in a requirement specification.

Supplier selection

The third stage is the selection of the supplier. This will generally be by means of a tender, requiring the issue of an invitation to tender, responding to questions and the evaluation of tenders which are received. The key here is consistency of information and approach. Any variation can lead to bidders essentially tendering for different pieces of work, with the possibility of a low bid being accepted but with the subcontractor being under the illusion that less is required of him than is actually expected. The evaluation of rival bids should be done in a systematic way which allows the assessment of the quality of the response not to be coloured by the price. The evaluation should also cover the managerial and financial stability of the supplier. Visits to reference sites can also shed illumination on a supplier's actual performance. At the end of this process, a preferred supplier should be identified, along with any special points requiring further attention.

Post-tender negotiation

The fourth stage involves post-tender negotiation culminating in the signing of contracts. The post-tender negotiation is intended to remedy any weakness in the approach adopted by the preferred supplier. The contracts themselves should ensure there are incentives for the subcontractor to perform in a way consistent with the aims of the organisation, and that there are penalties for non-conformance that are significant enough to represent a risk to the subcontractor.

Contract monitoring

The final stage is of course monitoring of the contract. At the most basic level this is to ensure that the subcontractor simply meets the minimum requirements. The intention, however, should be to make the exchanges mutually beneficial. Many improvements in service level will not be simply a matter of tighter control; they will arise from applying the principles of partnership sourcing the linking and co-ordination of the activities of the supplier and the customer. These can only arise if there is a spirit of co-operation. Furthermore the contract should provide for a reward to the supplier for successful co-operation, allowing the supplier to recover any increased short-term costs.

INFORMATION SYSTEMS AND TECHNOLOGY

Objective

During Step 3, *Radical Change,* a list of potential improvements to the information systems and technology was drawn up and a cost/benefit case developed. Some of these will involve a change to the information systems which will affect the whole company and need to be supervised by the task force responsible for the information systems. Others will have a narrower scope and can be supervised by the managers of the affected areas. The proposals themselves need no further development, other than their adoption by the appropriate manager. Once this is obtained they can be passed up for approval of funds, which is outlined in Step 5, *Sustainable Improvement*. In practice, the advantage of many of the changes involving localised improvments to the information systems and technology is that the investment required is small compared to the saving and therefore approval is often automatic.

We now discuss how these localised improvements to the information systems and technologies can assist in improving effectiveness, efficiency and economy.

Effectiveness

Information systems and technology enable the goods or services the customer receives to be aligned with that which is required, even if the systems and technologies are only deployed in a localised fashion. First, they allow a proper definition of the items, perhaps through direct entry of the requirements at a remote terminal. Second the ability to carry out on-line scheduling allows the provider of the goods or services to make firm commitments for the timing of delivery. Finally communication networks allow coordination of the delivery of the goods or services to the location required. In summary computing and communication assist in providing an internal or external customer with what is wanted, when it is expected and where it is required.

In many cases, the deliverable is information and electronic data interchange avoids the re-entry of information and the delays and imprecision this causes.

Efficiency

Improvement in efficiency is the area which is most typically associated with installing information technology. The automation of repetitive clerical tasks was one of the first applications of computing. While there will always be opportunities for additional efficiency improvements as the cost of processing power decreases, many of the substantial gains are only possible through applying the technology in an integrated fashion.

Localised installation of technology tends not to raise internal efficiency as it creates 'islands of automation', which are efficient in themselves but which still require clerical effort to operate at the interfaces. The implication is that in seeking efficiency improvements, as much attention needs to be paid to the interfaces of the activity to be automated, as to the activity itself. However in doing this, the change will frequently cease to be localised and will require co-ordinated change across the organisation.

The previous comments apply to increasing the internal efficiency of a department. The other aspect is the use of systems and technology to increase the efficiency of those under a department's control, say through better scheduling of resource. This is akin to making the department more effective in its operations, and is feasible even where the systems and technology is installed locally.

Economy

The economy with which resources are procured depends on the ability to execute the purchasing cycle outlined earlier. Information systems and technology can assist in each phase of the cycle; it can provide wider market research, specifications more closely matched to requirements, a more rigorous supplier selection programme, the use of electronic data interchange for ordering, closer monitoring and expediting, better inventory control of stored items and properly timed payments. Further savings can arise through better forecasting and scheduling, in order to avoid short lead time ordering which is usually relatively expensive and the costs of carrying excess inventory arising from over-ordering.

Many of these benefits cannot be implemented in a localised fashion; in particular electronic data interchange and inventory control are topics which impinge on functions outside the purchasing function. This should not discourage effort in this area, however, since bought-in costs frequently amount to half of the total costs of the company. Assuming a company is operating on a 10 per cent margin, to increase its profit by half either requires a 50 per cent increase in sales or a 10 per cent decrease in bought-in costs; the consensus is that the second course of action is far easier to achieve, especially given the application of systems and technology.

Conclusion

Many of the significant benefits of information systems and technology can only be obtained by considering the organisation, or at least processes, as a whole. Nonetheless, there will be benefits that can be obtained through installing systems and technology locally and these benefits can often be obtained relatively quickly with only a minor investment.

PREPARING FOR IMPLEMENTATION

Introduction

The project team will have been identifying various options for improvement throughout this step. The need is now to pull these together into a coherent plan for improvement to which the management is committed. This involves the collation of the various options and their associated cost/benefit analyses and the development of an outline plan.

The assumption is that, since the changes will be relatively localised (unlike those considered in Step 3, *Radical Change*), implementation and monitoring can be achieved through the existing managerial structures and systems, without recourse to separate structures, such as task forces.

Collation

Each of the options for improvement needs to be developed by the team to the point that the costs, benefits, risks and timescales are known; this should be done in conjunction with the manager of the affected activity centre. These analyses are then brought together and summarised so that the senior management can discuss which of the proposed changes are to be acted upon. This ensures that, although each of the changes may only have a localised effect a global view is available of the overall impact on the organisation.

Plan definition

The next step is to develop outline project plans for each of the options. Again, the project team needs to work closely with the management to ensure that there is full acceptance of the tasks proposed.

Next steps

The outline plans and their cost/benefit analyses are considered by the senior management in the project planning phase of Step 5, *Sustainable Improvement*. At this stage sanction is given for any expenditure involved and the corporate plans recast to account for the expected benefits.

ORGANISATIONAL EFFICIENCY CASE STUDY

Background

The organisation is engaged in the product support of major pieces of equipment. Product support is complex and requires four key skills:

- engineering skills, to diagnose problems in the equipment and authorise modifications;
- inventory management skills, to ensure components are available in the right place at the right time;
- contract management skills to negotiate substantial contracts with suppliers;
- financial skills to ensure that the operation is run to budget.

In the past these skills were undertaken within functional departments, as illustrated in Figure 5.6. This had severe problems, as the process of product support of a particular subsystem involved co-operation between four separate departments. There is currently a move to create groups of staff, combining all the necessary skills, to support a particular subsystem. The exact form of these groups has to be developed. This is being done against a background of a major cost reduction being imposed on the product support organisation.

Objective

The objectives of the work are to:

- adjust manning levels in the organisation, so as to accommodate the cut in resources;
- change the organisational structure so as to maintain service levels despite the reduction in resource.

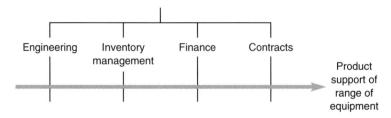

Figure 5.6 Original organisation

Approach

The basic activities of the product support process are defined and the role of the four key skills in each of these activities is defined. The method for modelling the resource requirements of these activities is then determined in order to calculate the resources required for each activity. The communication needed between each activity and the volume of information passed is then considered. From these two analyses an efficient organisation structure is then derived.

Identification of activity drivers

There are four broad categories of activity, which reflect the required skills defined above. Each of these has its own driver of cost. An understanding of these drivers is essential to the setting of resource levels. The activity drivers vary by the type of skill involved:

- Planned engineering tasks, in which the maintenance policies for the subsystem are reviewed with a view to preventing breakdown. This is proportional to the number of items, but each item can make very different demands on engineering time.
- Unplanned engineering tasks, where the engineer responds to faults being reported. Each fault report takes a different amount of time to resolve, but in general the time taken to resolve faults is proportional to their number.
- Inventory control tasks, whose resource requirement is proportional to the number of items being managed. These items fall into two categories, those low cost items, whose inventory levels are automatically managed, and high cost items, requiring individual attention.
- Financial and administration tasks, which are diverse, though mostly proportional to the complexity of the business, which in turn is reflected by the number of people employed.
- Contract-related tasks, whose resource depends on the number and value of contracts being issued.

These activity drivers are now used for resource modelling.

Resource modelling

The modelling of the planned engineering tasks requires identifying the items within each subsystem to be supported. This planned engineering input is then classified into bands according to the time required annually per item. While appearing straightforward, the difficulty is that in the past this work has often not been carried out because of shortage of resource and therefore there are no available records to support the classification. With this in mind, the bands have to be fairly coarse; nonetheless the method provides a means of estimating the resource required for the task. In future, during the design of the subsystem, a more precise estimate of the planned engineering time needed for product support to be made.

The modelling of the unplanned, or reactive, engineering time presents more of a problem. Ideally, the reliability of the subsystem requiring support could be estimated, along with the time needed to respond to each type of fault, thereby allowing the requirement for resource to be made for each subsystem; in practice this information is simply not available. As an alternative, the outputs of the reactive engineering work are measured for each subsystem, in terms of the instructions which are issued and their type. This is then used in a multiple regression to find the correlation between volume of output and the resources employed. The correlation is good, but the measures have two limitations:

- The resulting measures relating type of instruction and the resource requirements are relative only. They can only indicate apparent over or under-resource for particular subsystems.
- By only measuring the output from the function, the method is unable to detect if engineers are generating unnecessary work, i.e. if an area was over-resourced it is possible that to stay busy there is unnecessary intervention and generation of instructions.

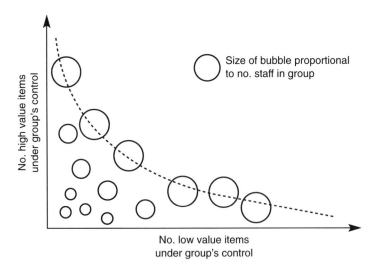

Figure 5.7 Boundary of supervisory control

The resources required for planned and unplanned engineering resource are then combined and used to redistribute engineering resource across the subsystems to be supported. Since the unplanned work is largely not carried out at present the total resource requirements amount to more than is available, and the levels will need to be trimmed back.

Inventory control is exercised through groups dedicated to particular subsystems. When the number of high and low value items is plotted on a graph we see a curve representing the natural boundary of supervisory control, as shown in Figure 5.7; a manager can supervise either a large number of low value items or a large (but lesser) number of high value items, but not both. There are however a number of groups which do not justify a section leader and are candidates for merger. The next step is to carry out a multiple regression, relating the number of clerks under a section leader to the number of high and low value items being managed by the groups. The correlation is good and shows that high value items require over ten times the resource required for low value items and gives an estimate of the resource required for both. When combined with the previous analysis on the limits on supervisory control, we can also deduce the natural span of control of a section leader in this organisation.

The organisation employs relatively few finance staff so resource modelling is less critical in this area. A simple approach is therefore used, and the average ratio of finance and administration staff to total staff complement is found. This will be used to apportion these staff across the organisation, subject to resource constraints.

The number of contracts staff required for each subsystem is estimated according to the number of contracts being issued. Allowance is also made for the value of the material being purchased, so that staff are not ineffectively deployed on dealing with large numbers of low value contracts.

It will be apparent that most of the resource modelling is directed towards equitably allocating resource according to need, as opposed to deriving the required resource from first principles. This is satisfactory in the context of a major cost reduction even if an ideal staffing level is derived it is scarcely relevant if the staff will not be available to meet it. The final stage of the resource modelling is therefore to adjust the resource levels needed for each subsystem to fit the total workforce which will be available following the staff reduction. A key issue is to balance, the need for additional resource for planned engineering work against additional reductions elsewhere; the increase in planned engineering resource is essentially a policy decision and this is done on a judgemental, not analytic basis.

Lower organisational structure

Once the resource levels have been set across the organisation, it becomes possible to consider the organisational structure. The aim is to integrate the four skills around particular subsystems.

For inventory control, the basic operating unit has already been defined: a section leader in charge of several control clerks. The scope of their responsibility is set by identifying subsystems with the appropriate number of high and low value items which can fulfil the working capacity of the clerks.

These subsystems will have an engineering workload associated with their planned and unplanned maintenance, which defines the number of engineers required. The engineers will report to an engineering manager. The number of managers required depends on the number of technical decisions which must be referred upwards for his approval, which in turn depends on the technical complexity of the subsystems, as opposed to the volume of the maintenance workload. In practice, this leads to relatively narrower spans of control.

The inventory control and the engineering units need to work closely together and are situated in the same area. The inventory control staff are much more numerous than the engineering staff and there is a need for an additional tier of management, with several section leaders reporting to an inventory control manager. This provides a structure as shown in Figure 5.8.

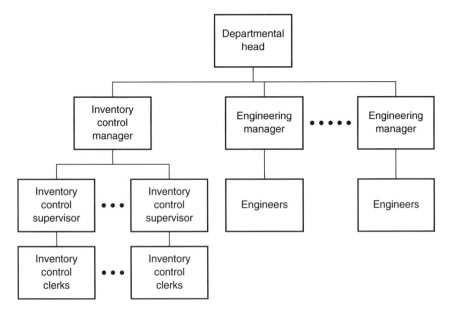

Figure 5.8 Lower organisational structure

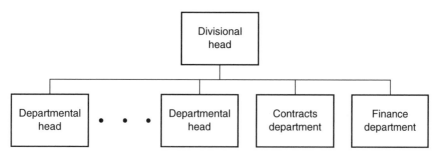

Figure 5.9 Organisational structure

Each inventory control unit is associated with an engineering unit and is responsible for a particular subsystem, which can now be supported without interdepartmental communication.

The department head can be drawn from either the inventory control or the engineering routes, since at this level the work is of a general managerial nature. He is responsible for the product support of an entire system.

Higher organisational structure

The financial, administration and contracts staff are less numerous and it is therefore only practical to integrate them with the other skills at the senior management level. The higher organisational structure is shown in Figure 5.9. Several departmental heads report to a divisional head, who is also responsible for a contracts department and the finance and administration staff.

Although these staff are not closely integrated with those with the inventory control and engineering skills, communication analysis illustrated in Figure 5.10, shows this to be acceptable. In terms of volume, the most significant communication is between the inventory control and engineering staff, who are now closely linked, and between finance and contracts, who can be located together. The divisional manager is now entirely responsible for the product support of the systems in major pieces of equipment. He has underneath him all the necessary skills for this support and can be held fully accountable for performance.

Conclusion

The new structure is far better suited to effective product support. Responsibility for the support of a piece of equipment is now concentrated in a single individual who has the necessary skills at his disposal. The groups of staff who need to communicate are situated together and can now

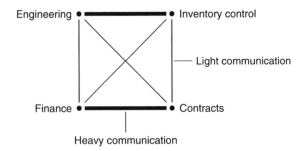

Figure 5.10 Contacts analysis

speak to each other without the need for formal and slow interdepartmental communication.

The conclusions from this product support case-study are equally applicable to organising for Concurrent Engineering.

6

SUSTAINABLE IMPROVEMENT

He that diggeth a pit shall fall into it . . .
ECCLESIASTES 10:8

INTRODUCTION

Objectives

The objectives of the final step are to ensure that the improvements in the control of overheads that have been identified in the project-orientated phase of the work can be implemented and sustained. This is one of the most difficult aspects of the whole programme and first requires the setting in place of a proper project control programme. We then consider the performance measures used by the organisation; these are crucial because the set of performance measures placed on a manager are probably the biggest influence on his behaviour. This leads naturally into a definition of the management reporting systems which are required by the organisation.

Finally, we consider 'total quality'. This is a very broad topic and one whose issues are notoriously intangible. However this should not dissuade the project team from tackling it, since in the long run, the ways in which staff relate to each other and the attitudes they have to their work, is amoung the biggest influences on sustainable improvement. It is also an excellent topic on which to conclude, because it brings together many of the issues raised by activity-based management techniques.

Deliverables

During this final step, illustrated in Figure 6.1, the project team will produce:

- a project control system for ensuring the progress of the improvements;
- proposals to change the organisational culture;

Figure 6.1 Step 5 Sustainable Advantage

- a review of the performance measures used by the company;
- proposals for enhanced reporting systems;
- a framework for implementing a total quality programme.

Issues

We have earlier referred to the advantages of a project-based approach, namely its ability to deliver reliable results in a short period of time. The disadvantage now has to be confronted, namely that the sheer speed and intensiveness of the approach usually means that the project team can move ahead of the organisation.

There should not be an intellectual gap, if proper use has been made of the steering group both to guide the team in the most practical approach and to inform them of the thinking of the project team. However, there is likely to be gap in attitudes and in appreciation of what is practical which needs to be bridged. This is the largest obstacle, and if it is not tackled there is the danger that when the team is disbanded at the end of programme the organisation will breathe a sigh of relief and lapse back into the familiar way of doing business.

PROJECT CONTROL

Need

By this stage the project team will have identified many potential initiatives for change; these are:

- several task forces, set up during Step 3, *Radical Change* to tackle projects of major importance;

- several projects defined in Step 4, *Focused Change*, which are to be monitored through the periodic reporting systems of the company.

The demands which the successful execution of these projects will place on the organisation should not be underestimated. There are two aspects the:

- Co-ordination of the various changes and the monitoring of their progress, so as to correct deviations which threaten their objectives, will have to be properly organised.
- Impact of the changes on the staff of the organisation may be significant. If not properly handled there will be the 'fud' problem: fear, uncertainty and doubt. Even without fud, change is not welcomed by those who have not experienced it for some years and this must be recognised and tackled.

The first of these issues relates to project management; the second deals with change management. We now enlarge upon both these topics.

Overview of project management

Successful project management requires diverse skills. On the one hand there is a need to maintain a wide perspective of the various changes taking place, so as to place differing priorities on projects. On the other hand, there is a need for attention to detail and an almost obsessive desire to meet targets.

In particular, it is important not to jump to the detailed stages of the process and begin drafting detailed project plans without first considering the higher aims of the project.

Furthermore, the structuring of all the projects needs to be carried out in unison. This is first to ensure that the goals, objectives and strategies of the projects are consistent and to identify any dependencies that may exist between the various individual projects.

Work breakdown structure

Good project control is assisted by identifying a clear structure to the work. The principle is to take a large complicated task, namely the project and break it down into smaller less complicated tasks. The first step is to take the overall project and to identify several parts of the project which are relatively self-contained and can be controlled independently.

If necessary each of these units can be further decomposed, and the process repeated until a hierarchy of small projects has been identified. This hierarchy is called the 'work breakdown structure'; some structures are better than others. The mark of a good structure is the relative independence of elements of work on the same level. The work can be broken down by different parameters: for example, time, geographic area, use of resource or the organisational structure. An example of a work breakdown structure is given in Figure 6.2.

The breakdown proceeds to a project plan which relates the individual activities together by means of a network, which we discuss later. First however, we consider the application of the structure to the project plans.

Collation of the project plans

At the start of this section we noted the broad scope of the change that will be taking place within the company. To ensure proper co-ordination it is necessary to collate the various outline plans for change, so that any dependencies between the various actions can be understood; this includes the changes to be made under both Step 3 and Step 4. Once the changes have been collated then the senior management can review the proposed changes and give approval, subject to the availability of financial and managerial resource. Following the approval the task forces can then be launched.

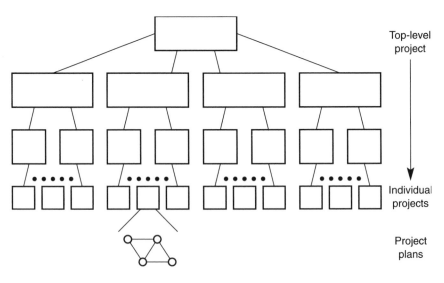

Figure 6.2 Work breakdown structure

The next step is to apply a work breakdown structure to the approved schemes for change. The structure should be split according to the terms of reference of the various task forces (for Step 3 projects) and the organisational structure (for Step 4 projects).

Once the breakdown structure has been established, it is necessary to develop a detailed project plan for every occasion where there is intended to be a change in activity, perhaps its cost, lead time or quality standards. The detailed plans will be amplifications of the outline plans, but recognising any interdependencies that have become apparent. In this way, the entire sum of change proposed for the company can be accounted for at the activity level and nothing will have fallen through the net.

Critical path network

The first step in detailed project planning is to define every task necessary for the completion of the project, along with its duration and resource requirements. This can be difficult, but nonetheless does more to guarantee a successful conclusion than any subsequent act.

There are always many dependencies between tasks and understanding these dependencies is a crucial element of project control. A very useful tool in identifying the dependencies is the critical path network. There are two types; 'activity on arrow' and 'activity on node'; we will deal with the latter though the choice between the two is finely balanced. The various activities are set down and the conditions between them are drawn in. The most common condition is that one activity cannot begin until another is finished, though there are others, e.g. that an activity cannot begin until another has begun or an activity cannot finish until another has finished. Once the network is complete it is then possible to define a 'critical path'.

The critical path is the sequence of activities that determines the minimum time within which the project can be completed. Any delay on the critical path will cause a delay to the project. A delay elsewhere will not cause a delay in the project, until it reaches a certain level. This level is called the 'slack' or 'float' in an activity.

Once the network has been defined, resource can be scheduled and a series of control documents produced, e.g. bar charts for project monitoring.

Parameters to monitor

Once the critical path of a project plan has been defined, the next stage is to summarise the:

- actual resource consumption;
- completion dates of activities;
- major milestones, which will show if the project is on schedule.

The last item is the key to monitoring the project. Significant steps in the project are identified and these can then be used for central monitoring of the progress of the project overall. For the Step 3 projects, the plans are for the benefit of the relevant task force; for the Step 4 projects, the plans are used by the manager of the appropriate activity centre.

Finally, there is a need to recast the corporate financial budgets and plans to account for the effects of imlementing the proposed plans.

Monitoring function

The form of project monitoring selected can vary. As a minimum, a small monitoring authority can be created, which holds copies of the project plans for each action, and the recast financial targets. The function then simply monitors the progress and when it is slipping, notifies the Chief Executive of the problem. Full responsibility for enacting the plans rests either with the task forces (for Step 3 changes) and with the line management structure (for Step 4 changes). This has the advantage of minimising the disturbance to the normal reporting relations; however, if progress is slow, the monitoring authority cannot act directly to remedy this.

The alternative is to set up a monitoring authority with executive power, effectively a Chief Executive's department, which can intervene where progress is not being made. This will have the effect of enhancing the ability of the company to force through change, but at the expense of potentially disrupting the normal operation of the business. The choice between the two will depend on the urgency for change.

Change management

So far the discussion of change has concentrated on the 'hard' side of project management, namely the identification of activities and their dependencies, establishing networks and so forth. There is also a 'soft' side, which can be equally important. We highlight here the main issues to be tackled in creating change in organisations.

First, the 'vision thing', as President Bush memorably called it, is crucial. There must be a simple clear vision, so that staff can see a guiding purpose for the change which is occurring. It may be to beat a competitor; one Japanese car company reputedly had as their corporate goal to 'kill Porsche'

and interestingly their cars resemble those of their named rival. Alternatively the goal is expressed as a set of values; this is particularly the case
with the younger, more dynamic industries where the management and staff
share a vision of creating a unique type of company.

Second, the simple goal needs to be quantified into objectives, e.g. a set
of clear aspirations necessary to meet a goal, which in turn cascade down
into strategies for achievement, plans and finally activities.

Third, a large emphasis needs to be placed on communication. This
would appear to be simple to achieve, though it is surprising how often there
is utter failure! Good communication can take many forms:

- Least imaginatively, there is the dreaded memorandum. Often used with a
  pompous introduction 'It has come to my attention' or 'To whom it may
  concern', it is a dry and one-way form of communication, which is
  unlikely to carry conviction. But, it is better than nothing.
- The pep talk. This at least gives the speaker a chance to express the message in a form best suited to the audience and to gauge the audience
  response. If the speaker is considered trustworthy, the message will also
  carry some conviction. Nonetheless, these events are usually treated with
  some cynicism by staff.
- The pow-wow. Here there is genuine two-way communication. Staff are
  invited to speak or even own the event. The higher the sense of ownership
  and openness, the more effective the event will be. These events do however place demands on the managers; they will have to deal with staff on
  a first among equals basis, while not falling back on rank.

These methods can be supplemented, if the money is available, by communication programmes; newsletters and social events; all help build relationships and a common understanding. Finally, the effect of the humble canteen
should not be forgotten. When studies are made of how information is
passed within organisations, it emerges that relatively little is passed through
the formal channels. Most information is exchanged in informal ways, perhaps in a corridor or, more congenially, in a dining-room or canteen. The
midday meal provides an excellent opportunity for communication; the significance of rank tends to decline and comments can be exchanged more
freely.

Involvement, the fourth issue, goes a step further than communication.
Here the staff are given the opportunity to influence their future. Not only
will they have a far higher sense of ownership of the plans, but also the plans
are likely to be improved. Despite the efforts of the project team to canvass as
wide an opinion as possible in creating the proposed plans, there will still be
opportunities for improvement. This is where the real pay-offs of good

change management occur, where staff realise that all is not a sham, but that their views are being taken into account.

Finally, there is the issue of cultural change. It is usually the case that some cultural change is required. It is far easier to bring about if staff are being treated in a way that assumes that it already has occurred. For example, if there is a reluctance to take initiative, this can only be remedied by allowing initiatives to be recognised and encouraged. We now discuss the topic of organisational culture in detail.

ORGANISATIONAL CULTURE

Context

In the previous steps of the programme we have touched upon the organisational and informal aspects of controlling overheads. We discussed the different options for the business, e.g. functional or process methods, and considered various measures of organisational efficiency. The responsibility for key parameters within a process has also been considered.

There is no doubt that having a sensible internal structure, which is efficient, orientated towards satisfying customers and provides clear responsibility for important decisions, is useful. However it is only the lesser part of the task of building an effective corporation. Most people can recall examples of outstanding performance being delivered despite corporate structures, simply because the managers and staff worked well. Alternatively, the most sensible corporate structure cannot compensate for a poor internal culture.

We now consider the internal culture of organisations, starting with a review of the ways in which organisations have been considered in the past.

Rational organisational theory

The earliest organisational theory is now termed the 'Rational school' and the foundation was laid in *'The Principles of Scientific Management'* (Taylor, 1911). An engineer by training, he adopted a very mechanistic view of the organisation. He advocated a very close definition of the tasks to be carried out, so as to separate out the intellectual discretion from the execution of the work. In this way the operators' task was to be purely mechanistic. The managers' task was also defined by sets of rules and guidelines, so as to identify the best way of operating the company.

Although Taylor's views have tended to fall from favour, the underlying assumptions are still dominant. In gaining control over a situation, most managers will automatically define the tasks to be carried out, allocate responsibility, set up reporting lines and create monitoring mechanisms. They will have created an organisational machine. This approach has the advantage that it ensures co-ordination and avoids dependence on particular individuals, but it can deny the opportunity for the individual to make a personal contribution, which may be valuable.

The Rational approach was developed further in *Economy and Society* (Weber, 1947), who expounded the advantages of bureaucracy. He identified three systems of authority, the rational/legal, the traditional and the charismatic; of these he recognised the first method as by far the most efficient and the keystone of the success of modern societies. The embodiment of the rational/legal system is bureaucracy, which he saw as thoroughly beneficial, particularly in the way it separated the post itself, from the individual who occupied it for a transitory period, since this detachment allowed decisions to be taken within rational rules without the interference of human frailty.

Although bureaucracy is now a detractive term, most people still expect managers and administrators to operate in a way that is bureaucratic in many respects. A manager is expected to detach himself from his personal prejudices and make a decision according to an accepted approach; people look for consistency in a way actions are taken, even if the staff in the posts change.

In summary therefore, we see a paradox surrounding the rational theories. Their limitations are recognised, but they still form the basis for most management behaviour.

Human relations organisational theory

Soon after the rational theories of organisational control were being developed, their limitations were also being recognised.

The view of workers as social, as well as economic, beings was developed; i.e. staff are not simply rational creatures motivated by economic gain, but their behaviour is also governed by their social and psychological needs. Few would deny this; for the manager, however, the alternative approach offers little practical guidance, apart from 'don't forget they are people'.

In doing so, and recognising that are influences are staff behaviour other than the purely economic, there are two aspects which need to be considered: individual motivation and the effect of groups.

The best known analysis of individual needs is the hierarchy given in *A Theory of Human Motivation* (Maslow, 1943). However, the concept of a hierarchy, consisting of physiological needs, a sense of security, social needs, the need for esteem and finally self-actualisation has been challenged. There are many examples where individuals place the need for esteem over the need for socialising, or even the need for self-actualisation over the need for security.

An alternative classification of human needs was provided in *The Achieving Society*, (McClelland, 1961). Here three basic needs were identified: power, achievement and affiliation. This is highly applicable to the workplace. When working with a group of people it can be useful to draw a triangle with the three parameters at the vertices and place individuals within the triangle according to the balance of their needs; different balances will lead to a given change being viewed quite differently.

Finally, this balance of needs will depend on the age of an individual. Various studies (typically of men) have sought to classify the different stages of adult life and their different priorities, generally noting a move from the need to strive and prove oneself in the twenties, to become established in the thirties, to acquire authority in the forties and a period of reassessment thereafter. A particular organisational change will be received differently by those in different stages of development.

The difficulty of accommodating this diversity of non-economic needs of individuals is perhaps the reason many managers resort to purely economic means of motivation. However there is one occasion when economic incentives cannot be solely relied upon: this is when teams are being formed. Teams will be of central importance to the change process; not only are the task forces required to function effectively as teams, but staff may well be put together into new groupings, either on a permanent basis, or to develop particular changes further.

This was examined in *Team Roles at Work* (Belbin, 1993) where nine team roles were identified: the Chairman, the Company Worker, the Completer/Finisher, the Monitor/Evaluator, the 'Plant' (an ideas man), the Shaper, the Team Worker, the Resource Investigator and the Specialist. Although some are glamorous, such as the 'Plant' and some are not, such as the conservative Company Worker, the conclusion was that for a team to work well, it had to be balanced; in particular it was found that teams with two or more 'Plants' fared no better than teams with none. In forming teams, where there is a choice of members, it is useful to consider whether all the necessary roles are being fulfilled in some way.

Finally, teams can have a tendency to assume an identity of their own which can over-ride that of their members. Sometimes this can be beneficial and managers can seek to encourage it, by arranging social events or having special clothes produced for members to enhance the group identity. The only danger is that this group identity can then obscure individual judgement, so independent assessment of the team becomes essential.

In summary, it is worth bearing in mind that nearly all the staff who come to work will have a private life that probably will not be passive. The staff could be running sports teams, organising political parties or raising funds for charity. All this requires initiative and competence, which are qualities that are available to the employer of the staff if he chooses to ask and provide the opportunity. While this may sound simple enough, it is the area of interpersonal skills which seems to represent the chief area of weakness in many managers. Managers usually rise to their post through an ability to master the technical side of the job and are often very task-orientated. When it comes to managing staff, however, they often apply this task-orientated 'product' approach, as opposed to process-orientated 'people' approach which can antagonise and demotivate their staff. The distinction between product and people approaches to management was made in *The Managerial Grid* (Blake and Mouton, 1964) where they also advocated a 'team' approach to gain the best of both approaches.

The environment

While the previous two approaches to controlling and motivating were very different, they had one element in common, namely they treated the company as a closed system. The implication is that the company is in control of its own fate; by designing either procedural or social systems in which its staff operate, then it will obtain the desired results.

Other theories stress that the corporation is not self-contained but exists in an environment. The environment is all-important. It is the source of staff, materials and customers. It will regulate the company either formally through legal means or through informal social norms. It will generate the technologies which affect the company. Therefore the company must be recognised as an open system.

This is consistent with the modern corporate view that companies need to be outward facing and not introspective. It is also very realistic. There are very few Western companies now that are fortresses, so strong as to dictate to the environment and not vice-versa.

Within this 'open systems' approach, a 'contingency' theory has been developed, in which the design of an organisation is viewed as dependent on the environment which affects it. There is no longer a view that a single structure is suitable for all companies. We now discuss some of the influences on corporate structure which the project team may wish to consider.

Design of organisation

The appropriate form of organisation was explored in *Designing Organisations A Decision Making Perspective* (Butler, 1991), where he defined the 'Principle of Requisite Decision Making Capability' as: 'an organisation needs to design a structure of the requisite capacity, that is, one which is sufficiently crisp to minimise decision-making costs and sufficiently fuzzy to achieve adaptability'.

The implication is that crisp structures, with clear roles and rules are associated with low decision-making capacity. The effect of rules is to reduce discretion and to mechanise decision-making processes; in effect the decision will have already been taken by the individual who defined the decision-making procedures. This path has the great advantage of economy; in the past low-paid clerks could be used to act in critical areas because the procedures were clear cut. Nowadays the clerks themselves may not be necessary because the processing could either be undertaken by conventional computer systems or artificial intelligence. However, crisp structures are not adaptable, and require clearly defined objectives and clearly defined means to satisfy those objectives. They do not function well in ambiguous or complex environments.

Fuzzy structures, which permit greater discretion, have a higher decision-making capacity. Decision making tends to be more interactive and collective, and the process can tolerate ambiguity in both objectives and the means of achieving them. There are costs associated with this however.

Butler also makes the point that the culture within the company is dependent on the balance between crispness and fuzziness. Crisp structures tend to encourage only a narrow range of ideas and opinions, are very efficiency-orientated and hold individuals responsible for shortcomings. On the other hand fuzzy structures permit a far broader range of differing opinion, are more concerned with the appropriateness of policies and are mutually supportive. These differences are often apparent in moving from the production facility of a company, with its very crisp structures, to its corporate strategy unit, with its emphasis on fuzzy decision making.

Empowerment and information technology

We are now in a position to consider the implications of empowerment and the major impact information technology has in this area. Following the 'Principle of Requisite Decision Making Capability', the aim is to design as crisp a structure as is feasible given the ambiguity, complexity and uncertainty of the environment in which a particular activity or process must operate. This, of course, is following the Rational school of organisational design, but accepting that there will be many cases where a fully rational approach to decision making is not possible; in these cases a bounded rational decision-making approach, which is associated with fuzziness, becomes necessary.

The effect of the five-step programme itself should be to increase the overall level of crispness and rational decision making that is possible within the company, because the level of information and understanding of the company and its processes will be far higher than when the programme started.

Where crispness is possible then information technology is applied to automate the tasks; as indicated earlier, this can now be carried out to a far greater degree than previously. There is now relatively little need for staff to carry out repetitive clerical or manual tasks. The remaining posts will therefore have a degree of fuzziness associated with them, which is currently beyond the ability of technology to accommodate. These are then filled with staff who all have some degree of decision-making authority. They have, in effect, been empowered. They will remain so until technology advances to subsume their decision making and then they will become redundant.

When these ideas are applied to companies there is automatically a need for cultural change. As was noted in the previous subsection; the culture in fuzzy structures differs from those in crisp structures. There will be a shift in culture and ways of dealing with staff away from that favoured by the Rational or Taylorist organisation design.

The paradox is that empowerment is not only the antithesis of Taylor's methods, but is the result of Taylor's methods, when all the low decision-making elements of the structure have been automated.

Implications for management

The emergence of a smaller empowered workforce has serious implications for the management of a company. These are most evident where a traditional company is being forced to adopt new technology in order to survive. While the workforce is changing, the management may not be. If this is the case, problems normally arise. The newer type of worker can soon resent the attitudes of the old guard management, leading to high labour turnover.

Sometimes the old guard anticipate the problems and refuse to change. Perhaps the most extreme example of this at the national level was in Romania, where the national industrial plan for the twenty-first century of the old communist government did not have any reference to electronics factories, only steelworks and the like. An advanced workforce would have implied a degree of national cultural change which could not be contemplated by the government. The government went bust, as will any other corporation where the management chooses not to adapt to the environment because the implications are too dreadful.

The ability of the company to change its management style ultimately rests with the Chief Executive. Even if a sole voice, the Chief Executive has the ability to initiate change. However, if the Chief Executive does not see the need for change, then progress will be difficult since the elements who are reactionary to change will always be able to appeal to the top to maintain the status quo.

Once commitment from the Chief Executive has been obtained, the next stage is to begin the training and development programmes. These should begin with management though as time progresses should encompass all the staff. In changing the culture within the company, which is a key part of many Total Quality programmes which are discussed at the end of this chapter, training and education will be a significant expenditure. This expenditure should include not only the time of staff but also the engagement of professional trainers.

The effectiveness of this investment can be monitored through the use of surveys of staff attitudes, to identify where change is being achieved and where attitudes remain which are an obstacle to change.

PERFORMANCE MEASURES

Past failure

We have already referred to the adage 'What you measure is what you get'. Most staff and managers are acutely aware of the few parameters on which they are measured. They are likely to concentrate on appearing good on paper, especially if there is an unsympathetic management style.

For this reason, the choice of performance measures a company chooses is critical. In the past there has been well-justified criticism of the performance measures which companies have adopted, or been forced to adopt. The main criticisms are:

- Short-term measures predominate over long-term measures. This seems to be a national, as opposed to an international, problem. Countries which use the banking system to discipline the efficiency of managers, such as Germany or Japan, seem to be able to take a longer view; those which use the stock market, such as the US and the UK, to ensure good corporate performance are forced into short-term decisions. The relative performance of the two systems speaks for itself and the cause is obvious. In the US and UK, it would be a foolhardy Chief Executive who cut dividends to increase inward investment: it would be a case of fattening the goose while simultaneously lowering the price.
- Proxies predominate over reality. The real corporate issues, e.g. the product lead over rivals, the delivery reliability, and the level of customer satisfaction are ignored. In their place there is the language of earnings

per share, return on capital; the senior managers therefore operate the business one step removed from reality. The irony is that these financial measures are themselves easily manipulated by skilled practitioners and are not a reliable guide. The dangers of the over-use of proxies were highlighted in *Management Rediscovered* (Curtis, 1990).

- Efficiency measures predominate over effectiveness measures. While it is sometimes possible to derive measures which show the efficiency with which operations are carried out, the measures neither address the relevance of the activities to the customers of the company, nor consider the quality of the work carried out. This can be a real hazard if efficiency measures are crudely applied; it is relatively easy to appear efficient under simplistic performance measures, if the quality and relevance of the output is ignored.

- Economy measures predominate over efficiency measures. Often it is not possible even to measure the efficiency of conversion of input into output. In this situation, the measures simply record the amount of resource expended in particular areas; most variance analysis of fixed costs is of this form, noting over or under-expenditure compared to the budget. By this stage in the five-step programme, this should be less of an issue, because there will at least be an appreciation of the relationship between the input of resource and the output of activities.

- Functional measures predominate over customer related measures. Senior managers frame measures for their juniors which are orientated around the functional performance of their department, as opposed to meeting the needs of customers.

The classic cases of inappropriate performance measures come to a spectacular climax in the manufacturing sector. The most common case is where the factory manager is given a *short-term measure* and a *financial proxy* to follow, say overhead recovery. Recovery of overhead requires sheer throughput, without regard to whether the operations are *effective* in meeting the needs of customers. While the efficiency of the manual labour and the raw material utilisation will have been measured, the same cannot be said for the significant overhead functions, where the only tracking is of the *economy* of overhead expenditure. The manufacturing personnel are likely to insist on *functional measures* such as high utilisation of labour and machinery from their subordinates to deliver the throughput, with the result that batch sizes will be extended and the production orders 'cherry-picked' for those most likely to provide good functional performance.

The net result is that the manufacturing operation will be pursuing an agenda which will no doubt result in good overhead recovery. What the customer thinks of it all, is a different matter.

Designing new performance measures

We have outlined the hazards of poor performance measures. More constructively, there is a need to design better ones. The basic information needed to do this has already been acquired by the project team.

The stakeholders of the business have been identified, the most obvious of which are the customers and those who own the business. Others may include those in the local community. The critical success factors have also been identified, and these have been translated into particular requirements. Wherever performance is required by a stakeholder, it should be measurable.

Given an understanding of the external performance parameters and of the process which delivers this performance, one set of internal performance measures becomes immediately apparent. The internal measures for each

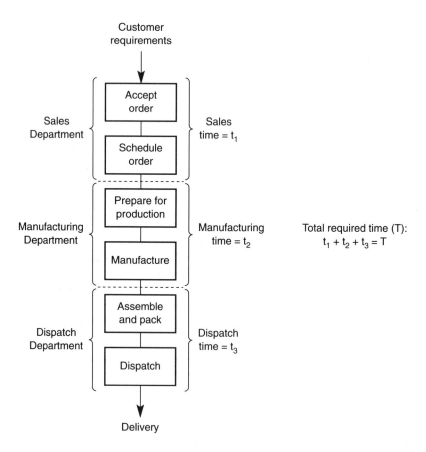

Figure 6.3 Process performance measures

activity in the process can simply be the external parameters broken down into several parts. The simplest example to visualise, shown in Figure 6.3, is lead time. If lead time is an important factor and the delivery process is linear, it is straightforward to stipulate the minimum queuing times and lead times necessary to met the customers' requirements. In practice there may be unforeseen iterations and delays; while these make a simple sequential model unsuitable for predictive purposes, it does not negate the use of lead time as a performance measure. Whatever the internal problems with meeting a given lead time, if lead time is a customer requirement then it remains a relevant performance measure for each activity in the supply chain.

The concept of process measures can also be applied to cost and quality. The costing of the activities within a process is particularly useful. As noted above many performance measures only reflect resource consumption, without addressing the efficiency of conversion. If the activity costs can be correlated with the level of activity that exists, then it is possible to use the activity costs as a performance measure. The understanding of the current levels of an activity is also of use in setting budgets, and lies behind the principle of activity-based budgeting.

In measuring quality within a process, the relevant parameters are the incidence of faults and their cost. The principles of quality costing have already been described, especially as regards the crucial point that the full cost of a quality problem may well be felt at a point far removed from where it was initiated.

Not all performance measures will be process measures, e.g. where an external measure for a process has been disaggregated into components for each activity. In some cases there will be an external measure which is not the result of any single process. For example, a critical success factor for a technological company may be the ability to retain and interest first-class research staff; this ability does not depend on a single process, but nonetheless measurement is important and might involve the proportion of graduates with first-class degrees recruited, the proportion of job offers declined and the average employment period. Alternatively, for many companies market share is important, not least because studies show that high margins and return on capital are only achieved by those with significant market share; although it does not depend on a single process, market share is clearly important and needs to be measured.

The measures will also have to reflect how the company is meeting the needs of its owners. The measures used to assess this have already been considered in Step 1, *External Review*. The owners are likely to be interested in the value of their asset. The two main influences are the level of earnings and the level of dividends. The level of earnings determines the overall value of the company, for a given price earnings ratio which in turn depends on the level of perceived risk attached to the earnings. The level of dividends is particularly relevant to minority shareholders, the value of whose shares equals the dividend stream divided by the yield, where the yield associated with the share is dependent on the risk attached to the dividends and the prevailing level of interest rates. While it is incontestable that companies need to make a profit and to pay dividends, there remains a tension between short-term and long-term performance; it is possible to increase dividends, and sometimes earnings, in the short term by lowering inward investment but at the expense of long-term performance.

Another very common measure is 'return on capital employed' (ROCE), popular with divisionalised companies because of the ability it offers to compare alternative uses of capital and its pivotal role in much of the theory of financial management. The problem with ROCE as a performance measure is that it discourages capital investment, by both lowering the numerator and increasing the denominator of the measure. Whatever its theoretical attractions, if it is applied to companies which are undercapitalised, as many US and UK companies are, and it discourages additional investment, it is not a particularly good performance measure. An alternative is 'residual income', which deducts a capital charge from the earnings of the company; this has the advantage of encouraging all investments whose earnings will exceed their finance charges.

A hierarchy of measures

There is a need for a hierarchy of measures. Even if all the measures originate from a consideration of the critical success factors, some of them are appropriate to the top level of the organisation, others to the middle managers and other to supervisors and junior staff.

The three levels can be classified as related to:

- *Strategic direction.* In the private sector, such measures may include market share, customer satisfaction, key staff retention, earnings and dividends. In the public sector, it will be necessary to measure how the organisation is meeting its basic objectives. In both cases, the purpose of the measures is to indicate to the senior management the areas in which the company is succeeding or failing.
- *Processes.* These measures are used by middle management to indicate the degree to which customers or other stakeholders are being satisfied or disappointed, on a day-by-day basis. The process measures indicating cost, timeliness and quality are all relevant here.

- *Activities.* These measures are used by junior managers who may lack the opportunity to judge how their performance affects the process as a whole. Concentrating instead on the internal operations of the company, the managers require measures of the effectiveness, efficiency and economy of the activities they control. Measures here may include, defect detailed costs, cycle and queuing times.

The challenge is to ensure that:

- There are no gaps in the performance measure framework, whereby higher level measures are not supported by measures at a lower level. If this happens the junior managers may not be working towards a higher level aim.
- The measures in use at the different levels remain consistent. If this is not the case managers will be pulling in different directions.

The last point is difficult to achieve. We now discuss how there is often a natural tension between the performance measures used in different departments.

Tension between different measures

In the absence of a process-based organisational structure, the different functions of the company will usually be pulling in opposite directions. To illustrate, in the finance sector, there will be a tension between:

- the marketing of lending services, where the emphasis will be on simplifying the procedures for loans to be granted and widening the lending base;
- the management of credit risk, with the emphasis on thorough examination of a borrower and the exclusion of those who present a bad risk.

In the manufacturing sector there will usually be a tension between:

- Sales and marketing who will generally be seeking maximum availability of product, flexibility of distribution and variety of design. Providing these will increase the costs of inventory holding, distribution and manufacturing respectively.

Figure 6.4 Performance measure tension

- Manufacturing and distribution, who seek stability of schedule, low variety coupled with high volume to provide the advantages of long batches with minimal set-up times, and substantial inventory which acts as a buffer against uncertainty. This will tend to lower the flexibility offered to customers and the high inventory will add to the capital costs of the company.

These tensions are illustrated in Figure 6.4, and are a feature of a functional organisation, where managers are concerned with only part of the overall process. If both a functional structure and the functional performance measures are retained, the resulting tension needs to be recognised. Once this is done any differences can be actively managed at the top level within the company and not simply allowed to degenerate into ongoing arguments which dissipate effort.

MANAGEMENT INFORMATION SYSTEMS

Maintaining programme information

The five-step programme itself has been highly information intensive; deriving the information necessary to bring the overheads under control will have been a significant part of the workload of the project team. It is now necessary to make arrangements for the routine collection of data to provide the enhanced management information after the project has concluded. Implementation of this will be the responsibility of the information systems task force.

There are two possible ways to achieve this:

- automate the data collection for the calculation of activity costs, by streamlining the processes which collect the information from the ledger and other systems before transferring it into the PC database application;
- modify the main information systems, to include the functionality of the PC support tool.

The first option is easier to achieve and allows greater flexibility in changing the system in the future, and is therefore often preferred. The second option does provide for a more efficient system in the long run, if the information requirements are unlikely to change.

We now discuss the issues to be considered in maintaining the corporate systems themselves.

System structure and output

The structure of the systems need to match the structure of the business, which by now has been well researched. The team will have defined:

- the major business segments, most notably products and customer groups;
- the major activity centres, which themselves may be divided geographically;
- the major processes and their component activities.

This division of the business developed during the five-step programme should be used for the main management information systems.

The output from the systems necessary for decision support were recorded during Step 2, *Activity Analysis*, and the proposals to change the systems, have already been encapsulated in the project plans for developing the information systems. One use of the systems is for planning, budgeting and monitoring, which are of course crucial to the longer term control of overheads; we now discuss these in more detail.

Planning systems

The ability to plan and forecast is one of the most basic business disciplines. It forms the difference between having to react to daily events and being prepared. Most difficulties can be overcome given enough notice and in the rare cases where this is not possible, then at least an exit from an intractable situation, while minimising losses can be made.

It is a relatively mature field, indeed some would say its heyday is now past. In the sixties and seventies, corporate planning was highly developed: large central staffs would produce analyses of alternative scenarios and strategic investment and divestment would be made on their basis. This form of planning has gone into decline along with the companies that practised it. It was noticed that companies which thrived were those who channelled their energies into being good at what they did.

Nonetheless a more focused form of planning is still necessary. It begins with the strategic planning, producing on an ongoing basis the type of information used in Step 1, *External Review*. This does not require a large staff; instead it requires the senior executives to devote some of their time away from the short-term issues. For this reason it is best if the long-term strategic planning is kept distinct in time and process from the detailed planning. Consequently the strategic planning process usually does not have an immediate impact on the management accounting systems.

However once the strategic planning is complete there will be a need to ensure that it is consistent with detailed planning. The time horizon for the latter varies, though two to three years is typical. There is a choice whether to have a new plan issued annually, or adopt a rolling forecast, whereby after each period, a quarter of a year say, a new period is added to the end of the plan. A rolling plan is undoubtedly the more developed planning method, but there is a cost associated with it. The detailed planning is best conducted within the framework used for the other management information; it should use the same classification.

Sometimes there is a distinction between the financial plan for the forth-coming year and the annual budget, which is the main control mechanism of the company. These usually arise out of timing differences and there is no fundamental reason why the two plans should differ, given they are covering the same topic and time horizon.We now discuss the budgeting procedure itself.

Budgeting

We finally arrive at the procedure most people associate with overhead control. As often practised, it has been seen as irrelevant to the directing of the overhead activities towards adding value to the business. Nonetheless it is certainly still relevant for the short-term control of organisations. Given this topic is so well covered in other management texts, we will concentrate here on the more recent developments in the area.

The quest in budgeting has to be to relate the funds allocated to a department to the quantity of work carried out and the relevance of the work to the corporate objectives. This is not new. 'Zero-based budgeting' sought to overcome the setting of budgets on a historical basis, by a detailed bottom-up re-examination of the needs for each activity; this was intended to replace a more subjective top-down approach, where judgements were made on the relative importance of areas of the business and funds allocated accordingly.

This programme itself, has laid the foundation for a rational setting of budgets. Most importantly, the basic activities within each activity centre have been identified and a view obtained of whether costs are genuinely fixed, proportional to volume or proportional to transactions. This is the basic information needed to conduct an activity-based budgeting exercise. This is related to variable budgeting, which is well established; activity-based budgeting is simply the extension of variable budgeting to encompass many activity drivers as opposed to a single variable.

The key to activity-based budgeting is to ensure consistency between the financial plans and the various operating plans which deal with the physical side of the business, and the assumptions made on the throughput of work and the expected productivity levels. In carrying out activity-based budgeting there is a need for the management information systems to integrate the financial and physical projections.

Once the planning process is clear the data requirements to support planning and forecasting out to the desired horizons will become apparent; usually more data are required to support the detailed short-term plans and forecasts than those for the longer term.

Monitoring

The monitoring of the company performance inevitably creates heavy demands for input data. It is necessary to:

- identify costs as they are incurred, classifying them as revenue or capital costs;
- allocate them; this allocation will almost certainly be a multiple allocation because:
  - the costs must be allocated to the lowest level of detail within the system and then 'rolled-up' for summary at a higher level, in several dimensions e.g. to calculate the costs of activity centres, the costs of a product line and the costs of a customer;
  - indirect costs may require reallocation, e.g. telephone costs may have been recorded as a single item within the system, but would require reallocating to different cost centres.

- allocate income to the various activity centres, products and customers;
- record the relevant non-financial parameters, both for use as performance measures and for possible use as allocation parameters.

These allocations are not simply a matter of arithmetic; implicit within them are policy decisions, e.g. on the costing of spare capacity.

The ledger systems which record much of this information are the hub of the organisation's information systems. Nearly all companies will already possess such a system and if a replacement is being considered, a packaged solution would probably be the natural choice.

The usual reason for contemplating a replacement of the ledgers at all is the lack of flexibility in reporting, especially as regards the multiple roll-up of costs and income so as to provide multiple views on costs and profitability. The prospect of replacing the ledger systems, or even modifying them, is often ruled out on the grounds of cost. In these cases the use of a PC database application with automated links to the main system has attractions. Where there is a move to replace the ledger systems, those using fourth generation languages and relational database technology are often favoured, because they offer the prospect of retaining flexibility and permitting changes to be made in the future while retaining the initial investment.

TOTAL QUALITY

Introduction

The improvement of quality within both the manufacturing and service sectors has been pursued with zeal in the past decade. Industries have been facing intense competition, much of it on a global level, and higher quality has been seen as one of the key areas of competitive advantage. Much of the competition has come from Japanese companies, whose reputation for quality has not relied on any grand innovation but on the patient application of quality measurement techniques developed in the West and an attitude that quality is paramount.

In the service sector quality is equally important; the customer comes in contact with the provider of a service and obviously the ability to rectify faults before they affect the customer is much reduced. Not surprisingly therefore, there is an emphasis on preventing errors before they occur.

Over time opinions on quality have also tended to evolve. They began with a prosaic view, namely good quality is defined as conformance to specification. Now the view is more philosophical, where quality is defined as the absence of waste, of getting it right first time and being, in short, perfect. These are not contradictory: the first view recognises that customer requirements are paramount and the company should be aiming to meet them; the second view is consistent with poor quality amounting to waste, which benefits neither the organisation or its customers.

Framework

The main philosophy underpinning the drive to improve quality, Total Quality Management (TQM), espouses the view that a company must identify and serve its customers. There is a great deal of literature on TQM; rather than duplicate this, we summarise the main points, illustrated in Figure 6.5:

- an identification of the internal and external customers of the corporation and how the activities of the company serve these;
- understand internal functions;
- estimation of the total cost incurred by poor quality within the organisation, namely 'the cost of quality';
- justification of a programme to reduce this amount, given its size, which is typically 30 per cent of total cost;
- use of this information to identify quality improvement programmes;
- creation of quality improvement teams;

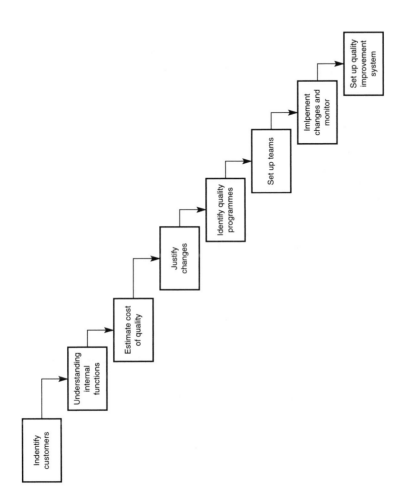

Figure 6.5 Total Quality Management (TQM)

- use of the quality improvement teams to change the organisation as a whole and monitor performance;
- the setting up of a quality management system.

Great emphasis is placed on the management of change within the organisation and especially on achieving a shift in attitudes. While this sense of priority is correct, it is also important not to neglect the quantitative aspects of total quality; without good quality costs, not only will the wrong priorities be set for the quality improvements programmes, but the subsequent monitoring will not be effective.

Relevance of the programme to total quality

Building on the five-step programme to bring about a total quality culture within the company is straightforward, since the programme has been totally compatible with the basic tenets of total quality. The common factors include:

- attaching a priority to understanding the needs of the customers, whether internal or external. Much of Step 1, *External Review* was concerned with just this point;
- understanding how the organisation currently operates to serve customers, and how it fails. This was the emphasis of Step 2, *Activity Analysis*; in quality programmes the contents of this step may be called 'function analysis';
- obtaining the staff's ideas for improvement, which was considered in Step 3, *Radical Change* and Step 4, *Focused Change* through challenge groups.

Therefore much of the work already undertaken has a natural place in a quality programme. This relation is shown in Figure 6.6. It can be seen that the main item not yet covered is the creation of a quality management system, which we now discuss.

Quality management system

There are very practical reasons for setting up a quality management system. During the five-step programme substantial changes will have been initiated; there is a need to define systematically the new state of affairs. Weaknesses in controls and procedures may well have been evident; these need to be corrected. Even after the period of change, staff will leave and there is a need for the new staff to be briefed on how the organisation actu-

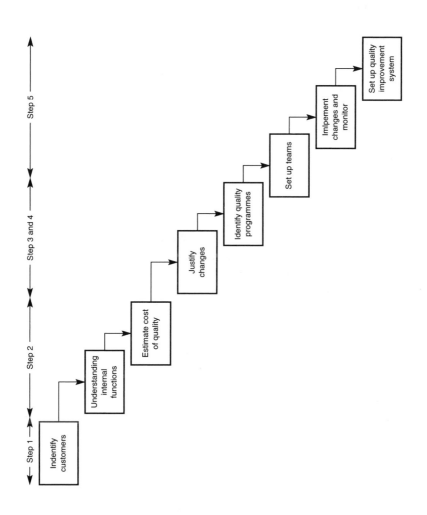

Figure 6.6 TQM and the five-step programme

ally works, as opposed to relying on the flawed and parochial view that comes from the 'sitting next to Nellie' approach to induction.

The quality management system seeks to overcome these problems by setting down how the company is expected to work. An important part of this account is how actions can remain traceable, so there is also an emphasis on defining the minimum level of documentation necessary to ensure that the company is functioning as it should. This need not lead to unnecessary bureaucracy: there is a proper way of carrying out the various activities, which should be defined, and the documentation is necessary to ensure that, at the main decision points, there is a record of who did what and when.

There is also provision made for sampling and internal audit. The use of sampling, or statistical process control, should not be confined to finding fault; on the contrary, the intention is that the operator should monitor the variability of the process, in order to trap problems before they become serious. In addition to this, however, there is a case for a more formal procedure to ensure that the system as a whole is being followed.

If the company undertakes to install a quality management system, it usually seeks to take credit for the achievement through applying for registration under the ISO9000 scheme. This can be a useful discipline, since it demonstrates both to the management of the company and to its customers that the quality management system conforms to best contemporary practice. It will also avoid the company having to undergo separate assessments from individual customers, as long as they accept the independent accreditation.

Having dealt with the procedural aspects of total quality, we now consider the less tangible aspects.

Customer care

Much of the substance of quality within the company will not be immediately visible to outsiders, instead the customers will gain many of their impressions in relatively superficial contacts. These contacts, while fleeting, can create lasting impressions and influence the overall perception of the company.

It is worthwhile tracing the various ways a customer will gain first-hand experience of the company and its staff and then training staff to leave a good impression at each of the points of contact. For example, the most prolific form of communication is almost certainly the telephone for most companies: therefore it is necessary to ensure that all those who will answer the telephone do so promptly and coherently. Written material is usually the next most frequent form of contact. Given modern word processing techniques it is relatively simple to produce correctly spelt material of good appearance.

Finally there is personal contact. Field sales staff rarely create problems here, since they are selected with personal appearance in mind. Where visitors visit the company site, it could be useful to 'walk through' their treatment and ask 'how it feels'. One public relations agency took a high risk approach in selling to the chairman of a company not reputed, at the time, for the courtesy of its staff. The chairman, on visiting the office was treated rudely, left for half an hour without refreshment in a dingy room. As he got up to walk out, the head of the agency appeared and announced that the chairman had just enjoyed a typical encounter with the staff of his own company! This, however, is not the recommended way to obtain customers.

Of all the aspects of overhead control, customer care is one of the most intangible. Apart from observing the basis courtesies, staff attitude is also important and we conclude on this point.

An attitude of mind

This last section apart, the tone of this book has been objective and analytical. The last words, however, need to refer to attitude. When applying any of the many methods to bring overheads under control, we should remember that overheads walk on two legs. With the right spirit, of wanting to please, to achieve, to be exceptional, almost every obstacle can be overcome. A superb infrastructure plus a stolid staff will only add up to a failure.

ORGANISATIONAL CHANGE CASE STUDY

Background

The final case study contains a useful summary of many of the techniques proposed in this programme, in particular the use of market research to guide overhead cost reduction. The preliminary stages involve an activity analysis of the operations and a benchmarking exercise. This is then followed by three programmes: the first is concerned with determining the customer requirements, the second reviews the organisational structure and the third examines the value and efficiency of the operations. The programme concludes with a workshop to initiate the change management process.

The company is a regional distributor of electricity seeking to make a 15 per cent reduction in its cost base over a period of five years. The change process has been proceeding well but the company is now finding difficulty in meeting its financial targets.

The company covers a wide area which encompasses both rural and urban populations. Its organisational structure is shown in Figure 6.7. The

Customer Service directorates are intended to deal with all aspects of the business which involve communication with the customer, so as to provide 'customer focus'. This includes fault repair of the low voltage circuits, arranging for connection to the network, supervision of meter reading and answering customer queries.

The Engineering function is responsible for all technical functions, including the maintenance of the higher voltage lines. The tasks of the remaining functions are self-evident from their titles.

Objectives

The purpose of the exercise is to identify the obstacles to further cost reduction and to identify ways in which this cost reduction can be achieved while minimising the impact on customer service.

A secondary objective is to ensure that any proposed programme for change is consistent with a current business process re-engineering programme that is under-way within the company, to redesign the customer-related processes. The timescales for this programme are longer than those which can be accommodated for the cost reduction exercise; nonetheless, since the two projects will run in parallel, they must be consistent.

Activity analysis

The foundation for all the work is a definition of the activities which take place in the operation of the distribution network. This is carried out through the interview of managers in the Headquarters and two Areas; these two Areas are then used as a proxy for all the Areas. The activity analysis produces about 150 activities in order to obtain the necessary detail; to illustrate, a list of maintenance activities is given in Figure 6.8.

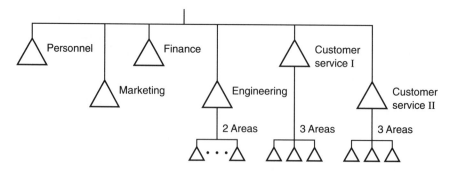

Figure 6.7 Organogram

Code	Activity	Description
RM01	Repairs	Performing repairs & overhaul servicing
RM02	Operating	Performing all high voltage switching
RM03	Condition Monitoring	Conditioning monitoring e.g. oil sampling, infra-red scanning
RM04	Routine Sub station visits	Regular visits to sub stations – including all readings & checking
RM05	33–132 kv lines	Line patrols & repairs
RM06	Clearing	Performing grass and tree cutting
RM07	Draughting	Maintain a graphical record of the distributor's base
RM08	Tower Maintenance	Tower maintenance, rust removal, foundation repairs
RM09	Building Maintenance	Maintenance to sub-stations
RM10	Transport	Activities associated with transportation of transformers
RM11	Live Line	Live line training and operating
RM12	Measurement & Control Mtce	Fault and preventative maintenance
RM13	Transmission & Switching Mtce	Fault and preventative maintenance
RM14	Engineering investigations/monitoring	Investigating power supply problems and network performance
RM15	Maintenance planning	Scheduling maintenance and outages
RM16	Cut-offs	Cutting off customers
RM17	Protection Maintenance	Fault and preventative maintenance
RM18	11–22 kV Line	Line patrols and repairs
RM19	LV Transformer Maintenance	Fault and preventative maintenance

Figure 6.8 Maintenance activity library

The detail is necessary to ensure that there is no ambiguity in the definition of Headquarters and Area activities and that the subsequent benchmarking exercises are valid.

Benchmarking

The benchmarking is carried out both on the core and on the support functions; for the former the benchmarking gives an indication of whether efficiency improvements are possible and the latter whether the provision of a given level of resource is appropriate to the business. Both national and international benchmarks are used.

The national benchmarks show the maintenance activities to have far more staff then expected. The larger number of maintenance staff seems to be the result of the supervisory structure, whereby two workforces are deployed in a particular Area, that is a Customer Service workforce and an Engineering workforce.

The international benchmarks are confined to ratio analysis, which indicates that there is scope for reduction in many of the support functions. The variations are accounted for by the differing quality of systems and diverse expectations on the level of employee support that exist between different countries.

Diagnosis

First, the most serious obstacle to meeting the targets is the duplication of physical and supervisory networks which exist within the company. For example, the Customer Service directorates maintain a series of premises across the company's area. There is a network of Depots, largely based in industrial estates, from which the maintenance crews for the low voltage network operate. Nearby to the depot, but in the commercial and retail area of town, there is a 'Customer Service Centre', where customers can visit. The Depots and Customer Service Centres report up to an Area office. The three Areas then report into a Customer Service directorate. There are two Customer Service directorates, one of which has premises outside the corporate headquarters, on a site distinct from an Area office, a few hundred yards away.

Furthermore the Engineering directorate has its own physical and supervisory network. There is a need to maintain a substantial higher voltage network and for this purpose they require their own workforce and Depots, many of which are adjacent to the Customer Service depots but independently managed. Apart from the administrative overhead this entails, there is a further disadvantage that each repair and maintenance workforce has to be staffed so as to deal with the peak workload in each function, with the result that excess direct labour is being carried.

Second, the company is incurring additional costs in order to provide increased access to the customer. This is the rationale for opening the Customer Service Centres. However, these costs are being incurred without any research into the value the customer places on physical access and the use which is made of it.

Third, many staff both in the Area offices and the Headquarters functions are engaged in activities which have little relevance to the supply of electricity.

Proposed plan

There is a need to recognise the difference between Area activities and Headquarters activities, to avoid the duplication of networks. This should also enhance customer service because at the moment although a Customer Service Area office is charged with maintaining customer service, in practice much of the resource to achieve this, including maintenance of the higher voltage networks, is outside its control.

Second, there is a need to measure the actual customer requirements, to understand if the additional money being spent on enhancing the customer interface is being spent in the right way, or whether it is justified at all.

Finally, there is a need to conduct a value added and efficiency review of the activities to understand which are essential to the supply of electricity and, if they are needed, their appropriate size.

These three strands of work are shown in Figure 6.9, along with the concluding project planning stage.

Headquarters/area structure

This is a critical part of the process to reduce the operating costs of the business. Each activity needs to be examined to determine whether it is properly

Figure 6.9 Project plan

an Area activity or a Headquarters activity. In applying this test there are two considerations:

- Area activities are those which require a knowledge of the locality, be it of customers, the network or the terrain;
- Headquarters activities are those for which an integrated view is essential, or for which, given an investment in systems, there are economies of scale to be derived from centralisation.

Most groups of activities fall into one category or another. Typically we see Area activities including the connection of new customers, the reading of customers' meters, the engineering work associated with connection of customers and the physical work on the network. Headquarters functions include the billing and collection of debt, the planning of the development of the high voltage network and the variety of corporate functions, such as marketing finance and personnel.

The clear division of Area and Headquarters functions ensures the avoidance of duplicated supervisory networks. The Area activities are placed under the control of an Area manager, given the spans of control this role entails, the number of Areas can be reduced from six to four.

An organisational structure which follows these principles is given in Figure 6.10. The decision to centralise the delivery of customer service is discussed below.

Customer service definition

A comprehensive market research programme shows the Customer Service Centres are not the best delivery mechanism for customer service. There are two clear market segments.

- Customers who only use centres to pay bills, which can be easily done through a bank. For general queries, these customers prefer the phone.

- Customers who wish to deal face-to-face, but who find difficulty in travelling to the centres.

The segmentation of the market needs to be recognised and the delivery mechanisms tailored accordingly. It is proposed to close the centres and replace them with a toll-free number and a series of mobile centres, which visit substantial populations of customers who cannot travel. In this way service is enhanced and costs are reduced.

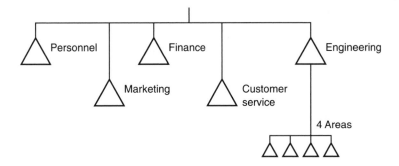

Figure 6.10 Proposed organisational structure

Value-added and efficiency analysis

The value-added analysis is carried out in the way described in Step 2, *Activity Analysis*. The value-added activities comprise both those essential for the operation of the network and those services which the customer service definition shows are valued by the customer. The efficiency study draws on the benchmarking exercise to identify over-staffing in these activities.

Non-value added activities occur to accommodate a particular policy or way of working. The purpose of the analysis is to establish the true cost behind these corporate policies and conventions. Armed with this information it is possible to establish the cost of these policies, and justify changing them. As a result economies are identified in the personnel and finance functions.

Project planning

The result of this work is condensed into some twenty project plans. Each plan is a proposal for change in the following format:

0.	Title
1.	Definition
1.1	Description of Change
1.2	Benefits of Change
1.3	Justification of Benefits
1.4	Constraints on Change
2.	Quantification
2.1	Affected Activities and their Costs
2.2	Proposed Activity Costs

The purpose of the plan is to gain approval at the management board for the change and, given this, to build the financial implications of the changes into the budgets and financial plans for the next year.

Relationship to business process engineering

The programme is fully compatible with the business process re-engineering project being undertaken by the company. The establishment of the customers' requirements is an important part of the project and the clarification of Area and Headquarters activities is also an essential step in the design of new processes.

REFERENCES

Belbin, M., *Team Roles at Work,* (Butterworth-Heinemann, London, 1993).

Blake, R.R. and Moutan, J.S., *The Managerial Grid: Key Orientations for Achieving Production Through People* (Houston, Gulf, 1964).

Booth R., 'Cost Leadership and Activity Analysis', *Management Accounting*, June 1992.

Brimson, J., *Activity Accounting*, (Wiley, New York, 1991).

Butler, R., *Designing Organisations*, (Routledge, London 1991).

Curtis, D., *Management Rediscovered*, (Dow Jones Irwin, Homewood Illinois, 1990).

Ferror, H., Dobler, D. and Killen, K., *The Purchasing Handbook* (McGraw Hill, New York, 1993).

Hauser, J. and Clausing, D., 'The House of Quality' *Harvard Business Review*, May–June 1988.

Hickey, G., 'Strategic IS/IT Planning' in Peppard, J. (ed), *IT Strategy for Business* (Pitman, London, 1993).

Maslow, A.H., 'A Theory of Human Motivation', *Psychological Review* 50, 1943, 370–96.

McLelland, D.C., *The Achieving Society* (Van-Nostrand, Princeton, NJ 1961).

Miller, J., and Vollman, T. 'The Hidden Factory' *Harvard Business Review*, Sept–Oct 1985.

Peppard, J., 'Using IT to Gain Competitive Advantage', in Peppard J. (ed), *IT Strategy for Business* (Pitman, London, 1993).

Pickwell, I., *Value for Money Audit* (CCAB Ltd, 1980).

Porter, M., *Competitive Strategy* (Free Press, New York, 1980).

Shillinghow, G., 'The concept of attributable cost', *Journal of Accounting Research*, Vol 1 No 1 Spring 1963.

Taylor, F., *The Principles of Scientific Management* (New York, Harper and Row, 1911).

Weber, M., *Economy and Society* (Bechminster, New York, 1947).

INDEX